IMAGINING CHILD WELFARE

in the Spirit of Reconciliation

Voices from the Prairies

Previous publications in the Voices from the Prairies series:

Putting a Human Face on Child Welfare (2007)

Passion for Action in Child and Family Services (2009)

Awakening the Spirit: Moving Forward in Child Welfare (2012)

Reinvesting in Families: Strengthening Child Welfare Practice for a Brighter Future (2014)

Transforming Child Welfare: Interdisciplinary Practices, Field Education, and Research (2016)

IMAGINING CHILD WELFARE

in the Spirit of Reconciliation

Voices from the Prairies

edited by

Dorothy Badry, H. Monty Montgomery, Daniel Kikulwe, Marlyn Bennett, and Don Fuchs

Suggested Citation: Badry, D., Montgomery, H., Kikulwe, D., Bennett M., & Fuchs, D., (Eds.). (2018). *Imagining Child Welfare in the Spirit of Reconciliation.* Regina, SK: University of Regina Press.

Printed and bound in Canada by Marquis. The text of this book is printed on 100% post-consumer recycled paper with earth-friendly vegetable-based inks.

Cover Design: Duncan Campbell, University of Regina Press
Text Design: John van der Woude Designs
Copy Editor: Alison Jacques
Proofreader: Dallas Harrison
Index: Patricia Furdek
Cover Art: Altered from the original by smartboy10 / stockphoto. Inspired by the promotional materials from the Imagining Child Welfare in the Spirit of Reconciliation conference.

Library and Archives Canada Cataloguing in Publication

Imagining child welfare in the spirit of reconciliation / edited by Dorothy Badry, H. Monty Montgomery, Daniel Kikulwe, Marlyn Bennett, and Don Fuchs.

(Voices from the prairies) Includes bibliographical references and indexes. Issued in print and electronic formats. ISBN 978-0-88977-575-6 (softcover).—ISBN 978-0-88977-576-3 (PDF).—ISBN 978-0-88977-577-0 (HTML)

1. Child welfare—Prairie Provinces. 2. Kinship care—Prairie Provinces. 3. Indian children—Care—Prairie Provinces. 4. Social work with children—Prairie Provinces. 5. Social work with Indians—Prairie Provinces. 6. Social service—Prairie Provinces. 7. Indians of North America—Kinship—Prairie Provinces. 8. Reconciliation—Social aspects—Prairie Provinces. 9. Prairie Provinces—Social conditions. I. Badry, Dorothy Eleanor, 1958-, editor II. Montgomery, H. Monty, 1962-, editor III. Kikulwe, Daniel, editor IV. Bennett, Marlyn, 1963-, editor V. Fuchs, Don, 1948-, editor VI. Series: Voices from the prairies

HV745.P73I43 2018 362.709712 C2018-903908-6 C2018-903909-4

10 9 8 7 6 5 4 3 2

University of Regina Press, University of Regina
Regina, Saskatchewan, Canada, S4S 0A2
TEL: (306) 585-4758 FAX: (306) 585-4699
WEB: www.uofrpress.ca

We acknowledge the support of the Canada Council for the Arts for our publishing program. We acknowledge the financial support of the Government of Canada. / Nous reconnaissons l'appui financier du gouvernement du Canada. This publication was made possible through Creative Saskatchewan's Creative Industries Production Grant Program.

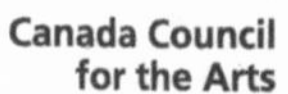

Conseil des Arts
du Canada

For the children. We dedicate this book to everyone involved with and striving toward a child welfare system that is caring and compassionate in the work of meeting the complex needs of children and families where child protection and family support are needed. The time for reconciliation and transformation has arrived.

Contents

Part III: Research

Part IV: Education

Foreword

Jeannine Carriere, Professor, School of Social Work, University of Victoria

I begin this foreword by acknowledging the territory on which I have the privilege to live, work, and play. I live on Vancouver Island, and more specifically I am allowed to teach among the WS'ANEC' (Saanich), Lkwungen (Songhees), and Wyomilth (Esquimalt) peoples of the Coast Salish Nation. My family and I live in the territory of the Cowichan Tribes near Duncan, BC, and every time I look out at the big cedars in my yard or hear the calling and chirping of eagles and ravens nearby I am grateful. I also wish to acknowledge my ancestors and the territory I come from. I am a Métis woman, and I grew up in southern Manitoba in the territory of the Anishinabe, Cree, Assiniboine, and historic Métis Nation. I acknowledge how my ancestors fought for our rights and the privileges we have today. I am also grateful for the experiences I had as a frontline social worker in Alberta. The Prairies will always be "home." As I write this foreword, I also acknowledge the many Indigenous children who have died in the "care" of child welfare or other authorities. May they be at peace knowing that there are people who remember them, including those who contributed to this book, and I am honoured to be part of this work.

As I ponder over the title and chapters of this book, I can't help but rethink the whole concept of reconciliation and how we are all working to "decolonize" and "reconcile." The "we" of course includes social work educators, administrators, and practitioners. It is enough to make my head spin most days; however, it is one of the most current and important discourses that we have before us as social workers and as people who live in Canada. How can we ignore the context that we have now come to, with our increased knowledge about the tragedies of residential schools, the impact of the Sixties Scoop or Indigenous child-removal system, and, for me as a Métis academic, the harsh reality that Dr. Catherine Richardson and I connected with in our research on Métis child welfare in 2017? Through our research, we discovered the lack of identification for Métis children in care is very problematic and renders them the invisible children of child welfare.

As Indigenous peoples, do we simply "move on," which is what a number of Canadians might wish us to do—and which raises the question, do settlers accept their role and complicity in these atrocities and "move on" as well? As Bopp, Brown, and Robb (2016) state, "the majority of Canadians, even those working in post-secondary institutions, know very little to nothing about Indigenous history, culture and current realities except for what they may have heard about in the media" (p. 3). I cannot imagine that we have arrived anywhere near that place of moving on yet, and in this foreword I ask the reader to imagine a world where there is no need for both decolonization and reconciliation. Imagine the peace, acceptance, and love of life we might all share in. Imagine how resources might be shared as well and how all of our children might be healthy, strong in their identities without having to fight for it, and able to walk freely in a world that does not discriminate every day against them and how they live. Imagine it. Is it comfortable? Is it where you wish you were, rather than sitting in the discomfort of knowing and not "knowing"? What can be done to reverse the tragedies and horrific actions toward Indigenous children and families in Canada to date? How can reconciliation truly happen when there is still so much work to be done in reversing the damage that has occurred? These are the questions I ask you to ponder as you move through this book and absorb its important information on promising practices with Indigenous children and families.

As you read these scholarly gems, I also ask that you consider some of the discourse on reconciliation. For example, I was truly inspired by Paulette Regan's (2010) book *Unsettling the Settler Within*, in which she describes the nature of colonialism as the gap between what non-Indigenous peoples think they are doing by engaging, with good intentions, in an intercultural dialogue and how Indigenous peoples experience that same event. She describes reconciliation as "regifting," where settlers have come forward with new promises, but she warns that the language of reconciliation can be a "regifting of the old package of settler promises wrapped in pretty paper" (p. 16). Regan states that "Canada has consistently sought bureaucratic solutions to a long list of 'Indian problems' such as poverty, low education levels, poor health and dysfunction" and that Canada has subscribed to a "peacemaker myth" (p. 34). Regan proposes that "challenging the peacemaker myth and critiquing reconciliation discourse requires us to be honest with ourselves about the actual impacts of colonial policies and practices upon the lives of Indigenous people" (p. 62). Following this line of critique, we need to consider the implications for child welfare work where policy and practice intertwine to have a great impact on the lives of Indigenous people. Deconstruction of the myth of "helping" is timely and necessary. Strategies that promote Indigenous values on child caring, on self-governance, and on relationality are some of the ways we can take a leap forward in truth telling and reconciliation. In this book, you will see examples of taking such a leap on behalf of children and families and learn about policies and practices that include restoration of Indigenous practices in caring for children and supporting their families.

All chapters in the book address some important aspects of policy and practice, and some are very specific as to how the decolonization of child welfare can be implemented. For example, Indigenous family reconnection is one of the implications of kinship care as described by Daniel Kikulwe and Julie Mann-Johnson. They examine kinship care as part of the 2010 UN Guidelines for the Alternative Care of Children's "global vision for the placement of children," and, in another chapter, these authors propose that we can understand the impacts of structural colonization on Indigenous children and families through kinship care assessments, policy, and legislation. Co-authors Shelley Thomas Prokop, Laura Hicks, and Rachel Melymick describe the importance of "community knowledge" and collaborative practices. Peter Choate and Gabrielle Lindstrom discuss how Indigenous peoples can be empowered to seek these new methodologies in ways that "respect their cultures" while protecting their children. Michelle Stewart, Lisa Lawley, Rachel Tambour, and Alexandra Johnson argue "for parents to be treated as experts in the care of their children" and that Indigenous mothers can "actively push back on colonial sensibilities that implicitly and explicitly facilitate the effacement of Indigenous families through the displacement of Indigenous children." Marlyn

Bennett and Ainsley Krone passionately highlight the need for access to Indigenous culture, knowledge, and teachings. Jennifer Hedges reminds us that "the proper education and training of child welfare workers is one of the Truth and Reconciliation Commission's calls to action." These are examples of strategies that can be implemented through some structural changes that demonstrate the will to fully engage in reconciliation with Indigenous peoples and child welfare. Rousseau (2015) proposes that,

> *within a reconciliatory framework, relationships and partnerships between Aboriginal communities and mainstream child welfare organizations can be developed to move the agenda forward for appropriate planning and development of Aboriginal child and family services (Blackstock et al., 2006). Basic principles for reconciliation involve acknowledging past mistakes through open communication, and establishing non-discriminatory practices within the child welfare system by affirming Indigenous families and communities as the best caregivers for Indigenous children and youth. Principles of reconciliation are intended to lead to improved systems of care for First Nations and Aboriginal children through strengthening child welfare professionals' capacity to respond to the needs of Aboriginal children and families and ensure that past mistakes are not repeated.* (p. 49)

I also wish to highlight that, in our research on Métis child welfare, Cathy Richardson and I imagine a landscape where Métis children are no longer "invisible." We encourage huge steps forward to ensure that Métis children are recognized consistently and significantly in child welfare legislation, standards, and policy. Some of us were heartbroken to see the outcome of the Sixties Scoop settlement as another form of exclusion for Métis people. This should be of particular relevance to an audience that is involved with the Prairie Child Welfare Consortium, and I encourage ongoing dialogue to address this huge gap in policy and practice. Reconciliation includes the work that has to be done with the Métis peoples of Canada.

In closing, I remain with some sense of discomfort, as I am sure some of you are experiencing as well. We need to remain vigilant and continue on this path to repair damage and restore healthy relationships to better serve Indigenous children and families and to acknowledge how this work matters to everyone. We are not asking that you feel shame, guilt, or sorrow. We are asking that we work together to ensure that events such as residential schools and massive adoption strategies never reoccur for Indigenous peoples of Canada. There are many ways that social workers can get involved as strong allies in activism and advocacy. For example, we have a desperate need to protect our lands and water. A number of Indigenous peoples have struggled in those deliberations, and joining their voices is something tangible that can occur on behalf of all our children. If you are an educator teaching social policy, you might want to consider a unit on environmental policy and its linkages to social work practice. Community engagement can lead the way to important relationship building that will impact our practice in significant ways and demonstrate the will to walk together as allies.

I leave you with these thoughts and wish you all the best in your work and life. I have always said to my students that child welfare work is "not for everyone," but if you can get involved you may be surprised and rewarded by the difference you can make in one child's life. I still believe that and reach out to you in respect.

All my relations.

References

Bopp, M., Brown, L., & Robb, J. (2016). Reconciliation in the academy: Why is Indigenization so difficult? Unpublished presentation. Vancouver, BC: University of British Columbia. Retrieved from https://teachingcommons.lakeheadu.ca/sites/default/files/inline-files/bopp%20brown%20robb_Reconciliation_within_the_Academy_Final.pdf

Carriere, J., & Richardson, C. (2017). The invisible children of child welfare: Legislation, policy, and governance models for Métis child welfare. In J. Carriere & C. Richardson (Eds.), *Calling our families home: Métis peoples experiences with child welfare* (pp. 50–73). Vernon, BC: J. Charlton Publishing.

Regan, P. (2010). *Unsettling the settler within: Indian residential schools, truth telling, and reconciliation in Canada*. Vancouver, BC: UBC Press.

Rousseau, J. (2015). The elusive promise of reconciliation in British Columbia child welfare: Aboriginal perspectives and wisdom from within the BC Ministry of Children and Family Development. *First Peoples Child & Family Review 10*(2). Retrieved from http://journals.sfu.ca/fpcfr/index.php/FPCFR/article/view/276

From the Editors

We are pleased to present the book *Imagining Child Welfare in the Spirit of Reconciliation: Voices from the Prairies*. The sixth publication of the Prairie Child Welfare Consortium (PCWC) in our Voices from the Prairies series, it emerges from the eighth biennial symposium, Imagining Child Welfare in the Spirit of Reconciliation, held in Winnipeg, Manitoba, on October 26, 27, and 28, 2016. To date the PCWC has hosted eight symposia—in Saskatoon in 2001; Winnipeg, 2003; Edmonton, 2005; Regina, 2007; Winnipeg, 2009; Edmonton, 2012; Saskatoon, 2014; and Winnipeg, 2016—with attendance increasing on a regular basis. The PCWC reflects a partnership between the faculties of social work at the University of Calgary, University of Manitoba, and University of Regina, as well as the Saskatchewan Federation of Indigenous Nations, the First Nations University of Canada's School of Indigenous Social Work, and child welfare directors in Alberta, Saskatchewan, Manitoba, and the Northwest Territories. The title of the book reflects the theme of imagining child welfare in the spirit of reconciliation at a time when public awareness of the work of child protection has increased, and the need for change remains ever constant. The PCWC conferences gather people together to share information, to share a vision of moving child welfare forward for all children in the spirit of reconciliation, to give voice to children, youth, and foster parents, and to acknowledge and honour child welfare concerns unique to Indigenous peoples of Canada.

The chapters in the book represent a selection of some of the outstanding presentations at the 2016 PCWC conference in Winnipeg. The conference was a community event that was supported by the Social Sciences and Humanities Research Council of Canada through a Connection Grant, our partner universities, Alberta Human Services, PolicyWise for Children & Families, the Government of Saskatchewan, Manitoba Families, the Thomas Sill Foundation, RedMane Technology, and Booth University College, reflecting a rich collaboration of government, university, and community partnerships. The conference program was infused with Indigenous tradition and culture and was guided by the wisdom of Elders.

The theme, "Imagining Child Welfare in the Spirit of Reconciliation," reflects important movements happening in child welfare, including a response to the recommendations of the Truth and Reconciliation Commission of Canada (TRC). The symposium focused on current trends and issues in child welfare through the lens of reconciliation and on moving an action plan forward. Its intention was to inspire and ignite action through discussion and planning. This book has attempted to capture the spirit and commitment of the symposium in imagining a child welfare system that moves forward in the spirit of reconciliation through co-operative, collaborative, and innovative interdisciplinary and intersectoral policy, program, and practice initiatives.

The keynote presentations by Cindy Blackstock, Robert Joseph, and Karen Joseph were highlights of our conference. Dr. Blackstock's advocacy and human rights work on behalf of and for First Nations children has been instrumental in shifting policy and practice in Canada, and the implementation of Jordan's Principle is making positive differences for children in need of supports. The Voices of Youth panelists were identified as the "heart and soul" of the conference, serving to confirm the need to always hear the voices of children and youth in our gatherings. The active involvement of the Office of the Children's Advocate and reflections on its rights-based work were critical aspects of the conference. This gathering of policy-makers, advocates, scholars, community members and leaders, frontline service providers, families, foster parents, and caregivers in order to engage in dialogue and promote understanding of the care and protection of children is a key value of the PCWC symposia. We all need to work together in this important work for children and families who represent the future of our Canadian society.

The symposium provided an opportunity to acknowledge and honour child welfare challenges unique to Aboriginal peoples and to learn about Aboriginal ways of knowing and practice. Further, the symposium provided a mechanism to promote and foster specific cross-sectoral collaboration among child welfare providers, as well as promoting scholarly research and human resource development. An initiative that was new at the 2016 symposium also recognized the contribution of students engaged in the child welfare system. Three scholarships, each worth five hundred dollars, were awarded to successful social work student applicants. Previous symposia have identified the need for developing innovative programs based on Indigenous knowledge and methods, and have pointed out the need to develop evidence-based, culturally appropriate, anti-oppressive practice to ensure that well-intentioned policy, programs, and intervention do no harm but continue to evolve to provide effective services to children and families at risk of child maltreatment.

The PCWC is a tri-provincial and northern multisector, cross-cultural child and family services network representing university educators, government, First Nations, and Métis in service training and service delivery administrators. Members of the network are dedicated to working together for the purpose of strengthening and advancing education and training, policy, service delivery, and research in aid of children and families in need. The development of the PCWC remains deeply influenced by Aboriginal and Métis peoples and agencies, concerned with the escalating numbers of their children and youth in the care of the state. This influence permeates the PCWC's vision, mission, and goals, which are directed toward ensuring that child and family services in the Prairie provinces and the North meet the needs of the children, families, and communities they support. Working together across many levels and sectors, the PCWC partners seek to influence, advocate, and change education, training, research, policy, and practice/service delivery through collaboration, innovation, and partnerships. Ensuring respect for the needs of Indigenous communities in the delivery of child welfare services is fundamental. In this quest, the PCWC seeks affiliation with other national child welfare bodies for joint initiatives that would further the PCWC mission and present a Prairie/northern perspective at the national level.

The book has four sections: (1) Policy; (2) Practice; (3) Research; and (4) Education. In each of these four sections, the authors provide scholarly observations and imaginings of child welfare practice, policy, and education as guided by a spirit of reconciliation. There is much work to be done as we move toward supporting and enacting the recommendations of the TRC. Consistent with the mandate of the PCWC, this book conveys the work of presenters at the 2016 conference in Winnipeg who were able to dedicate time and energy to the difficult task of presenting their experiences, ideas, and research in print form for publication purposes. The outstanding contributions reflect the dedication, commitment, and passion of the authors to co-create and renew a child welfare system that effectively helps children and families grow and thrive. It is the intention of the editors and the authors of this book to help strengthen the child welfare community in Canada by adding to its distinctive body of child welfare knowledge. Further, it is our hope that the perspectives contained within this book will contribute to child welfare transformations that lead to effective collaborative and co-operative interdisciplinary and intersectoral policy, programs, and practices that work to strengthen families in supportive communities. As always, the ultimate goal is to provide safe and healthy environments for children to live free from the risks of maltreatment.

The work of the Saskatchewan First Nations Family and Community Institute is profiled in a chapter in this book, and we have aligned ourselves with the values of this organization, including respect, love, bravery, wisdom, humility, honesty, and truth. We believe that these values are reflected in the chapters of this book, which sets the stage for the 2018 conference and our next publication, focused on a theme of change in the child welfare system in Canada.

—Dorothy Badry, H. Monty Montgomery,
Daniel Kikulwe, Marlyn Bennett, and Don Fuchs

Acknowledgements

This book represents the interprovincial collaboration among the Prairie Child Welfare Consortium (PCWC) partners: the Universities of Manitoba, Regina, and Calgary, and the First Nations University of Canada. It would not have been possible without the contributions of many people, and as editors we would like to thank each of them for their hard work and support. We must begin by acknowledging the outstanding contributions of the chapter authors, whose expertise, wisdom, and patience with the editing process have created a manuscript that will benefit the field of child welfare research and practice. The chapters reflect the breadth of the authors' considerable experiences as social work practitioners in the field of child welfare and as researchers, program planners, curriculum developers, and academics. Readers can learn more about the chapter authors in the Contributors section of the book.

The following people served as peer reviewers and provided feedback and suggestions on the chapters. Their comments helped sharpen the focus of and the key messages emerging in each chapter, and we are sincerely grateful for their input: Jason Albert, Dorothy Badry, Marlyn Bennett, Peter Choate, Don Fuchs, Deb Goodman, Gwen Gosek, Tom Grinnell, Daniel Kikulwe, Regine King, Brad McKenzie, Bruce MacLaurin, Denise Milne, H. Monty Montgomery, Vicki Russell, Christine Wekerle, and Alexandra Wright. We also offer our deep appreciation to Dr. Jeannine Carriere for writing the foreword for the book and to Monty Montgomery for writing the epilogue. We also acknowledge the contributions of Dr. Jackie Sieppert, Dr. Kathleen Kufeldt, and Les Jerome for their comments for the book's cover.

We are grateful to Bruce Walsh, director and publisher of University of Regina Press, who agreed to publish and distribute the hard copies of the book. We are greatly indebted to Donna Grant, senior editor at University of Regina Press, for her ongoing support and encouragement with the Voices from the Prairies series. We would also like to thank Karen Clark for her support over the past few months as we worked toward the manuscript submission. We would like to acknowledge the fine work of Marlyn and Raven Bennett on the artwork for the conference, which inspired the cover design of this book, and Alison Jacques for the detailed work of copyediting. Staff members from University of Regina Press meticulously corrected all of the inconsistencies across chapter formats and contributed substantially to the overall quality of the book.

We wish to acknowledge the time and commitment of the planning committee members of the PCWC's eighth biennial symposium held in Winnipeg, Manitoba, on October 26, 27, and 28, 2016. In particular, we would like to acknowledge Don Fuchs, Jennifer Hedges, and all those involved in organizing the Manitoba symposium. We encourage readers to visit the website (http://pcwcsymposium2016.ca/), where many of the presentations that formed the bases of the chapters contained in this book can be found.

We wish to thank the faculties of social work at the University of Calgary, University of Manitoba, and University of Regina, and First Nations University of Canada, for providing us with the encouragement and administrative infrastructure support to carry out much of the work of this book. The editors had valuable assistance from a number of people within their universities. The First Nations University of Canada hosted a face-to-face meeting of the PCWC steering committee on November 1 and 2, 2017, that included representation from the National Directors of Child Welfare and the deans and directors of our partner universities.

As well, we would like to thank the core partners of the PCWC for their co-operation and support: Faculty of Social Work, University of Manitoba; Faculty of Social Work, University of Calgary; Faculty of Social Work, University of Regina; First Nations University of Canada School of Indigenous Social Work; Manitoba Family Services; Alberta Human Services; Saskatchewan Child and Family Services; Federation of Sovereign Indigenous Nations; and Métis Association Alberta.

Introduction

Don Fuchs

Reconciliation means working together on what is best for Our Children.
—Dr. Chief Robert Joseph

The Truth and Reconciliation Commission of Canada (TRC) provided an opportunity for residential school survivors to tell their stories and a voice for their stories to be heard. Indigenous peoples in Canada are still living every day with impacts of the "cultural genocide" perpetrated by the assimilationist policies of the federal government that established the residential schools. The TRC challenged all of Canadian society to move forward in the spirit of reconciliation. The first five recommendations of its report address needed changes in child welfare (TRC, 2015). Realizing that opportunities to gather together in person are limited, the organizing committee of the eighth biennial Prairie Child Welfare Consortium (PCWC) symposium, held in Winnipeg, Manitoba, in 2016, sought to provide an opportunity for a wide range of individuals who are collectively committed to the safety, health, and well-being of children and youth to work collaboratively on imagining a child welfare system as one that is moving forward in the spirit of reconciliation.

Specifically, the aim of the symposium was to identify and support efforts that have been in place to address the recommendations of the TRC. The program therefore featured research, innovative programs, projects, and practices that are making a difference for at-risk children and families. It also placed special emphasis on supporting vulnerable Indigenous families and developing capacities in the Prairie child welfare system, through sharing innovative programs and building linkages to foster increased community engagement and collaboration. The symposium provided unique opportunities for both youth in care and foster parents to participate and share their perspectives.

In addition, symposium participants had opportunities to reflect on the changes that have taken place and to imagine the possibilities that still lie ahead for our organizations, our communities, our children and families, and ourselves. Many outstanding efforts are involved in the ongoing transformative initiatives being pursued within the field of child welfare on the Prairies at the practice, academic, and policy levels in a variety of settings—governments, academia, First Nations, Métis, and the non-profit sector—that are vital to the well-being of children and families.

In his plenary address to participants of the 2016 PCWC symposium, Dr. Chief Robert Joseph indicated that reconciliation is about our relationship with one another as we work together on what is best for our children and a core value in child welfare as a continuing way of being. He indicated that we all need to learn about the histories of the Indigenous children of Canada and to learn more about traditional ways of parenting. He called on child welfare professionals to love with courage and daring as they provide service to children and youth. Chief Joseph pointed out that it is important to acknowledge the barriers within the child welfare system. He went on to state that, as part of reconciliation, non-Indigenous people need to acknowledge that Indigenous children are not their children, and they need to learn to work alongside Indigenous families and communities to enable Indigenous children to grow and thrive. Finally, and of major importance, he indicated that non-Indigenous people must find ways of transforming responsibility back to the Original Peoples.

In a recent opinion piece, Cindy Blackstock (2017) notes that Minister of Justice Jody Wilson-Raybould had unveiled a set of ten principles intended to govern the relationship between the federal government and the Indigenous peoples. The minister affirmed that reconciliation will be achieved only through recognition of rights, respect, co-operation, and partnership. Ottawa now recognizes that Indigenous self-government and laws are critical to the country's future. Blackstock contends that these principles—even though they reflect the United Nations Declaration on the Rights of Indigenous Peoples only in part—are a step in the right direction. However, she goes on to point out that our country's success will be measured not by the formulation of these principles, but by their realization, maintaining that such a declaration of principles is meaningless if the old colonial, bureaucratic ways are perpetuated on the ground (Blackstock, 2017). She indicates that, currently, the federal government funds child welfare services for Indigenous children living on-reserve. Through decisions made by government officials in Ottawa about what is funded and what is not, the federal government effectively makes policy unilaterally and sets the level of service. She contends that there is no clearer example of the "colonial systems of administration and governance" that the statement of principles vows to discard (Blackstock, 2017), which extends colonialism beyond the Indian Act system, as the government cannot even be held to standards and rules set by Parliament.

Blackstock (2017) observes that the federal government's statement of principles affirms that Indigenous self-government is an inherent right and that this requires "space for the operation of Indigenous jurisdiction and laws." Yet current federal child welfare policy does the opposite. Indigenous child welfare agencies are funded only if they agree to comply with existing provincial laws (Blackstock, 2017). Blackstock points out that provincial laws were not designed with Indigenous culture in mind. Her incisive analysis indicates that there is much reconciliation work that needs to be done to find ways of transforming responsibility for child welfare services for Indigenous children and families back to the Original Peoples.

The theme of the PCWC symposium, "Imagining Child Welfare in a Spirit of Reconciliation," was most appropriate and timely for bringing together researchers, Indigenous and non-Indigenous practitioners, educators, and policy-makers for an opportunity to reflect on if, and how, the recommendations of the TRC relating to child welfare are being implemented.

The sense throughout the PCWC symposium was one of connectedness and appreciation for the opportunity to come together in a shared commitment to the spirit of renunciation and the well-being of children and families. The experience shed light on the important reconciliation work being done in child welfare and helped to mobilize participants. Overall, the symposium was inspiring and hopeful, igniting participants into action—to take the knowledge and experience gained from this symposium onward as we move forward in the spirit of reconciliation.

Following upon the success of the 2016 symposium, the PCWC steering committee collectively agreed to support the development of a sixth volume in the Voices from the Prairies book series that would draw upon the conference's overarching theme to discuss multiple dimensions of the reconciliation. The PCWC symposium presentations had spoken to the transformational power of healing and truth telling among service users and practitioners alike. Youth in care and foster parents shared their stories directly with service providers and policy-makers, some for the first time. Other presentations demonstrated how scholarly research can document evolving social phenomena and provide evidence in support of innovative reconciliation policies, programming, and practices to address the intergenerational trauma faced by many Indigenous children, families, and communities. Some presenters spoke to changes in policy directions that have occurred over time and their visions for future improvements. Still others spoke to the potential for transformation that can occur through well-designed training, professional development, and higher education. The range of reconciliation activities occurring within social policy, interpersonal relationships, scholarly research, and adult education is also used as a guiding framework for this book. The four thematic tracks established for the 2016 symposium naturally replicated themselves in the submissions that were received in response to the invitations distributed by the co-editors of this volume to the symposium presenters following the conclusion of the event. Accordingly, the chapters of this book have been grouped into four sections: (1) Policy; (2) Practice; (3) Research; and (4) Education.

Each section contains two or more complementary chapters that introduce and discuss varying dimensions of contemporary research and thinking relating to reconciliation initiatives taking place within the child welfare domain. Individually, each chapter articulates its authors' distinct subjective positioning with, knowledge of, and philosophical orientation to reconciliation in child welfare. Although chapters have been grouped together for presentation in this book, each chapter presents the authors' own scholarly imaginings relating to reconciliation within child welfare. Academic peers who possess subject-matter expertise on the topic have reviewed each chapter. Readers are encouraged to engage in the visions and imaginings portrayed in the following chapters to articulate progressive approaches to child welfare policy, standards, and practice that are guided by a spirit of reconciliation as set out in the vision outlined by Chief Joseph in his plenary address.

The first section of the book features two chapters that provide direction on moving policy forward into action so as to foster progressive change in the child welfare system. The directions put forward in these chapters are based on the first five recommendations of the TRC, which aim to engage and mobilize communities in strengthening their approaches to caring for children in their own communities.

In Chapter 1, Daniel Kikulwe and Julie Mann-Johnson examine how the United Nations' global visioning of kinship placements is being implemented in the Canadian Prairie region. The chapter examines the policy strategies used by the Prairie provinces to promote the concept of kinship care and their implications for social work practice. Through an examination of the UN legislative frameworks, they conclude that the use of kinship placements should be considered by child welfare authorities not only as preferable placements but also as a right for children whose needs cannot be met within the care of their parents. The assertion that kinship care should be a right for every child is based on the idea that children need cultural permanency, as this connects children to their historical roots.

In Chapter 2, Shelley Thomas Prokop, Laura Hicks, and Rachel Melymick share some of the promising practices that the Saskatchewan First Nations Family and Community Institute (SFNSCI) utilizes to develop and create ownership of culturally relevant training processes and products that enhance and build professionalism in First Nations child welfare in Saskatchewan, while maintaining alignment to the SFNSCI vision, its mission, and the many First Nations cultures in Saskatchewan.

The second section of this book presents four chapters whose aim is to foster progressive transformational changes in the actions and practices of child welfare practitioners, managers, and administrators in the spirit of reconciliation.

In Chapter 3, Julie Mann-Johnson and Daniel Kikulwe discuss the use and findings of a study to honour the voices of people who have shared their perspectives at public consultations and information-gathering events. Their use of existing qualitative data helps to amplify the voices of the Indigenous community with the hope of influencing policy and practice to support these traditional kinship caregiving networks. The authors grounded their data analysis in anti-colonial and critical ecological frameworks in an attempt to understand the impacts of structural colonization on Indigenous children and families through the current use of child welfare kinship assessments policy and legislation. Crucial elements in kinship care home assessments are identified and examined in relation to advance practice and for consideration in policy and program development.

Anne Marie McLaughlin, Richard Enns, and Deena Seaward highlight in Chapter 4 both the serious challenges and the opportunities that are frequently overlooked in designing policy and practices within standardized approaches. They present results of their research that identified rural-specific issues such as role ambiguity, resource inequity, and resource depletion; in addition, they identify broader systemic issues that hinder the healthy development and future success of youth as they leave care.

In line with the TRC's calls to action, Peter Choate and Gabrielle Lindstrom argue in Chapter 5 that First Nations, Inuit, and Métis peoples must be empowered to seek new methodologies in assessment of First Nations parents involved with child protection, in ways that respect their cultures and engage Indigenous communities while still enhancing the protection of children.

In Chapter 6, Michelle Stewart, Lisa Lawley, Rachel Tambour, and Alexandra Johnson argue that the TRC's calls to action outlined the need for a fundamental reordering of how child welfare is being enacted in Canada while bringing into sharp focus the ways that Indigenous children have been, and continue to be, impacted by settler colonialism through child welfare practices that aggressively displace children through removal from their families and communities. The authors contend that contemporary child welfare practices continue to justify the forced separation of families and children. Grounded in qualitative research, this chapter focuses on the resiliency of families who are raising children with a complex disability and the perspectives of two mothers in particular as they discuss the challenges of identifying culturally safe(r) programs/practices and the strategies they deploy to protect themselves and their children from unsafe practices. The authors argue for parents to be treated as experts in the care of their children—to be treated as paraprofessionals—and for a focus on the unique perspectives of Indigenous mothers as paraprofessionals.

The third section of this book draws attention to contemporary research associated with a range of phenomena, practices, and experiences that address specific aspects of reconciliation in the field of child welfare. This research has much to say about the past, present, and future of child welfare across the Prairie provinces, nationally, and internationally. The editors maintain that this current research may have significant impacts on child welfare service users currently and in the future. More well-designed studies that are culturally and ethically based are needed to create evidence that can monitor current efforts at responding to the calls to action by the TRC and be a catalyst for undertaking and examining new innovative reconciliation activities.

In Chapter 7, Marlyn Bennett and Ainsley Krone passionately argue that, for reconciliation in child welfare practice with girls and young women, a strong need for access to culture and to Indigenous knowledge and teachings must be recognized. They highlight the role of a healthy community in child welfare practice and identify what is missing in Manitoba's current public structures. Their chapter, which draws upon the words, wisdom, and guidance shared by community leaders, offers some groundbreaking recommendations directed at child welfare in Manitoba.

In Chapter 8, Bruce MacLaurin, Hee-Jeong Yoo and Morgan Demone offer an analysis of the Alberta Incidence Study of Reported Child Abuse and Neglect (AIS-2008), which is a provincial study that examined incidence and characteristics of child maltreatment in Alberta. These Incidence Studies are critical to informing policy and practice. Neglect, exposure to intimate partner violence, emotional maltreatment, physical abuse, and sexual abuse are the leading reasons for child welfare investigations, in that order, with a total of 14,403 substantiated investigations. This research remains critical and the Incidence Studies continue to make important contributions to the landscape of child protection in Canada.

David Este and Christa Sato, in Chapter 9, examine the perceptions of and experiences of South Sudanese refugees with Canada's child welfare systems. Using a thematic analysis, they explore specific issues that have made the relationship problematic. The chapter presents a series of strategies recommended by the study's respondents, which, the authors contend, are designed to improve the relationship between child welfare authorities and the South Sudanese community in the two respective urban centres.

Dorothy Badry, Christine Walsh, Meaghan Bell, and Kaylee Ramage indicate in Chapter 10 that there is a great need to examine the intricate link between fetal alcohol spectrum disorder (FASD) and youth leaving the child welfare system who move into unstable, often tenuous housing with an outcome of homelessness as young adults. The authors argue that the needs of youth with FASD who are leaving the child welfare system are not well understood, and their vulnerability places them at increased risk for exploitation. They provide the insightful results of their interviews with homeless youth who have aged out of care and discuss the implications for policy, programs, and practices of recommendations that would support better outcomes for homeless youth with FASD.

The final section of this book focuses broadly on the transformative potential of education (teaching) and training within child welfare. In keeping with one of the key purposes of the Prairie Child Welfare Consortium—namely, pre-professional education and practitioner training—the editors have devoted the concluding section of this volume to authors whose writing speaks to the education and training domains of child welfare service delivery. When practitioners and instructors engage with one another using purposefully selected curricular resources, practice can indeed shift. It is no surprise that many of the calls to action and recommendations arising from external child welfare practice and program reviews explicitly call for better training of helping professionals. This concluding section presents two chapters that detail the critical necessity of creating and utilizing accurate and timely curricular materials and teaching methods as catalysts for self-reflective and self-reflexive individual learning. These, they contend, are necessary to bring about the transformative change needed to foster imaginative reconciliation practices in the child welfare system.

In Chapter 11, Cathy Rocke and Judy Hughes maintain that a recognized gap exists between the social work classroom, where knowledge and skills about practice are taught, and the field placements where students are expected to apply these skills. They describe the development of a training video and instructor's and student's manuals for child welfare practice intended to reduce this gap. The instructor's and student's manuals were developed collaboratively with experienced child welfare workers to highlight the skills needed in this challenging social work field. Rocke and Hughes discuss future plans for the use of this teaching resource to bring about innovative and reconciliation-focused practice.

Child welfare workers are responsible and accountable for providing a variety of services that require a vast array of knowledges and skills related to complex individual, family, and community situations. In Chapter 12,

Jennifer Hedges contends that there is a gap in the research on how social work education programs are helping to prepare social workers to make a difference and be successful in this field of practice. Child welfare services are delivered through a highly legalized and bureaucratic system that presents unique challenges for social workers that highlight a tension between helping and controlling. Hedges points out that Indigenous children and families and other racialized minorities are highly overrepresented, and there is a great need to identify more effective, and culturally appropriate, ways to improve the preparation of social workers. The proper education and training of child welfare workers comprise one of the TRC's calls to action. Hedges maintains that barriers continue to exist between anti-oppressive frameworks and child welfare practice. Her chapter presents a review of the literature, exploring the relationship between social work education and preparation for work in child welfare through a critical Indigenous theory lens.

Collectively, the twelve chapters in this book provide significant insight into some of the most pressing issues for child welfare research, policy, practice, and training across Canada. We have also included discussion questions with each chapter as a means to support deepening knowledge on the topics addressed in the book. We believe these questions could be helpful in teaching and learning activities in the areas of social work and social justice. The work of the editors and the contributing authors has documented a range of significant dimensions and innovative practices that may well help to shape the child welfare theories, practices, and services of tomorrow. It is not a road map for change that is presented here but rather a snapshot of where child welfare scholarship currently stands in relation to imagining child welfare as permeated by the spirit of reconciliation and in relation to the call to action emerging from the testimony of the TRC.

It is the intention of the editors and the authors of this book to extend the dialogue on implementing the calls to action and recommendations of the TRC, in a spirit that promotes reconciliation with a focus on decolonizing the child welfare system. Collaboratively, our goal is to work toward strengthening the child welfare community in Canada by adding to its distinctive body of practical child welfare knowledge.

Throughout the PCWC symposium of 2016, the event's participants were prompted to reflect on ways of moving the TRC's recommendations pertaining to child welfare forward. Particularly, the symposium provided participants with an opportunity to reflect on whether, and how, the recommendations are being implemented in the ongoing transformative initiatives being pursued within the field of child welfare at the practice, academic, and policy levels in a variety of settings: governments, academia, First Nations, Métis, and the non-profit sector. We hope that this book will prompt ongoing reflection and dialogue and promote decolonization, social justice, and reconciliation policy, programs, and practices in child welfare in Canada. We hope that the imagination and dialogue collectively shared in the 2016 symposium, and in this book, will in some way assist in the implementation of the TRC's recommendations. In this work, we all aspire to create environments where children are safe, healthy, and thriving.

References

Blackstock, C. (2017, August 1). Reforming child welfare first step toward reconciliation: Opinion. *Toronto Star*, A11.

TRC (Truth and Reconciliation Commission of Canada). (2015). *Truth and Reconciliation Commission of Canada: Calls to Action*. Winnipeg, MB: TRC. Retrieved from http://www.trc.ca/websites/trcinstitution/File/2015/Findings/Calls_to_Action_English2.pdf

PART I

Policy

CHAPTER 1

Exploring Human Rights Approaches to Kinship Care Provision in the Prairie Provinces: Implications for Social Work Practice

Daniel Kikulwe and Julie Mann-Johnson

Introduction

Based on a large body of literature, it is clear that kinship placements are becoming an important part of child welfare practices around the world, including in Canada (Burke & Schmidt, 2009; Kroll, 2007; Stoner, 2006; Trocmé, Knoke, & Blackstock, 2004). This global shift in focus toward kinship care as a placement option for abused and neglected children is in line with the 2010 United Nations Guidelines for the Alternative Care of Children (hereafter, UN Guidelines). In this policy, the UN defines kinship care as a formal or informal family placement that includes the child's extended family or close friends. This definition of kinship assumes that a family network would provide support to a child who is at risk of harm by the parents.

The main purpose of this chapter is to examine how the UN's global visioning of kinship placements is being implemented in the Canadian

Suggested Citation: Kikulwe, D., & Mann-Johnson, J. (2018). Exploring human rights approaches to kinship care provision in the Prairie provinces: Implications for social work practice. In D. Badry, H. Montgomery, D. Kikulwe, M. Bennett, & D. Fuchs, (Eds.), *Imagining child welfare in the spirit of reconciliation* (pp. 3–26). Regina, SK: University of Regina Press.

Prairie region, which includes Manitoba, Saskatchewan, and Alberta. Research in the Prairie region identifies that an increasing number of Indigenous children are in care (Blackstock, 2007; Galley, 2010; Lavergne, Dufour, Trocmé, & Larrivée, 2008; Trocmé et al., 2004). Also increasing is the concern regarding placement of immigrant and racialized children in state care in various jurisdictions in Canada (UNCRC, 2012). The care and placement of Indigenous and racialized children in Canada warrant a review from a human rights perspective that considers the use of kinship care as a cultural safety net when parental care is not an option.

In order to explore this topic, we completed a literature review, focusing on the UN's global vision of kinship placements and an examination of the child welfare policies and legislation that the Prairie provinces have adopted to promote kinship care. We use children's rights as articulated in the United Nations Convention on the Rights of the Child (UNCRC) and the UN Guidelines as a lens through which to examine the promotion of kinship care in Manitoba, Saskatchewan, and Alberta. The child-centred philosophy inherent in both the UNCRC and the UN Guidelines provides insights into the global visioning of the UN, as well as into the work being done in the Prairie region to promote and implement kinship care in child welfare practice.

The chapter is organized into four sections, beginning with the review of the core values undergirding the UNCRC and the UN Guidelines as they relate to the topic of kinship care. The second section focuses on existing child welfare legislation and policies in the Prairie region that promote kinship care. Included in this section is a discussion that advances the idea of applying a child rights approach in promoting the use of kinship placements in child welfare practice and in identifying limitations of child welfare kinship policies. The third section focuses on the implications of kinship placements in child welfare–focused social work practice. The last section summarizes the key ideas of the chapter.

The UN Convention on the Rights of the Child and Guidelines for the Alternative Care of Children

In this section, the central argument posed is that kinship homes are not simply placements but sites that provide cultural permanency for children who cannot be cared for by their biological parents. Denby (2016) defines cultural permanency as a belief that children need to maintain a connection to their historical roots, language, ethnicity, traditions, and heritage. In connection with the central argument, we also claim that kinship as an alternative form of care must be supported to achieve the best outcomes for children. In this section, our discussions of kinship care and our focus on cultural permanency and support for kin caregivers are consistent with children's needs and priorities as identified in the UNCRC, which was adopted by the UN General Assembly on November 20, 1989.

Canada became a signatory to the UNCRC in 1990 and ratified it in 1991. The UNCRC is the most widely and rapidly ratified international human rights treaty in history, and, as of 2016, it has been ratified by 196 nations (Bernstein, 2016). Under Article 20(2) of the UNCRC, States Parties are obligated to provide alternative care for children who are temporarily or permanently removed from family environments in which their best interests cannot be met. This provision under the UNCRC is strongly supported by the resolution on Guidelines for the Alternative Care of Children adopted by the UN General Assembly (2010), which clearly identifies the measures that should be taken by States Parties to strengthen the care for children outside of parental care. It is important to note that Canada has obligations and commitments associated with being a signatory that include minimizing disruption of the child's educational, cultural, and social life, as noted in paragraph 11 of the UN Guidelines.

Cultural Permanency

Kinship care tends to be a common parenting practice used among racial and ethnic communities and needs to be the first option on the permanency plan and in child welfare practice (Goodley, 2011). Article 20(3) of the UNCRC recognizes the importance of cultural continuity for a child, including a strong focus on the child's ethnic, religious, cultural, and linguistic background (Wright, Hiebert-Murphy, Mirwaldt, & Muswaggon, 2005). The UNCRC recognizes that a child's cultural permanence can be achieved through the extended family networks or kin of the child. A child's culture, religion, and familial and social relationships are more likely to be maintained when a child is placed in kinship arrangements. Gonzales-Mena (2001) takes the position that "children's identities [including their cultural background] should be preserved and kept intact" (p. 368). Guided by the principles of the UNCRC, preserving children's identities should be both a goal and an issue of equity and social justice because children need to be rooted in their culture and attached to their families. It is important to note an Indigenous cultural belief that the responsibility for a child's well-being extends beyond the immediate family to the extended family (Pringle, Cameron, Durocher, & Skelton, 2010). The Indigenous view of family places the child within kinship systems through clan, band, and tribal membership. Ideally, children are cared for within a cultural community, with their grandparents, aunts, uncles, and older cousins all responsible in some part for child rearing (Pringle et al., 2010). This belief—that the entire community shares the responsibility of child caring—is in line with the UNCRC. Canadian researchers Gough (2006) and Cuddeback (2004) emphasize the importance of children being supported to maintain family relationships while other permanency options are being considered for them, arguing that family members promote greater cultural and spiritual affiliations for children.

In African American communities, families play a pivotal role in the nurturing, socialization, social functioning, competence, and success of adolescents (Hopps, Tourse, & Ollie, 2002). The family is a place where youth learn to cope and gain the survival skills necessary for dealing with an external environment that is hostile and noxious to the extent that it is raced, gendered, and classed (Hopps et al., 2002). This view is complemented by Chipungu and Goodley (2004), who argue that for youth developing coping skills involves active participation in community—including spiritual and family rituals such as naming ceremonies and rites of passage that emphasize the children's racial identity—and having a place within a family and community that connects them to a larger historical and contemporary reality. Family homes hold history, culture, and identity, and Chipungu and Goodley (2004) state that such connectedness provides a stable force that can foster resilience in a child during difficult times. Therefore, if the best interests of children cannot be served within their families and histories, alternatives that promote and maintain kinship ties must be considered.

According to the UN Committee on the Rights of the Child (2012), "the principle of the best interests of the child is neither widely known, nor appropriately integrated and applied in Canadian legislative, administrative and judicial proceedings, and in policies" (p. 7). The committee expressed "serious concern regarding the frequent removal of children from their families as a first resort within the Canadian child welfare system" (p. 12). Investment in kinship placements was noted as lacking within the Canadian child welfare system (UNCRC, 2012). Canada's practice contradicts the underlying philosophy of the UN Guidelines, which gives due respect to cultural continuity. The same philosophy and focus on the continuity of the child's upbringing and ethnic, religious, cultural, and linguistic background also underlie Article 20(3) of the UNCRC.

Even when removed from their homes, children can have meaningful access to their families; this can result in a sense of belonging and hence further the best interests of the child (Kikulwe, 2014). Wensley (2006) argues that children's cultural and family backgrounds cannot be treated as abstract concepts, meaning that good outcomes for children are related to cultural and community connections. The less abstract the cultural/family background is for workers, the greater the opportunity for them to change practices and knowledge to ensure better outcomes for children, including their cultural permanency.

Bernhard (2012) comments that the celebration of diversity in Canada is still superficial because there is often an underappreciation of the importance of culture in terms of the family and child functioning. Bernstein (2016) adds that the UNCRC is a resource that can be used to create a child welfare infrastructure that promotes cultural permanency for children in care. He argues that part of the problem in using the UNCRC as an advocacy tool is that it is not well publicized or used as a pivotal children's rights international treaty. In other words, a greater emphasis needs to be placed on the role and use of the UNCRC in advancing the idea that children are individuals with their own rights. Such an approach will help ensure that children become visible members of society and that their social, cultural, physical, educational, and emotional needs become a higher priority in government policies, legislation, and budgets.

To summarize, a sustained focus on children's rights fits with Goodley's (2011) idea of the need for a culturally based strategy to promote child welfare practices that preserve families and the connectedness between children and their communities. This view of cultural permanency for children in need of protection can be achieved by supporting kin caregivers, as discussed in the next section.

Support for Kin Caregivers

The UNCRC's philosophy that children should be cared for by kin is rooted in an understanding that a child's biological parents may not always have the ability to provide care, implying that children need to be protected from abusive and neglectful parents. Paragraph 56 of the UN Guidelines indicates that both kin caregivers and children in those placements should receive any necessary financial and other support that would promote the child's welfare and protection. Canada, as a signatory to the UNCRC, has committed to the obligation of care and protection of children. The issue of who cares for children in need of protection requires examination through a human rights lens that focuses on the best interests of children and families, which by extension should include kin. Other scholars emphasize that protecting children within kinship systems means also protecting and preserving their families (see Bennett, Blackstock, & De La Ronde, 2005; Leschied, MacKay, Raghunandan, Sharpe, & Sookoor, 2007). Supporting kin caregivers is another important facet of UNCRC Article 20(2) because kin caregivers not only make possible the safety, health, and well-being of children in their care but also help maintain their culture, heritage, and religious beliefs.

In examining the American kinship system, Denby (2016) writes that kin caregivers frequently do not receive the services they need, indicating that many placements are poorly supported by government and the child welfare system. The underlying expectation is that relatives are supposed to care for children without the same supports afforded to foster care homes that are licensed and fall within the scope of child welfare placement services. In Australia, the term "granny burnout" has been coined because so many elderly grandparents are caring for their children's children (Hammill, 2001). In Canada, Fuller-Thomson (2005) as well as Callahan, Brown, MacKenzie, and Whittington (2004) have noted a high incidence of poverty among kinship caregivers and a belief that the family is an independent unit that should take care of its own. Denby (2016) indicates that many kin caregivers are women and elderly. It is clear that the UNCRC's ideals of maintaining the child's identity cannot be implemented without solidifying support for kinship caregivers. In the next section of the chapter, we explore the existing child welfare legislation and policies in the Prairie region that promote the use of kinship care.

Provincial Kinship Policies

In this section, we review ten policy documents in order to determine whether the UN's ideals of alternative care have been translated to the child welfare contexts of the Prairie provinces. Each of the three Prairie provinces—Manitoba, Alberta, and Saskatchewan—has its own child welfare legislative framework, which therefore requires that we examine how kinship care policies in each jurisdiction, separately, are harmonized with the ideals of the UNCRC. For the purposes of this chapter, we reviewed the following Saskatchewan provincial documents:

- The Child and Family Services Act (CFSA)
- *Children's Services Manual*
- Ministry of Social Services Regulations, Chapter-5.1 Reg 145 (2007), as amended by Saskatchewan Regulations 75/2010.

For Alberta, we looked closely at the following documents:

- Child, Youth, and Family Enhancement Act (CYFEA)
- *Kinship Care Review Report*
- "Immediate Kinship Placement."

We reviewed three policy documents for the province of Manitoba:

- The Child and Family Services Act (CFSA)
- The Child and Family Services Authorities Act
- *Child and Family Services Standards Manual.*

In this review of the existing child welfare legislation and kinship policies, we examine whether the Prairie provinces' policies and practices have linkages to the UNCRC's ideals of kinship care with local child welfare policies when it comes to extended family care for children who are at risk of abuse and neglect. Two key questions are addressed in this section: (1) What are the policies and legislation that apply to kinship care in the three Prairie provinces? (2) What are the limitations of these provincial kinship policies and child welfare legislation? As noted below, each of the three provinces has taken steps to adopt the use of kinship care in its child welfare policies and legislation.

Child Welfare Policies

Saskatchewan

On December 11, 1991, the Saskatchewan legislature declared its support of the UNCRC, stating that the UNCRC was in line with the province's commitment to and responsibility for the care and well-being of all children in the province (Legislative Assembly of Saskatchewan, 1991). In June 2002, Saskatchewan introduced a children's services model that supported the use of kinship care as a placement priority. Subsequently, in June 2003, amendments to the Child and Family Services Act were passed by the legislature to provide a framework for kinship care (Sandstorm-Smith, 2004). Under section 53 of the Act, children are to be maintained, wherever possible, within their families and kinship networks. In 2007, Saskatchewan passed Chapter-5.1 Regulation 145, and part of the objectives of this legislation included (1) building and maintaining strong families and communities; (2) maintaining children, wherever possible, within their families and kinship networks; and (3) supporting the stable, long-term attachment of children to their families and kinship networks. In 2010, the province amended Chapter-5.1 Regulation 145, with the main change being to ensure monitoring of Saskatchewan government programs, services, and initiatives to determine their impact on women and families, but the legislative objective of keeping children within kin networks was maintained.

Saskatchewan's *Children's Services Manual* requires child protection workers to explore extended family placement regularly as part of the ongoing case planning for a child in care, which is a commendable child welfare practice. However, scholars such as Geen (2004) have suggested that early identification of kin caregivers in the placement of children is ideal. There are several reasons for this. Early kinship placement can minimize the trauma a child experiences when removed from the family home. With prolonged in-care child placements, the identification of a kin caregiver becomes more difficult. Furthermore, there may be tensions within families, reluctance on the part of parents to share information regarding available extended family, or hesitancy on the part of relatives because they may have tried in the past and failed due to ongoing struggles with addiction or mental health.

Regarding the future of relative (kinship) placements, the Saskatchewan government faced strong public criticism following the tragic death in

2012 of a four-year-old child and serious harm to her two-year-old sister at the hands of Kevin and Tammy Goforth (Fraser, 2017). Kevin and Tammy were extended family/kin caregivers under the program known as "Person of Sufficient Interest" (PSI), which is part of the Saskatchewan Child and Family Services Act. The couple were sentenced to prison terms after a jury found that their actions had led to the severe malnourishment of both girls (Fraser, 2017). In light of this tragedy, and of the review conducted by the Saskatchewan Child Advocate, it is anticipated that government changes will be made to the "Person of Sufficient" program, which currently provides relative placement opportunities for children. When such tragic incidents occur, there is often a public outcry, demanding that children in kinship placement deserve the same level of protection as those in the regular foster care system.

Alberta

In Alberta, the inclusion of extended family and significant others as the first placement option for children in need of protection was legislated for the first time in 2004, with the Child, Youth, and Family Enhancement Act (CYFEA; Alberta, Children and Youth Services, 2009). Section 2 of the provincial Act, also known as the "Matters to Be Considered," requires that any child welfare decision should take into account the benefits to the child if placed with the extended family.

According to Alberta's Immediate Kinship Placement policy (Alberta Human Services, 2014a), children or youth in kinship care are entitled to receive the same services, basic maintenance per diem, and supports as children in foster care. While training is not required for kinship care providers beyond the initial orientation, they are encouraged to access foster care training or other training that would support their ability to care for the child placed in their home. If a child is placed in the care of relatives, those kinship care providers are reimbursed for costs associated with orientation training, including babysitting and transportation. The kinship caregiver also has ongoing contact with child welfare workers (Alberta, Children and Youth Services, 2009). The Kinship Care Policy also requires that attention be paid to family history and that poverty not be considered a barrier to placement unless risks are such that they cannot be mitigated through the kinship care support plan or other supports. One interpretation of the Alberta kinship policy is that it incorporates the idea of social justice and strongly emphasizes the notion of the child belonging to the family, in line with Article 20(3) of the UNCRC.

To support its implementation of the Child Intervention Practice Framework in Alberta, the government released *Principle Based Practice Strategies* in 2014 with a goal of strengthening kinship connection by ensuring that children and youth are placed first in kinship care homes. The intent of the Alberta Practice Strategies was to highlight the importance of providing immediate support to kinship caregivers to ensure both best practices and best interests of the child (Alberta Human Services, 2014b).

Manitoba

The placement of children and youth in kinship care placements is articulated in Manitoba's Child and Family Services Act (CFSA) of 1985. The Act explicitly indicates that extended families and communities have both a right and a responsibility to care for their children and a right to receive preventive and supportive services directed to preserving the family unit. In 2003, Manitoba also proclaimed the Child and Family Services Authorities Act, which led to the creation of four authorities: First Nations Authority of Northern Manitoba, First Nations Authority of Southern Manitoba, Metis Authority, and General Authority. Each of the four authorities has the mandate to provide services to families and children from its own cultural group anywhere in the province (McKenzie & Wharf, 2016). Ethnicity, spirituality, language, and culture are among the many factors that these authorities are required to recognize when serving families and children under the Child and Family Services Authorities Act.

The Manitoba *Child and Family Services Standards Manual* also directs child welfare workers not only to consider family residences (kin homes) but also to follow specific safety procedures prior to placing children in the homes of extended family. What stands out in the manual is the onus placed on child welfare workers to determine the suitability of the family placement, as well as the inclusion of the community through Community Committees (individuals, groups, and organizations that may assist in meeting the needs of families) in approving the home placements for children at risk.

Based on our review of the existing policies, kinship care is valued and supported differently in all three Prairie provinces. Overall, relational permanency is emphasized in the provincial child welfare legislation of Saskatchewan, Alberta, and Manitoba, which is consistent with the

UNCRC. Through legislation and policies, provincial governments have provided child welfare agencies with a broad mandate to place children with kin caregivers as the first placement option, but this is not a guaranteed right, an idea that will be further explored in later discussions but nonetheless is raised here to demonstrate its importance in connection to the principles of the UNCRC. Alberta has developed specific policies that treat kinship foster care differently than non-kin foster care. Saskatchewan's and Manitoba's child welfare legislations also articulate relative placement as a preferred form of permanency for children, which is critical not only for policy and practice but also to ensure children's rights and is a practice that recognizes the importance of cultural continuity for children who cannot be raised in their parental homes. Although child welfare legislation is in place in all three Prairie provinces, we cannot lose sight of the policy limitations and their impacts on children and their families, which form the main discussion in the next section.

Policy Limitations

This section discusses four key limitations of the current child welfare policies:

1. Use of kinship placements, which raises concerns of underutilization and questions of cultural permanency and overrepresentation of Indigenous children in care.
2. Underutilization of kinship placement assessments, which are used to determine the appropriateness of relatives' homes and the potential risks to the child. (In discussing kinship assessments, we address the ongoing debates in child welfare of whether kinship care providers must meet all legislated requirements to qualify as an approved home.)
3. Lack of cultural understanding and of confidence in the capacity of Indigenous and racialized families to raise their children.
4. Tension between federal and provincial/territorial governments and its impact on the implementation of the UNCRC.

We will begin with concerns about the underutilization of kinship placements.

Underutilization of Kinship Placements

Although Manitoba, Saskatchewan, and Alberta have each taken steps to introduce policies and legislation on the utilization of kinship placements, these measures have limitations, and many child rights issues have still not been adequately addressed by the provinces' statutory placement requirements. Chief among these is the overrepresentation of Indigenous children in care. A report by Kozlowski, Sinha, Petti, and Flette (2012) indicated that 85 per cent of all children in the care of Manitoba's Department of Family Services and Labour on March 31, 2006, were Aboriginal (70 per cent of all children in care were First Nations, and 9 per cent were Métis). In 2017, it was reported that 69 per cent of all children and youth in care in Alberta were Indigenous (Alberta, 2017). In its 2012 report "Concluding Observations: Canada," the UNCRC noted a lack of Canadian data on the number of children aged fourteen to eighteen years who were placed in alternative care facilities (see FNCFS, 2012). Swift and Callahan (2009) and Blackstock, Trocmé, and Bennett (2004) have recognized as unacceptable the overrepresentation of racialized and Indigenous children in foster care and report that no viable plan appears to be in place to change this trend. According to the UNCRC (2012), Canada needs to put in place "urgent measures to address the overrepresentation of Indigenous and African-Canadian children in the criminal justice system and out-of-home care" and to take "immediate steps to ensure that in law and practice, Indigenous children have full access to all government services and receive resources without discrimination" (para. 33[a], [d]). These UNCRC recommendations mean that child welfare authorities need to consider the wide variety of permanency options available, particularly for those populations that are overrepresented in the system.

Kinship Assessments

The preceding discussion of the underutilization of kinship foster homes also links to kinship assessments. This underutilization could potentially be attributed to the requirement that child welfare agencies complete assessments of potential kinship caregivers to determine the appropriateness of their homes and the risks they may pose to the children needing care. Within child welfare, kinship care assessments can be justified for a number of reasons: they can help to determine the ability of the kinship caregivers to manage access with the birth parents; to determine what type of supports or information are required; and to reduce future risk of harm or abuse to the child. However, in a number of jurisdictions, the many requirements demanded by home assessments (criminal background and child welfare checks, as well as references and medical checks) are a deterrent for kin caregivers.

One of the ongoing debates in child welfare is whether kinship care providers must meet all legislated requirements that apply to foster parents in order to become an approved home that is ready to receive children (Stoner, 2006). For example, in Manitoba, these provincial standards and home approvals have become barriers to potential kin caregivers because medical backgrounds and checkups are to be completed by family doctors, yet many of the families do not have a family doctor (Marks, 2015). A medical reference from a walk-in clinic is not accepted, and thus some very loving and responsible people are disqualified from caring for children (Marks, 2015). The Child Welfare League of America (2000) argues that some flexibility should be exercised in terms of compliance and standards that are unrelated to child protection and safety, such as physical space requirements for children's sleeping arrangements. Some of this flexibility is articulated in the Alberta kinship policy and practice strategies that require child welfare workers not only to preserve the family unit but also to sensitively engage the family, using a strengths-based approach, when completing home assessments.

Lack of Cultural Understanding

While kinship placement has become one of the fastest growing placement options in North America because of legislative changes, it remains an underutilized option for children in need of protection. This is particularly true for Indigenous children. Bobbi Pampana, CEO of the Southern First Nations Network of Care, argued that the inability to use kinship placements suggests that traditional values and cultural beliefs have been de-prioritized within the child welfare system (Marks, 2015). McKay (2009) argued that "Present-day child welfare policies and practice continue to fuel historical harms by failing to understand the significance of culture and community to indigenous identity and well-being" (p. xx). Mullaly (2010) states that the ability of marginalized populations, including Indigenous peoples and immigrants, to parent is always being questioned, that these groups are regularly under surveillance, and that their rights are less well protected than the rights of parents of the dominant group. Mullaly goes on to note that these marginalized groups live in constant fear of being separated from their children.

The lack of understanding of the importance of cultural permanency has meant that mainstream Canadian society still has little confidence in the capacity of Indigenous and racialized families to raise their children, which points to the conclusion of the UN Committee on the Rights of the Child that the UNCRC is not solidly embedded in Canadian law, policy, or the national psyche, including social work practice. Part of the problem of the underutilization of kinship placements is not only in the issue of espousing the ideas of the UNCRC and implementing them in our practices but also in the concerns over the lack of trust of racialized and Indigenous kinship caregivers by social workers. Burke (2009) argues that some child welfare workers may perceive foster care placements as the first choice because they need not give much consideration to the placement suitability and the safety of the home.

Tension between Federal and Provincial/Territorial Governments in Implementing the UNCRC

Another policy limitation noted by Bernstein (2016) is linked to Canada's inadequate implementation of the UNCRC. In Canada, the federal government is responsible for ensuring compliance with the UNCRC within its sphere of jurisdiction, but many of the UNCRC directives fall under provincial jurisdiction (e.g., social services, health, education, and child welfare). This division of jurisdictional responsibility creates a significant challenge in terms of coordinating, implementing, and monitoring progress in the area of children's rights, including placement options. Bernstein concludes that stalemates are frequent, with federal officials maintaining they cannot do more to advance children's rights because of provincial jurisdiction. Similarly, provinces/territories are sometimes reluctant to assume any direct responsibility for meeting international commitments undertaken by Canada at the federal level.

Bernstein (2016) also points to "Concluding Observations: Canada" by the UNCRC (2012), in which the committee recommended that Canada address disparities in the treatment of Indigenous children. Similarly, in January 2016, the Canadian Human Rights Tribunal ruled (in *First Nations Child and Family Caring Society of Canada et al.*) that the federal government discriminates against Indigenous children on reserves by failing to provide the same levels of child welfare services and funding that exist elsewhere in the country. The tribunal ruling was an important development in the child welfare field because it reaffirmed the UNCRC, which guarantees children the right to non-discrimination under Article 2. This ruling supports the need to strengthen equitable service provision for Indigenous families and communities. In an interview with CBC News, Grand Chief Derek Nepinak of the Assembly of Manitoba Chiefs noted that less funding to support Indigenous families has meant more children ending up in the child welfare system ("First Nations Leader," 2016). We have yet to see the steps the federal government will take regarding this ruling by the tribunal—or the direction those steps will take.

Implications for Social Work

In this section, we discuss how kinship placements can be promoted and supported through social work practice at both micro and macro levels. At the micro level, the discussion focuses on the adoption of a child's rights approach to meet the needs of children and the potential kin caregivers, while the emphasis at the macro level is on the increasing number of children in care and the decreasing number of foster beds. The discussion of social work support for kinship placements at the micro and macro levels is intended to explore the use of alternative care, according to human rights approaches.

The Micro Level

At the micro level, Canada's commitment to the UNCRC means, as Bernstein (2016) aptly puts it, that children are to be placed at the centre of social work and perceived as belonging to their families, their communities, and their cultures. In the context of the UN Guidelines, the option of children being placed with kin caregivers when experiencing maltreatment should not be mere rhetoric but rather the reality of their lives. As in many other Canadian jurisdictions, child welfare legislation in the Prairie provinces has created a legal opportunity to shift social work practices to enhance and influence better outcomes for children at risk by using family placements. Although the kinship policy shift in the Prairies is a positive gesture by those three provincial governments, there is an equal need to fund social work positions that are specifically designated to recruit kinship caregivers and maintain kin caregivers' homes. For example, Shlonsky and Berrick (2001) note that kin caregivers need social work attention and support, but they regularly have less contact with social workers than do foster parents. Existing research also confirms the need to focus on the financial, emotional, and material assistance of kin caregivers because, when children are placed with kin, it is often due to a crisis, unplanned situation, or emergency, thus creating monetary demands on those relatives (Scannapieco & Hegar, 2002). Further, social workers' kinship recruitment work and training could also focus, in part, on researching new types of kinship placements, which, according to Denby (2016), include older siblings raising their brothers and sisters, male relatives as caregivers, and other circumstances.

Embracing a child's rights approach would also mean prioritizing the needs of the potential kin caregivers. Stoner (2006) argues that taking on the role of a kinship caregiver is not simply about taking on the financial and emotional responsibility of child care; it also involves a shift in family relationships. This shift means divided loyalties for the caregiver who now has to ensure the child welfare requirements of child safety and at the same time has to maintain relationships with relatives and parents if no safety concerns are present.

Further, we argue that child rights as human rights must not only be understood and defined but also realized in social work practice. Insisting on children's rights in order to achieve cultural permanency would mean meeting children's needs in order to maintain their family relationships. Available research strongly indicates that kinship care is significant to a child's social and emotional functioning because extended family placements increase stability and cultural continuity for children (ACS, 2007–2008). For social work, such placement stability can influence children's emotional security, safety, sense of belonging, and likelihood of healthy self-esteem, as well as lifelong relationships (Burgess, Rossvoll, Wallace, & Daniel, 2010; OACAS, 2010).

When it comes to placement and child permanency, Denby (2016) states that children in non-kinship placements long for a sense of belonging, which means that their needs extend beyond a place to stay to include cultural permanency. Children in non-kinship placements are faced with questions of who they are, to whom they belong, and to what home they belong, and these are permanency questions that are often overlooked in social work (Denby, 2016). Using a rights-based approach means that a moral and ethical imperative exists and that social work should seek to advance social justice (Ife, 2012) and to address children's questions of identity and sense of belonging. Social work cannot lose sight of children's vulnerability and powerlessness, which are heightened when they are not connected to their families and communities. A strong and compelling argument can therefore be made that the use of kinship placements deserves social work attention because it represents a viable placement option for children and youth at risk of harm as it enables them to maintain their identities. The practice of placing at-risk children in the safety of kin caregivers points to a child's rights–based social work practice, because it clinically takes into account the notion of cultural permanency.

The Macro Level

At the macro level, kinship placements are critical because of the increasing number of children in care and a decreasing number of foster beds. The shift by child welfare agencies and provincial governments toward favouring kinship placement options is a relatively new phenomenon, having emerged in the 1980s (Geen & Berrick, 2002; Gleeson, 1996; Ingram, 1996). Appearing to be directly associated with this shift in Canada is the increasing number of children in care, beginning in the early 1990s and continuing to today. In 1991, approximately 27,567 children were in care across the Canadian provinces and territories (Federal/Provincial/Territorial Working Group, 2001). In 2007 (the most recently recorded data), the number of children in care was 67,024, which reflects an increase of 41 per cent from 1991 (Swift, 2011). In Saskatchewan, the number of foster homes decreased from 626 in 2011 to 498 in 2015, while the number of apprehended children increased from 5,117 in 2011 to 6,493 in 2015 (Pringle, 2015). Callahan et al. (2004) noted that the increasing number of child placements is costly and unsustainable for the Canadian child welfare system. According to Fuchs, Burnside, Marchenski, and Mudry (2007), the rising child welfare costs in Manitoba are partly due to the increasing number of children in care who have medical, physical, intellectual, and mental health disabilities. Children with disabilities in Manitoba also remain in care for long periods of time, "not because of ongoing risk of maltreatment, but due to their intensive needs that their families are unable to fully meet" (Fuchs et al., 2007, p. 128).

There is also an indication that the foster system cannot continue to support the increasing number of children. The rapid growth in child welfare intervention has resulted in significant challenges for child protection services in placing all children and youth in environments adequate to meet their immediate and long-term needs (Canadian Press, 2012; OACAS, 2004, p. 4). The Child Welfare League of Canada recently indicated that repeated efforts to recruit foster families have met with limited success and that child advocates disagree on solutions to this shortage (Canadian Press, 2012; Farris-Manning & Zandstra, 2003). Twigg (2009) draws attention to the fact that the shortage of foster care spaces means that a growing number of children are placed in hotels—and that, while support and supervision may be provided in these settings, hotel life is not family life, nor is a hotel an environment that nurtures and fosters a child's cultural identity. Family-based care models including kinship care are supported by the recommendations found in the Truth and Reconciliation Commission of Canada's *Calls to Action* (TRC, 2015); by the Assembly of Manitoba Chiefs' report *Bringing Our Children Home* (AMC, 2014); and by the Hughes (2013) report on the Phoenix Sinclair inquiry, *The Legacy of Phoenix Sinclair: Achieving the Best for All Our Children.*

Conclusion

The main ideas in this chapter were inspired by the UN Convention on the Rights of the Child, which was signed twenty-eight years ago by almost every country in the world, and the UN Guidelines for the Alternative Care of Children. The UNCRC is based on the assumption that children, no less than adults, deserve specific rights and protections. Considerable progress has been made in the advancement of children's rights in areas of protection; however, as Bernstein (2016) persuasively argues, much advocacy work needs to be done in order to create a culture in Canada for children in which their rights are respected.

The central objective of this chapter has been to draw the connection between the UN legislative framework and kinship placement policies in the Prairie provinces. The UNCRC and the UN Guidelines provide a solid ground upon which a strong claim for children's rights can be made in the discussion and implementation of kinship care in Canada. By using the UN legislative framework, it becomes increasingly clear that utilization of kinship placements is not only preferable but also a right of every child whose needs cannot be met by the parents. Specifically, Article 20(3) provides a platform for a compelling argument for the utilization of kinship placements to ensure cultural continuity, the maintenance of a cultural identity, and a sense of belonging for children who have been removed from parental care. Braye and Preston-Shoot (2006) argue that international conventions, covenants, and declarations are important tools for social workers seeking to engage in a human rights–based approach to practice. The child's rights approach is also consistent with core social work values and with the code of ethics regarding the inherent worth of the individual that recognizes one's cultural identity (CASW, 2005).

What we propose, therefore, are kinship policies and practices that not only treat family/relative placements as preferred options for children but also emphasize the right of children to be placed within a kin home. Giving children the right to be placed with kin would help to address the ongoing challenge to their sense of belonging and the loss of their cultural identity. Maintaining healthy cultural identities for children is in line with the principle of "the best interests of the child" that is strongly promoted by all provincial child welfare legislations. In proposing a child's rights approach to kinship placement, our goal is to promote social justice and better outcomes for all children.

Discussion Questions

1. Discuss some of the ways that kinship care can be utilized to address the overrepresentation of Indigenous and racialized children in care.
2. Discuss the importance of social workers' understanding and application of the UNCRC.
3. How are you incorporating human rights–based approaches into your social work practice?

References

ACS (Alberta Children's Services). (2007–2008). *Annual report 2007–08*. Calgary: Government of Alberta. Retrieved from https://open.alberta.ca/dataset/67aaa3a0-2fe9-4a1f-a0f9-537eed9c365b/resource/7fece209-4799-4555-8d15-cbb4524cf70a/download/2007-08-CS-Annual-Report.pdf

Alberta. (2017). *Child intervention information and statistics summary: 2016/17 fourth quarter (March) update*. Retrieved from http://www.humanservices.alberta.ca/documents/child-intervention-info-stats-summary-2016-17-q4.pdf

Alberta. Children and Youth Services. (2009, November). *Kinship care review report*. Retrieved from http://www.humanservices.alberta.ca/documents/kinship-care-review-report.pdf

Alberta Human Services. (2014a). *Immediate Kinship Placement*. Retrieved from https://www.alberta.ca/documents/MPCI-ebinder.pdf (see pp. 99–103 of PDF)

Alberta Human Services. (2014b). *Principle based practice strategies*. Retrieved from https://www.alberta.ca/documents/MPCI-ebinder.pdf (see pp. 82–86 of PDF)

AMC (Assembly of Manitoba Chiefs). (2014, June). *Bringing our children home: Report and recommendations*. Retrieved from https://turtletalk.files.wordpress.com/2014/10/241508864-amc-report-and-recommendations-on-cfs-bringing-our-children-home-1.pdf

Bennett, M., Blackstock, C., & De La Ronde, R. (2005). *A literature review and annotated bibliography on aspects of Aboriginal child welfare in Canada* (2nd ed.). First Nations Research Site of the Centre of Excellence for Child Welfare and First Nations Child & Family Caring Society of Canada. Retrieved from http://cwrp.ca/sites/default/files/publications/en/AboriginalCWLitReview_2ndEd.pdf

Bernhard, J. (2012). *Stand together or fall apart: Professionals working with immigrant families*. Halifax, NS: Fernwood Publishing.

Bernstein, M. (2016). Transforming child welfare in Canada into a stronger child rights–based system. In H. Montgomery, D. Badry, D. Fuchs, & D. Kikulwe (Eds.), *Transforming child welfare: Interdisciplinary practices, field education, and research* (pp. 3–26). Regina, SK: University of Regina Press.

Blackstock, C. (2007). Residential schools: Did they really close or just morph into child welfare? *Indigenous Law Journal, 6*(1), 71–78.

Blackstock, C., Trocmé, N., & Bennett, M. (2004). Child welfare response to Aboriginal and non-Aboriginal children in Canada: A comparative analysis. *Violence against Women, 10*(8), 901–916.

Braye, S., & Preston-Shoot, M. (2006). Broadening the vision: Law teaching, social work, and civil society. *International Social Work, 49*(3), 376–389.

Burgess, C., Rossvoll, F., Wallace, B., & Daniel, B. (2010). "It's just like another home, just another family, so it's nae different": Children's voice in kinship care: A research study about the experience of children in kinship care in Scotland. *Child & Family Social Work, 15*(3), 297–306.

Burke, S. (2009). *Exploring kinship care: A newly recognized age-old practice* (Master's thesis). University of Northern British Columbia, Prince George, BC.

Burke, S., & Schmidt, G. (2009). Kinship care in northern British Columbia. *Child Welfare, 88*(6), 127–142.

Callahan, M., Brown, L., MacKenzie, P., & Whittington, B. (2004). Catch as catch can: Grandmothers raising their grandchildren and kinship care policies. *Canadian Review of Social Policy, 54*(Fall), 58–78.

CASW (Canadian Association of Social Workers). (2005). *Code of ethics 2005*. Retrieved from https://www.casw-acts.ca/sites/casw-acts.ca/files/documents/casw_code_of_ethics.pdf

Canadian Press. (2012, February 19). Canadian foster care in crisis, experts say: Some children placed in homes before safety checks made. *CBC News*. Retrieved from http://www.cbc.ca/news/canada/canadian-foster-care-in-crisis-experts-say-1.1250543

The Child and Family Services Act, CCSM c C80 (1985) (Manitoba).

The Child and Family Services Act, SS 1989–90, c C-7.2 (Saskatchewan).

The Child and Family Services Authorities Act, CCSM c C90 (2003) (Manitoba).

Child Welfare League of America. (2000). *Standards of excellence: CWLA standards of excellence for kinship care services*. Washington, DC: The League.

Child, Youth and Family Enhancement Act, RSA 2000, c C-12, s 2 (Alberta).

Chipungu, S., & Goodley T. (2004). Meeting the challenges of contemporary foster care. *The Future of Children*, *14*(1), 75–93.

Cuddeback, G. S. (2004). Kinship family foster care: A methodological and substantive synthesis of research. *Children and Youth Services Review*, *26*(7), 623–639.

Denby, R. (2016). *Kinship care: Increasing child well-being through practice, policy, and research*. New York, NY: Springer.

Farris-Manning, C., & Zandstra, M. (2003). *Children in care in Canada: A summary of current issues and trends with recommendations for future research*. Ottawa, ON: Child Welfare League of Canada.

Federal/Provincial/Territorial Working Group on Child and Family Service Information (2001). *Child and family services statistical report, 1996–97 to 1998–99*. Ottawa, ON: Human Resources and Skills Development Canada.

First Nations Child and Family Caring Society of Canada et al. v. Attorney General of Canada (for the Minister of Indian and Northern Affairs Canada), 2016 CHRT 2.

First Nations leader calls Manitoba a "child apprehension machine." (2016, January 26). *CBC News*. Retrieved from http://www.cbc.ca/news/canada/manitoba/first-nations-tribunal-discriminates-ruling-1.3420182

FNCFCS (First Nations Child and Family Caring Society of Canada). (2012, October). UNCRC concluding observations Canada. Retrieved from https://fncaringsociety.com/sites/default/files/UNCRC%20Briefing%20Note%202012.pdf

Fraser, D. (2017, March 14). Children's advocate wants child welfare changes to move faster; province has no timeline in place. *Leader-Post* [Regina]. Retrieved from http://leaderpost.com/news/politics/childrens-advocate-wants-child-welfare-changes-to-move-faster-province-has-no-timeline-in-place

Fuchs, D., Burnside, L., Marchenski, S., & Mudry, A. (2007). Children with disabilities involved with the child welfare system in Manitoba: Current and future challenges. In I. Brown, F. Chaze, D. Fuchs, J. Lafrance, S. McKay, & S. Thomas Prokop (Eds.), *Putting a human face on child welfare: Voices from the Prairies* (pp. 127–145). Prairie Child Welfare Consortium/Center of Excellence for Child Welfare.

Fuller-Thomson, E. (2005). Canadian First Nations grandparents raising grandchildren: A portrait in resilience. *International Journal of Aging & Human Development, 60*(4), 331–342.

Galley, V. (2010). *Summary review of Aboriginal overrepresentation in the child welfare system*. Regina, SK: Saskatchewan Child Welfare Review Panel.

Geen, R. (2004). The evolution of kinship care policy and practice. *The Future of Children, 14*(1), 130–149.

Geen, R., & Berrick, J. D. (2002). Kinship care: An evolving service delivery option. *Children and Youth Services Review, 24*(1–2), 1–14.

Gleeson, J. (1996). Kinship care as a child welfare service: The policy debate in an era of welfare reform. *Child Welfare, 75*(5), 419–449.

Gonzales-Mena, J. (2001). Cross-cultural infant care and issues of equity and social justice. *Contemporary Issues in Early Childhood, 2*(3), 368–371.

Goodley, T. (2011). Regulating the lives of children: Kinship care as a cultural resistance strategy of the African American community. In J. Schiele (Ed.), *Social welfare policy: Regulation and resistance among people of color* (pp. 25–42). New York, NY: Sage.

Gough, P. (2006). *Kinship care* (CECW Information Sheet #42E). Centre of Excellence for Child Welfare. Retrieved from http://cwrp.ca/sites/default/files/publications/en/KinshipCare42E.pdf

Hammill, J. (2001). Granny rights: Combatting the granny burnout syndrome among Australian Indigenous communities. *Development, 44*(2), 69–74.

Hopps, J., Tourse, W. R., & Ollie, C. (2002). From problems to personal resilience. *Journal of Ethnic and Cultural Diversity in Social Work, 11*(1–2), 55–77.

Hughes, T. (2013, December). *The legacy of Phoenix Sinclair: Achieving the best for all our children* (Vol. 1). Retrieved from http://www.phoenixsinclairinquiry.ca/rulings/ps_volume1.pdf

Ife, J. (2012). *Human rights and social work: Towards a rights-based practice* (3rd ed.). Cambridge, UK: Cambridge University Press.

Ingram, C. (1996). Kinship care: From last resort to first choice. *Child Welfare, 75*(5), 550–566.

Kikulwe, D. (2014). *This is what we know: Working from the margins in child welfare* (Doctoral dissertation). York University, Toronto, ON.

Kozlowski, A., Sinha, V., Petti, T., & Flette, E. (2012). *First Nations child welfare in Manitoba (2011)* (CWRP Information Sheet #97E). Canadian Child Welfare Research Portal. Retrieved from http://cwrp.ca/infosheets/first-nations-child-welfare-manitoba

Kroll, B. (2007). A family affair? Kinship care and parental substance misuse: Some dilemmas explored. *Child & Family Social Work, 12*(1), 84–93.

Lavergne, C., Dufour, S., Trocmé, N., & Larrivée, M.-C. (2008). Visible minority, Aboriginal, and Caucasian children investigated by Canadian protective services. *Child Welfare League of America, 82*(2), 59–76.

Legislative Assembly of Saskatchewan. (1991). *Routine proceedings: Presenting reports by standing, select, and special committees*. Retrieved from http://docs.legassembly.sk.ca/legdocs/Legislative%20Assembly/Hansard/22L1S/911211.PDF

Leschied, A., MacKay, R., Raghunandan, S., Sharpe, N., & Sookoor, M. (2007). *Empowering families, strengthening and protecting children: Introducing kinship program and family group conferencing program at the Children's Aid Society of London and Middlesex*. London, ON: Faculty of Education, University of Western Ontario.

Manitoba. (n.d.). *Child and Family Services Standards Manual*. Retrieved from http://gov.mb.ca/fs/cfsmanual/index.html

Marks, D. (2015, June 14). "Kinship care" program needed to fix broken child welfare system: There's too much bad press about Child and Family Services, First Nations welfare worker says. *CBC News*. Retrieved from http://www.cbc.ca/news/canada/manitoba/kinship-care-program-needed-to-fix-broken-child-welfare-system-1.3112954

McKay, S. (2009). Introduction: Voices of passion, voices of hope. In S. McKay, D. Fuchs, & I. Brown (Eds.), *Passion for action in child and family services: Voices from the Prairies* (pp. xvi–xxiv). Regina, SK: Canadian Plains Research Center.

McKenzie, B., & Wharf, B. (2016). *Connecting policy to practice in the human services* (4th ed.). Don Mills, ON: Oxford University Press.

Ministry of Social Services Regulations, 2007, RRS c G-5.1 Reg 145 (Saskatchewan).

Mullaly, R. (2010). *Challenging oppression and confronting privilege* (2nd ed.). Don Mills, ON: Oxford University Press.

OACAS (Ontario Association of Children's Aid Societies). (2004). *Ontario kinship model consultation report*. Toronto, ON: OACAS.

OACAS (Ontario Association of Children's Aid Societies). (2010). *Ontario child welfare survey on kinship services: Responses and findings*. Retrieved from http://www.childwelfareinstitute.torontocas.ca/sites/childwelfareinstitute/files/09%20Ontario%20Child%20Welfare%2C%20Survey%20on%20Kinship%20Services.pdf

Pringle, B. (2015). *Addressing challenges in out of home care. Saskatchewan Advocate: 2015 annual report*. Saskatoon, SK: Saskatchewan Advocate for Children and Youth.

Pringle, B., Cameron, H., Durocher, A., & Skelton, C. (2010). *For the good of our children and youth: A new vision, a new direction*. Saskatchewan Child Welfare Review Panel report. Retrieved from http://cwrp.ca/sites/default/files/publications/en/SK_ChildWelfareReview_panelreport.pdf

Sandstorm-Smith, L. (2004). *Overview of child protection proceedings in Saskatchewan and the amendments for kinship care*. Saskatoon, SK: Saskatchewan Legal Education Society.

Saskatchewan. Ministry of Social Services. (2016). *Child protection services manual*. Retrieved from http://publications.gov.sk.ca/documents/17/88038-Child-Protection-Manual.pdf

Saskatchewan. Ministry of Social Services. (2018, February). *Children's Services Manual*. Retrieved from http://publications.gov.sk.ca/documents/17/17090-Childrens-Services-Manual.pdf

Scannapieco, M., & Hegar, R. L. (2002). Kinship care providers: Designing an array of supportive services. *Child and Adolescent Social Work Journal, 19*(4), 315–327.

Shlonsky, A. R., & Berrick, J. D. (2001). Assessing and promoting quality in kin and nonkin foster care. *Social Service Review, 75*(1), 60–83.

Stoner, K. (2006). *Kinship care as a viable care option: How agencies in the Hamilton Niagara region use this service* (Master's thesis). Brock University, St. Catharines, ON.

Swift, K. J. (2011). Canadian child welfare: Child protection and the status quo. In N. Gilbert, N. Parton, & M. Skivenes (Eds.), *Child protection systems: International trends and orientations* (pp. 36–59). New York, NY: Oxford University Press.

Swift, K. J., & Callahan, M. (2009). *At risk: Social justice in child welfare and other human services*. Toronto, ON: University of Toronto Press.

Trocmé, N., Knoke, D., & Blackstock, C. (2004). Pathways to the overrepresentation of Aboriginal children in Canada's child welfare system. *Social Service Review, 78*(4), 577–600.

TRC (Truth and Reconciliation Commission of Canada). (2015). *Truth and Reconciliation Commission of Canada: Calls to Action*. Winnipeg, MB: TRC. Retrieved from http://www.trc.ca/websites/trcinstitution/File/2015/Findings/Calls_to_Action_English2.pdf

Twigg, R. (2009). Passion for those who care: What foster carers need. In S. McKay, D. Fuchs, & I. Brown (Eds.), *Passion for action in child and family services: Voices from the Prairies* (pp. 165–184). Regina, SK: Canadian Plains Research Center.

UNCRC (United Nations Committee on the Rights of the Child). (2012, October 5). Concluding observations: Canada. *Consideration of reports submitted by states parties under article 44 of the Convention*. CRC/C/CAN/CO/3-4. Retrieved from http://www2.ohchr.org/english/bodies/crc/docs/co/CRC-C-CAN-CO-3-4_en.pdf

UN (United Nations) General Assembly. (1989, November 20). *Convention on the rights of the child*. A/RES/44/25. Retrieved from http://www.un.org/documents/ga/res/44/a44r025.htm

UN (United Nations) General Assembly. (2010, February 24). *Guidelines for the alternative care of children: Resolution / adopted by the General Assembly. A/RES/64/142*. Retrieved from http://www.unicef.org/protection/alternative_care_Guidelines-English.pdf

Wensley, H. K. (2006). *Aboriginal children and child welfare: An overview of recent changes*. (PowerPoint presentation). Victoria, BC: University of Victoria Faculty of Law.

Wright, A., Hiebert-Murphy, D., Mirwaldt, J., & Muswaggon, G. (2005). *Final report: Factors that contribute to positive outcomes in the Awasis Pimicikamak Cree Nation kinship care program*. Ottawa, ON: Centre of Excellence for Child Welfare and Health Canada.

CHAPTER 2

Working with First Nations Child Welfare to Build Professionalism

Shelley Thomas Prokop, Laura Hicks, and Rachel Melymick

Introduction

It is widely recognized that First Nations Child and Family Services (FNCFS) agencies have been systematically underfunded compared with their provincial counterparts (Office of the Auditor General of Ontario, 2015). This underfunding has contributed to a situation in which the capabilities of many First Nations organizations are underdeveloped in areas such as program planning, applied research, and evidence-based policy development affected by local factors such as agency remoteness, technological limitations, and cultural and linguistic variability.

This chapter will share promising practices utilized by the Saskatchewan First Nations Family and Community Institute (SFNSCI) to develop and create ownership of culturally relevant training processes and products that enhance professionalism in First Nations child welfare in Saskatchewan, while maintaining alignment to the SFNSCI vision and mission and to the many First Nations cultures in Saskatchewan. An example of

Suggested Citation: Thomas Prokop, S., Hicks, L., & Melymick, R. (2018). Working with First Nations child welfare to build professionalism. In D. Badry, H. Montgomery, D. Kikulwe, M. Bennett, & D. Fuchs, (Eds.), *Imagining child welfare in the spirit of reconciliation* (pp. 27–42). Regina, SK: University of Regina Press.

work undertaken by SFNSCI is presented here as evidence of emerging best practice in First Nations–led child and family services professional development and training. This material was initially prepared for and presented at the 2016 Prairie Child Welfare Consortium Symposium in Winnipeg, Manitoba.

This chapter will share SFNSCI experiences of successes and learnings of adapting standardized training material for use by Saskatchewan First Nations, as well as our experiences in articulating select standards and developing curriculum. The chapter begins by describing the realization of SFNSCI and the values, mission, and principles that guide the work of its board and staff. To support SFNSCI's goal of growing professionalism within Saskatchewan FNCFS, we introduce and discuss the process the institute uses in developing training programs and curricular material. We then illustrate this work by describing the implementation of a training program associated with the Saskatchewan rollout of the Structured Decision Making (SDM) model.

The Saskatchewan First Nations Family and Community Institute

SFNSCI started in 2002 as an idea by Saskatchewan First Nations. At the time, Saskatchewan had sixteen FNCFS agencies providing child welfare services on-reserve. Many agencies had begun operations in the 1990s. The FNCFS executive directors wanted to develop a service that could provide culturally relevant training and support, coordinate policy and standards development, and facilitate strategic partnerships. Both the federal and provincial governments were approached, and an agreement was established to fund SFNSCI in 2007. SFNSCI is governed by a board of nine professional representatives with backgrounds in First Nations child and family services, human resources, financial services, and the legal sector. The institute's office is located near Saskatoon on English River Reserve, with a large training space and eleven staff who provide services including research, curriculum development, training, and support services in multiple areas, such as group homes, human resources, finance, prevention, caregivers, youth, and SDM. SFNSCI (2017) is guided by its vision—"Be the leading, innovative, sustainable, holistic center of research and professional learning to organizations serving children, youth and families"—and by the following mission: "To build capacity within organizations serving children, youth and families based on First Nations values." The institute's seven values—respect, love, bravery, wisdom, humility, honesty, and truth—are based on widely accepted First Nations values and ten guiding principles defining the nature of processes and relationships of those we serve, including youth, Elders, First Nations government, employees, members, community, environment, professional organizations, funders, and government.

When SFNSCI began operations in 2007, initial services focused on the flow-through delivery of "off the shelf" programs, where third-party organizations developed the curricular resources and SFNSCI organized the training. This way of delivering training reflected SFNSCI capacity at the beginning stages of the organization. A formative stance was important to help develop an understanding of the most effective types of curricular approaches and to determine the types of support needed by those attending training, for which an established audience already existed. We gathered feedback on a consistent basis at each training event, in order to determine additional needs, strengths, and challenges. The evaluation process was embedded in conversations with participants and focused on readiness, willingness, and offering honest feedback on the effectiveness and value of the training. SFNSCI uses the word "conversations" rather than calling it research because the word "research" is not fondly recognized by those we serve.

This initial approach to training supported SFNSCI to move toward training development that better reflected the distinct needs of First Nations child welfare workers in the province. SFNSCI has since moved away from coordinating the delivery of "off the shelf" training and is moving toward a blend of customized programs that best meet the needs of First Nations organizations. This approach helps to develop capacity within SFNSCI and those we work with, who receive culturally relevant training and standards. The institute is recognized as an emerging leader in the field of FNCFS curriculum development and has consistently been positively recognized for its training programs, as indicated in feedback forms, yearly member surveys, and the move toward program certification.

SFNSCI has utilized a co-operative approach in the development of standards and professional training. Our co-operative approach includes focused conversations with First Nations agency staff and learning of community knowledge(s) as the foundation of development within our training. Having discussions with those planning to attend the training and working with standards of practice are critical components of assessing readiness and willingness to participate, as both are key to ownership and implementation of training and standards. Readiness and willingness also contribute to a better understanding of the why, how, and who involved in staff development. We recognize and acknowledge that those being served are the subject-matter experts in First Nations child welfare.

Once a training or service delivery project is given the green light internally, a project charter is established with key performance indicators. The approach begins with a review of existing knowledge and literature related to the communities involved, their histories, and their cultures, as well as an understanding of child welfare and how it relates to the topic at hand. This process is critical and lends itself to a relational approach (Kovach, 2009), which, when working with First Nations, supports a better understanding for all involved in the development and delivery of programs and services. Although a lengthy process, this approach ensures that the training reflects and recognizes the communities and the realities of the people it serves.

Given the histories of First Nations people in Saskatchewan, SFNSCI is committed to providing training that is culturally relevant, sensitive to individual experiences of trauma, and considerate of the steps communities are taking toward decolonization and reconciliation. "Culturally relevant" means that curriculum is developed to be flexible and inclusive of variability among the First Nations in Saskatchewan. Rather than emphasizing any one particular tribal group (e.g., Plains Cree, Sioux, Dene), the curriculum and resources developed reflect commonly held values and practices. Learners take the information and correlate it with their own understandings of community culture in the implementation of the learning. Curriculum that is culturally sensitive fosters and facilitates an appreciation of each person as a learner who is working with emotional intelligence. This means including activities and exercises that help learners to be sensitive to the experiences and histories of those they work with and to respond in ways that are respectful and based on strengths. Trauma-informed approaches to this work are valued by SFNSCI, and this means developing curriculum that includes activities and exercises that recognize the trauma carried by or still being experienced by the people with whom learners work. All three approaches are interconnected and recognize the history of First Nations people. Culturally relevant, trauma-informed, and decolonizing curriculum upholds the spirit and intent of the calls to action set forth in the 2015 report of the Truth and Reconciliation Commission of Canada (TRC, 2015).

Implementing the Structured Decision Making Model with FNCFS Agencies in Saskatchewan

The collaborative and culture-based approach taken by SFNSCI in the development of standards and professional training was initiated with the implementation of standardized procedures for child welfare decision-making by the FNCFS agencies in Saskatchewan. Implementing the SDM model with FNCFS agencies in Saskatchewan was a unique project for SFNSCI in that the "off the shelf" model of Structured Decision Making came with an established set of policies and procedures, as well as a fixed training curriculum. The challenge for SFNSCI and the FNCFS agencies became how to implement a Western model of decision-making in a way that still honoured the approach and values of the agencies and of SFNSCI as a First Nations organization.

When the Saskatchewan Ministry of Social Services (MSS) first introduced its preferred model for improving child welfare decision-making to the province's FNCFS agencies, SFNSCI became involved in the discussions concerning the implementation of the SDM system for child welfare in the fall of 2010. Structured Decision Making was presented as a replacement of the Saskatchewan Risk Assessment tool (Pennsylvania Risk Assessment) then being used by child protection workers. This earlier tool was used to assess both risk and safety during the investigation process according to four broad levels of risk: no risk, low risk, moderate risk, and high risk (Pennsylvania Child Welfare Resource Center, 1996). The MSS had begun customizing the "off the shelf" SDM system for use within the Saskatchewan jurisdiction, and it was in 2013 that SFNSCI became engaged in this process.

The SDM system was originally developed by the Children's Research Center (CRC), a branch of the US National Council on Crime and Delinquency (NCCD), itself established in 1907. The CRC is an organization that strives to improve outcomes for children, youth, and families through partnerships with child-serving agencies through direct practice and organizational operations, by developing models that integrate evidence-based assessment, family-centred engagement strategies, and implementation science (NCCD Children's Research Center, 2008). The MSS presented SDM as a reliable and valid model, incorporating a set of evidenced-based assessment tools and decision guides designed to provide a higher level of consistency and validity to assessment and decision-making processes in the context of child welfare.

The key SDM tools include (1) Intake assessment, (2) Safety assessment, (3) Family risk assessment of child abuse/neglect, (4) Family strengths and needs assessment/reassessment, and (5) Family risk reassessment and family reunification assessment (NCCD Children's Research Center, 2017). The SDM system for child protective services is well articulated in a policy and procedures manual for agencies that was initially published in October 2011 and updated in February 2015. This document specifically addresses the Saskatchewan context and was created in collaboration with the NCCD Children's Research Center.

It is not the intent of the authors to comment in any way upon the experience of Saskatchewan FNCFS agencies with the SDM system. We can only speak to our experience in the process of supporting the implementation of the SDM system with the FNCFS agencies. SFNSCI began this work in 2013, where our initial work sought to understand the scope of implementation and what supporting a project of such magnitude may look like. A significant amount of care and attention went into determining if there was a role for SFNSCI and if this project fit within the vision and mission of the institute. Through research and discussions with the FNCFS agencies' executive directors and key stakeholders, it was determined that SFNSCI was well suited to house an SDM consultant, whose job it was to support the agencies by training and supporting their staff on the use of the SDM system. Thus, SFNSCI developed a job description for the future SDM consultant, highlighting the importance of being able to project-manage and assess agency needs during the implementation process. The hiring process was competitive, involving thorough reference and background checks and requiring applicants to deliver a presentation, complete a written evaluation, and undergo a panel interview.

The first SDM consultant was hired in December 2013 and began the early steps of building relationships with the FNCFS agencies associated with SFNSCI. Specific messaging and communication on the role and position of the SDM consultant were provided early on, to ensure that all agencies understood how the SDM consultant position had come to be housed and to work out of the SFNSCI office. This communication also included consulting with the agencies and assessing their readiness, resources, and plans for SDM implementation. The SDM consultant was also tasked with undertaking assessments (when requested) and providing ongoing consultation and support to workers on complex or unique situations arising with the implementation of SDM within FNCFS agency environments. SFNSCI provided instruction, guidance, coaching, and encouragement to FNCFS agency staff as workers developed the skills required to implement SDM standards and practices. This supportive outreach practice, as described above, was critical to creating a training environment that respects, values, and encourages the expression of First Nations and cross-cultural content through a process of constructive and supportive dialogue.

The development of relationships through conversation was critical throughout SDM implementation, and the power of dialogue and discussion cannot be underestimated in this process. Conversations would introduce SDM consultants to new understandings of the unique environment of each FNCFS agency working with SFNSCI. SDM consultants took time to hear individuals' concerns and hesitancies about implementing the SDM model at their agency. Frequently the concerns raised were about staff capacity to add to an already burdensome workload—the need for additional resources for implementation, the impacts on the agency as a whole and on the communities served (e.g., children being removed due to poor housing conditions). Other concerns were also raised: the cultural relevance of the tool, the need for a computer database system, and the fear that the SDM tools could take away worker and supervisor decision-making autonomy. It was important to understand each concern; simply to not respond to the concern with an immediate answer but to digest the concern and look for potential solutions if they existed; and then to support the agency through the concern. This approach recognizes that responding to agency concerns is a process that takes reflection and time.

One of SFNSCI's strategies for addressing some of the FNCFS agency concerns was to develop an SDM frequently asked questions (FAQ) document. This document was distributed to various FNCFS agencies and was also posted on the SFNSCI website. The SDM FAQ attempted to address issues around customization and adaptation, data ownership, case-management systems, implications for staff and agency, and the nature and extent of supports available from the SFNSCI SDM consultants.

A key step in responding to and supporting agency workers was identifying strategic partners with respect to building local SDM-implementation support teams. Because there were potentially seventeen FNCFS agencies to support, a model that relied on one trainer/consultant for all agencies would not be sufficient. Pre-implementation research undertaken by SFNSCI identified additional latent support team members, including local FNCFS agency supervisors, the MSS First Nations and Métis Services unit,[1] and the MSS Provincial Training Team,[2] as well as the staff from the Children's Research Centre (CRC). The agencies were involved in identifying and clarifying roles and responsibilities among the team members.

The SDM consultant initially started working with two FNCFS agencies in the first year, partnering with the MSS Provincial Training Team as a pilot for year one of the SDM system rollout. However, as FNCFS agency demand for support in using the SDM system increased, it became clear that a strategy was needed that recognized the level of support required by agencies to carry out implementation and ongoing skill development of SDM. In the first year of implementation of SDM with First Nations, five agencies that adopted SDM were supported by SFNSCI. In response to increasing demand for SDM system support, a second SDM consultant was hired by SFNSCI in September 2015.

In conversations SFNSCI was having with FNCFS agencies about the support required with system implementation, multiple sources identified a range of different perceptions of the SDM system. These perceptions were based on observations of MSS's SDM system rollout that had gradually been taking place in ministry offices for years. There was significant concern about many areas related to the SDM system, including the potential impact on agency staff and reputation, as well as the customizability and adaptability of the tools, specifically regarding cultural

1 The MSS First Nations and Métis Services unit is a team within Saskatchewan MSS staff that oversees and supports the delegation with Saskatchewan FNCFS agencies and MSS.

2 The MSS Provincial Training Team is the training staff that supports the ministry's workers and offices.

relevance. The SFNSCI process incorporated different pieces of an anti-oppressive practice when meeting with the agencies, including "integrating cultural knowledge, [and] drawing on practices that exist within customs, traditions and language of Indigenous peoples" (Freeman, 2011, p. 116). Significant time was spent in conversation with FNCFS agency stakeholders (board members, executive directors, frontline staff, Elders, and other community members) in order to develop and clarify the cultural relevance of the SDM model. While the SDM tools are uniform for Saskatchewan, SDM consultants worked with agencies to ensure that the practice around their use reflected the language, priorities, and social dynamics of the individual communities served.

SFNSCI demonstrated its organizational commitment to humility—a core First Nations value—by engaging respectfully with the FNCFS agencies and communities (SFNSCI, n.d.). SFNSCI continually consults with agencies as to what cultural relevance looks like for each community that they serve. This humble approach continues to define the way in which workers apply and understand the relevance and adaptability of SDM tools within specific cultural contexts. By acknowledging the centrality of social connection, SDM consultants are able to develop supportive relationships based on humility rather than dominance.

Feedback received early on in the system's implementation process was readily accepted by the SFNSCI SDM consultants. For example, several agencies indicated their interest in adapting the SDM tools to be more culturally relevant to their community. The CRC had created the SDM tools to "ensure that critical case characteristics, safety factors, and domains of family functioning are assessed for every family, every time, regardless of social differences" (NCCD Children's Research Center, 2017, p. 1). The SDM consultants quickly understood that a rigid, defensive insistence on the universal utility of the system might hamper the uptake of the tool among FNCFS agency staff. Instead, the institute's approach recognized, and continues to recognize, that workers apply and understand the SDM tools within their own cultural context—that they bring their own culture, and the culture of the person they are working with, into the conversations. The role of the SDM tools is designed to be that of a guide for these worker-client conversations.

Currently, SFNSCI's SDM consultants offer three levels of support to FNCFS agencies: implementation, training, and onsite support.

Implementation Support

Implementation support starts with a basic needs assessment completed via close co-operation and collaboration with an agency's executive director and supervisors. Some of the areas discussed during the needs assessment phase are designed to gauge the level of familiarity with SDM that agency staff have, which staff will be needing training, and what languages staff communicate in. Prior to SDM implementation, the consultants also discuss what potential gaps or challenges might exist with respect to training and how best to support agency staff, based on their unique organizational and geographic dynamics. While the needs assessment is occurring, relationships are being built along with an understanding of the FNCFS agency's infrastructure; how each SDM tool will be used within the agency is formed through this process.

Adapting to unique community needs is a critical aspect of this work. For example, during an initial meeting with several FNCFS agencies regarding the implementation stage of the SDM system, a significant gap regarding use of the tool was identified. At this meeting, several agency staff indicated that the standard SDM policy and procedures manual would not meet the needs of agencies that were not using the Saskatchewan MSS Linkin electronic case-management system. The FNCFS agencies in Saskatchewan as a whole do not use the same case-management system as the MSS. An unforeseen conflict emerged when it was discovered that the MSS had collaborated with the CRC to adapt the off-the-shelf version of SDM tools to meet the specified needs of MSS employees and offices rather than of agency staff based in First Nations communities. Accordingly, the SDM policy and procedures manual and the training manual that had been produced to correspond with the MSS Linkin case-management system were not always relevant to the FNCFS agency environment. In order to remedy this discrepancy, CRC developed an SDM policy and procedures manual specifically for agencies that did not utilize the Linkin case-management system. This new manual reflected the format of the original SDM policy and procedures manual.

After the basic needs assessment has been completed, the FNCFS agencies inform the SFNSCI SDM consultants of who they want involved in the implementation support plan for their agency and the communities they serve. In some cases, members of the support plan have included community Elders or a designated worker based out of the MSS First Nations and

Métis Services Unit. At this point, the rollout plan for the agency becomes customized depending on how the agency has chosen to implement the SDM tools. Some agencies have decided to initially roll out only the first three SDM tools, to get comfortable with them prior to implementing the last three, whereas others have implemented all six SDM tools at once.

Once the SDM tools to be implemented within the agency are identified, how these tools will be adapted into the agency's existing record-keeping workflow (i.e., its paper trail) is discussed. In support of this workflow adaptation, the SDM consultants can assist agency staff in customizing their forms to integrate the SDM assessment outcomes and processes, such as when an agency staff member fills out a Child Assessment Development Plan (CADP) for a child in the agency's care. The purpose of the CADP is to record important information related to the child's case plan. The SDM Child Strengths and Needs Assessment (CSNA) tool provides a conversational guide that helps workers to systematically assess and document the child's strengths and needs as of that particular date and time. This information is used to develop the child's case plan and to establish benchmarks for regular progress reviews. By adapting the CADP format to enable agency staff to date-stamp their entries and input a narrative of comments arising from the SDM CSNA, a clear understanding of a child's case plan is established. Doing so frees agency staff from unnecessary duplication of work and reduces the risk of data entry errors. Any type of change to agency forms is done only upon the request of the agency, and all drafts of agency-adapted forms are reviewed by the agency's executive director and supervisors prior to any SDM training sessions taking place.

Customized Training

The second level of support that SFNSCI provides to First Nations agencies upholds the importance of the value of love within our professional practice: "Demonstrating our belief (as professional services) that all organizations can and will succeed through their commitment to their communities" (SFNSCI, n.d.). With respect to the implementation of the SDM system, the principle of love is reflected in the ways in which training is customized to each FNCFS agency's infrastructure and respective culture.

Within the MSS, SDM training is delivered in a central urban location over a quick two and a half days. The training is formatted according to the structure of the ministry. For example, the MSS training references the Linkin case-management system and the regionalized organizational structure. In contrast, SFNSCI-customized SDM training is offered onsite at locations convenient to the FNCFS agency's staff, not in a centralized training facility. This creates more accessible learning opportunities. The duration of the training is customized, based on what the agency has requested. Well in advance of training sessions, resources for training are discussed with key decision-makers within the FNCFS agency, including the executive director, supervisors, and culturally informed individuals (e.g., Elder, interpreter). The impact of having training in the community versus coming to a shared location has had a positive impact on the application of the SDM tools. Agencies are able to have larger groups of staff trained at once, allowing staff to be trained and to grow in their learning as a team. When community Elders partake in the training sessions, they bring with them wisdom of the community and culture in which the agency staff both work and live. Community Elders open the training sessions with local cultural practices: for example, prayer, song, and smudging. Elders are then present throughout the training to provide input and insight and to be available to participants who may desire additional support. Training within their communities limits the time that agency staff are required to spend away from the families they are working with. This demonstrates the belief that all organizations can and will succeed through their commitment to their communities through the SFNSCI's value of love.

The institute's core value of honesty—"accepting that we have a requirement to be transparent and accountable to our members, communities, funders, stakeholders and each other" (SFNSCI, n.d.)—is also demonstrated in the SDM consultants' approach to supporting FNCFS agency staff. Before ever delivering training support to an agency, the SDM consultants discuss with the agency's executive director exactly who and which functions within the agency will be using the SDM tools. It was discovered after these discussions that some agencies required the training to be partialized in relation to the different positions within it. Based on this information, the training can be adapted into partialized versions in a way that offers varying levels of curriculum for specific roles within the agency, such as frontline protection staff, prevention workers, supervisors, and on-call (emergency duty workers or EDW) staff. For example, the

SDM consultants will offer training for the first two SDM tools (Intake and Safety) specifically to on-call/emergency workers, allowing the training to focus on the needs and requirements of these workers.

Part of our customized training is that the SDM consultants develop different training aids to assist agency staff in learning when to use tools. Depending upon the pre-identified needs of each agency, curricular resources and visual aids are developed to map out the steps of the SDM tools alongside existing agency forms, to show how the process flows together. Workers are provided with these materials during training and/or onsite support sessions. The customization and improvements continually being made by SDM consultants are derived from the post-training feedback of agency staff. SDM consultants hand out feedback forms during every training session. From the feedback they receive, SDM consultants make any alterations needed prior to the next session. SDM consultants follow SFNSCI's value of honesty to members and stakeholders by completing an evaluation of all of the feedback from SDM training and support from the year in SFNSCI's annual report.

Onsite Support

Onsite support is the third level of support and the focus of SFNSCI SDM consultants. As with implementation and training support, onsite support is likewise customized to the specific needs of each agency. A value of SFNSCI that is highlighted in onsite support is wisdom: creating internal capacity through ongoing professional development (SFNSCI, n.d.). SDM is embedded in social work practice and is more than extra paper work. Part of the SDM consultants' role with onsite support is strengthening social work practice at the agencies. Since onsite support varies among individual agencies, there is no one way to explain what this looks like. However, some aspects are one-on-one staff coaching, facilitation of case consultations and/or SDM case readings, group supervision/mentoring, and refresher/follow-up training.

In part, building capacity within the agencies comes through supporting agency supervisors. The SDM Supervisors Working Group, launched in early 2014, is another avenue created to support supervisors. Its main intent is to provide a space where FNCFS agency supervisors can receive the support they require to implement and supervise SDM at their agencies. The working group aims to provide a venue for supervisors to share their SDM-related experiences, promising practices, and challenges. Supervisors are able to learn and share best practices with one another, and group meetings are intended to be a place for communicating and sharing SDM policy-related questions and changes. The working group provides SDM consultants an opportunity to share information from MSS and to keep agencies informed on SDM-related projects. The consultants also help to bring in guest presenters, ministry supervisors, CRC representatives, and others to present or share information relevant to the working group's requests and priorities.

The SDM consultants try to support requests for additional training whenever possible and work closely with agencies to provide direction on training needs. Part of the process with SFNSCI is identifying—through feedback and needs assessments with SFNSCI members—where research and curriculum development should focus in order to address training gaps that currently exist in child welfare. If SFNSCI is unable to develop the training at the time due to other projects or internal capacity, our organization will help plan and host requested trainings. For example, many agencies were requesting training in suicide awareness and self-harm support/education; in response, SFNSCI organized a group to present and provide a certificate of training for agency staff.

The CRC has been involved as a strategic partner since the beginning of our engagement with the SDM tools. The relationship between SFNSCI's SDM consultants and the CRC has been consistent. The CRC expressed an interest in and a commitment to supporting those agencies implementing SDM through potential site visits. The initial site visits were underutilized for various reasons, including a lack of communication from the CRC on its availability and the structure of potential site visits, as well as agencies being in the very early stages of implementation and thus not in a position to identify what CRC support for SDM may look like. SFNSCI's SDM consultants currently act as coordinators and liaisons between the CRC and the agencies, helping site visits to be successful.

Conclusion

All of the work done by the SDM consultants and SFNSCI to date could not possibly have been done without the essential element of relationship. The process of supporting FNCFS agencies in the implementation of the SDM system maintained alignment with SFNSCI's vision, mission, and values, which reflect First Nations culture in Saskatchewan. The agencies are the ones that have guided and supported this process. SDM consultants continue to build these relationships by spending time collaborating and meeting with individual agency staff at different community events and taking every opportunity to have conversations, learning more about FNCFS agency practices and communities. SFNSCI is grateful for the opportunity to continue working with Saskatchewan FNCFS agencies and those who serve First Nations children, youth, and families. This very important work is helping us to operationalize our vision, mission, principles, and values and to continually support the TRC's calls to action.

Discussion Questions

1. What are the unique needs of Indigenous communities in relation to training and preparation for working in distinct communities?
2. What are the key values driving the work of SFNSCI, and why are these values important in child welfare training?
3. Why is it important to adapt tools and customize training for communities?
4. What are the processes that are important to undertake when determining a community's need for training?

References

Freeman, B. (2011). Indigenous pathways to anti-oppressive practice. In D. Baines (Ed.), *Doing anti-oppressive practice: Social justice social work*. Halifax, NS: Fernwood Publishing.

Kovach, M. (2009). *Indigenous methodologies: Characteristics, conversations, and contexts*. Toronto, ON: University of Toronto Press.

NCCD Children's Research Center. (2008). *The structured decision making model: An evidence-based approach to human services*. Madison, WI: National Council on Crime and Delinquency.

NCCD Children's Research Center. (2017). *Policy and procedures manual for agencies not on LINKIN*. Madison, WI: National Council on Crime and Delinquency.

Office of the Auditor General of Ontario. (2015). *Annual report 2015*. Toronto, ON: Office of the Auditor General of Ontario.

Pennsylvania Child Welfare Resource Center. (1996). *A reference manual for the Pennsylvania Model of Risk Assessment*. Updated April 2015 for CPSL amendments. Mechanicsburg, PA: School of Social Work, University of Pittsburgh. Retrieved from http://www.pacwrc.pitt.edu/Curriculum/CTC/MOD5/Hndts/HO07_ARfrncMnlFrThPAMdlOfRskAssssmnt_CPSLRevision2015%20(2).pdf

SFNSCI (Saskatchewan First Nations Family and Community Institute). (n.d.). *Vision, mission, values.* Retrieved from http://www.sfnfci.ca/pages/organizational-structure.html

TRC (Truth and Reconciliation Commission of Canada). (2015). *Honouring the truth, reconciling for the future: Summary of the final report of the Truth and Reconciliation Commission of Canada.* Winnipeg, MB: TRC.

PART II

Practice

CHAPTER 3

Exploring Decolonization through Kinship Care Home Assessments

Julie Mann-Johnson and Daniel Kikulwe

Introduction

The United Nations Guidelines for Alternative Care of Children supports the use of kinship care, and literature suggests that children placed in kinship care achieve positive outcomes (Farmer, 2010; Messing, 2006; O'Brien, 2012). In this chapter, we use the definition of kinship care as the "placing of a child with a caregiver who is an extended family member of a child, or a person who has a significant relationship with the child, or is a member of the child's cultural community" (Alberta Human Services, 2011, policy 2.0). With Indigenous children being overrepresented in government care and often placed with non-Indigenous caregivers, the issue of kinship care and assessment is particularly crucial for Indigenous families and communities. In Alberta, 69 per cent of children in care are Indigenous (Alberta, 2017), yet Indigenous people represent only 6 per cent of the provincial population (Statistics Canada, 2011). Various calls to action from the Truth and Reconciliation Commission of Canada (TRC) and the United Nations Declaration on the Rights of Indigenous People

Suggested Citation: Mann-Johnson, J., & Kikulwe, D. (2018). Exploring decolonization through kinship care home assessments. In D. Badry, H. Montgomery, D. Kikulwe, M. Bennett, & D. Fuchs, (Eds.), *Imagining child welfare in the spirit of reconciliation* (pp. 44–68). Regina, SK: University of Regina Press.

propose that child welfare systems address these colonizing actions through fundamental changes to their relationships and interactions with Indigenous peoples. More broadly, these are calls for our collective obligation and effort to incorporate decolonizing approaches into child welfare practice, including use of kinship care placements.

This chapter will discuss the use and findings of a secondary data analysis to honour the voices of people who have shared their perspectives at public consultations and information-gathering events. The findings suggest crucial elements to consider and approaches to decolonizing practice in the area of kinship care home assessment. The discussion will explore opportunities and consideration for integrating a decolonizing approach into the practice of kinship care home assessments. This is done through exploring directions suggested by community members who participated in the public consultations on kinship care in Alberta, identifying what they considered important in terms of family placement practice.

Organization of the Chapter

In the first section, we identify our interests in the topic of kinship care. The second section provides the theoretical perspective that informs the chapter discussion. Next we provide an overview of the impacts of colonization on Indigenous peoples followed by an examination of the calls for change to colonial legacies both locally and internationally. These compel us to action toward meeting the needs of Indigenous children, families, and communities. Included in section four is information on the current state of kinship care in Alberta, with a summary of the key literature. Section five provides an overview of the methodology informing the secondary qualitative data analysis used to inform the discussion in section six. This analysis becomes a consideration in decolonizing kinship assessments. The final section concludes the key points of the chapter.

Locating Ourselves

The principal author and co-author, who have different ethnocultural backgrounds, share a commitment to child welfare work and preservation of families and therefore a focus on kinship care, which forms the main focus of this chapter. The principal author identifies herself as a settler woman and an ally. As a social worker in the child welfare system, she worked closely with Indigenous families, communities, and agencies. However, there was always an overwhelming barrier to meeting the needs of children, youth, and families. Rules, regulations, policies, procedures, forms, optics, perceptions, and many other words that suggest the status quo had to be maintained. This tension is something that she has been keenly interested in challenging. The co-author grew up in Uganda, a former British colony where communal parenting is common. It is a cliché to say that it takes a village to raise a child, but the reality for the co-author was that children are cared for within a cultural community, with grandparents, aunts, uncles, and older cousins all having responsibilities in child rearing. During his fourteen years of child protection work, the co-author was keenly interested in the notions of family preservation and family placements. This is the personal and professional background that draws the co-author to the topic of kinship care as an important placement option for children in care.

Theoretical Frameworks

With the history of structural colonialism in the child welfare system, an anti-colonialist perspective must be adopted. This perspective is the most appropriate approach in addressing the overrepresentation of Indigenous children in care (Hart, 2009; Pon, Gosine, & Phillips, 2011). It differs from anti-oppressive approaches, which have failed to address overrepresentation because they have failed to recognize the continuing issue of white supremacy in the dominant culture (Pon et al., 2011). An anti-colonialist approach considers colonialism to be persistent. Because colonialism continues, anti-colonialism should not be confused with post-colonialism, a concept that considers colonization as an event in the past (Hart, 2009). Rather, anti-colonialism is the embracing of an alternative or oppositional paradigm as well as "cultural revitalization" (Hart, 2009, p. 32). In practice, anti-colonialism focuses on the recovery of traditional Indigenous knowledge (Hart, 2009, p. 32). An anti-colonialist approach would suggest a reorganization that embraces the Indigenous traditional ways of knowing, helping, doing, and being. This perspective recognizes traditional Indigenous knowledge and proficiency and is applicable to both social work practice and kinship home assessment practice.

This chapter is also grounded in critical ecological systems theory. This theoretical approach integrates principles of social justice through questioning and self-reflective application of theory. Ecological theory gives "equal weight to the individuality of our clients as people and to the social environments that determine their well-being," recognizing that the person and environment are intricately connected and "reciprocally sustaining and shaping one another" (Rothery, 2008, pp. 90, 91). This theoretical approach has significant influence not only on child intervention practice but also on the practice of approving caregivers for children in care. Assessment practices for caregivers often use an ecological framework (Scannapieco & Hegar, 1996). However, to ensure a socially just approach to typically marginalized populations, adding a critical lens to the consideration of kinship caregivers is of significant importance.

Colonization and Child Welfare

In considering any aspect of child welfare practice, it is important to understand the colonizing impacts of legislation and policy. Starting in the sixteenth century (Ing, 2006) and formalized in 1876 through the Indian Act (Greenwood & de Leeuw, 2006), Indian residential schools were established and typically operated by various religious organizations. With a goal of cultural assimilation, these institutions contributed to severed ties between children and their families. Children were forbidden to speak their Indigenous languages, and they suffered a number of other atrocities and indignities (Ing, 2006). At the height of these schools' operations, in the 1940s, approximately 8,900 children were attending residential schools for the purposes of assimilation (Milloy, 2009). By numerous reports, many of these institutions were fraught with physical, emotional, sexual, and spiritual abuse, as well as high rates of death due to preventable causes—disease and negligence (Thobani, 2007). Residential schools introduced multi-generational dysfunction as Indigenous communities learned to cope with the trauma they experienced in the residential schools and from the loss of community, culture, and family (Blackstock, Clarke, Cullen, D'Hondt, & Formsma, 2004).

Some of these schools started closing in the 1950s, but legislative changes at the time allowed for the delivery of child welfare services on federal reserve land by provincial authorities (Kozlowski, Sinha, & Richard,

2012). These services were often delivered by social workers "who had little or no knowledge about colonization and residential schools [and] who often mistook symptoms of systemic discrimination as parental failure" (Blackstock, 2011, p. 188). This led to the Sixties Scoop, where numerous Indigenous children were apprehended and placed with non-Indigenous families who, in most cases, eventually adopted them. This practice led to another generation of Indigenous children who were not raised with their families or communities and were further colonized.

The contemporary manifestation of colonization has been the overrepresentation of Indigenous children in care (Trocmé, Knoke, & Blackstock, 2004). The issue of overrepresentation is complex, and its exploration is outside the scope of this chapter. It is important to note, however, that the recruitment and assessment of culturally appropriate and connected caregivers is a substantial issue for Indigenous children because of their overrepresentation in the child welfare system.

Calls for Change

Truth and Reconciliation Commission

After years of silence on Indigenous issues, the Canadian government created the TRC, which set out to hear the truth from Indigenous people across Canada about their experiences. The TRC (2015) aimed to address two important aspects: (1) legacies of colonialism and its practices through the child welfare, education, health, and justice systems, as well as language and culture; and (2) a road map to reconciliation, which included education, professional development, and training for public servants, church apologies, finding missing children and burial information, and the adoption of the United Nations Declaration on the Rights of Indigenous Peoples framework.

Relevant to this discussion, the TRC (2015) found the current policies and practices of the present-day child welfare system—which includes disproportionate funding for First Nations children and the overrepresentation of Indigenous people in child welfare and prison systems—to be a legacy of colonization and the residential school system. The commission heard that "the doors are closed at the [residential] homes, but the foster homes are still existing and [Indigenous] children are still taken" (TRC, 2015, p. 138). The overrepresentation of Indigenous children in care is important to the discussion of kinship assessments because the TRC recommended that Aboriginal children in temporary and permanent care be placed in culturally appropriate environments. Furthermore, it recommended in its calls to action that frontline child welfare staff be properly trained about the potential for Aboriginal families to provide more appropriate family healing (TRC, 2015). This call to action recognizes that Aboriginal families have the skills to address their own challenges. Aboriginal families possess the expertise. This notion aligns with the anti-colonizing approach and theoretical approach outlined above.

United Nations Declaration on the Rights of Indigenous Peoples

The United Nations Declaration on the Rights of Indigenous Peoples (UNDRIP) is another key starting point from which to move toward a decolonizing framework in Canada. Specific to the issue of kinship care and assessment, UNDRIP's Article 7 refers to the right for Aboriginal communities not to have their children removed on large scales (UN, 2008). If children are removed, they should still have access to their culture. Furthermore, according to Article 18, Indigenous people have the right to participate in decision-making that is characterized by free, prior, and informed consent and includes the ability to participate in any decision that affects their lives (UN, 2008).

Alberta Kinship Care: Current State

In this section, we discuss the benefits and challenges of kinship care. We also examine the kinship home assessment policies to contextualize how social work can engage in a decolonizing kinship caregiver screening process, using Alberta as a case example.

When children come into the care of child welfare, they are placed formally in various caregiving arrangements, as in the example of foster care, which is temporary, family-based care (Alberta, Ministry of Children's Services, 2016). These families are typically unknown to the child or the child's family. Children or youth can also be placed in group or residential care (Alberta, Ministry of Children's Services, 2016). These settings range from being community based to more institutional. However, as indicated in our introduction, kinship care is considered to be the "placing of a child with a caregiver who is an extended family member of a child, or a person who has a significant relationship with the child, or is a member of the child's cultural community" (Alberta Human Services, 2011, policy 2.0). Currently in Alberta, kinship care is the preferred placement option, in recognition that placement with family or community members ensures the strongest possible connection for that child to the culture and community (Alberta, Ministry of Children's Services, 2016).

Benefits of Kinship Care

Through the strong connection to culture and community offered by kinship care, children are raised in a familiar way. Research highlights a number of benefits of kinship care placement as compared to other placements. Children placed in kinship care experience a higher degree of placement stability (Farmer, 2010; Koh, 2010; Messing, 2006), as well as increased and more fluid contact with family (O'Brien, 2012). More so than their counterparts in non-kinship placements, these children experience healthy and natural identity formation (Ban, 2005; O'Brien, 2012; Shlonsky & Berrick, 2001). The literature also describes a reduction in trauma and stigma for children placed in kinship care (Berrick, 1997; Messing, 2006). An additional finding is that, for children placed in kinship care, there is a lower rate of recidivism. This means that following their return to parental care from kinship care, they are less likely to be re-apprehended and returned to government care (Berrick, 1997; Koh & Testa, 2011; Perry, Daly, & Kotler, 2012).

Challenges for Kinship Care

Kinship care also has its unique challenges. Demographically, kinship caregivers are generally older women, are less educated, are ethnic minorities, live in compromised communities, and experience health challenges (Berrick, 1997; Christenson & McMurty, 2009; Keller et al., 2001). Kinship caregivers also often have challenges with poverty (Falconnier et al., 2010; Farmer, 2009; Shlonsky & Berrick, 2001). These structural disadvantages suggest that kinship caregivers may need additional support, financial or otherwise, to make these placements successful. Yet research shows that they receive less contact from caseworkers and less services than non-kin caregivers (Fuentes-Palaez, Amoros, Pastor, Molina, & Mateo, 2015; Keller et al., 2001), further marginalizing kinship caregivers and the children they are caring for.

Generally, kinship caregivers have received less preparation and training prior to placement (Christenson & McMurty, 2009). Often the decision to become a caregiver happens in a state of crisis, whereas foster parents typically take two years to make the decision to become caregivers (Coakley, Cuddeback, Buehler, & Cox, 2007). The kinship caregiver's time for and degree of preparation should be considered in the system's expectations of families.

Further complicating the dynamics of kinship care placements are caseworker attitudes. Caseworkers may hold beliefs that the relative of an abusive or neglectful biological parent is also likely to be abusive or neglectful. Such beliefs have been found to create a barrier to kinship placement and practice. Research has found that some caseworkers sampled felt that, if grandparents, for example, were "responsible for creating or participating in the problematic behavior by having raised adult children who abused or neglected their children, why should they be supported in raising a new generation of children?" (Lorkovich, Piccola, Groza, Brindo, & Marks, 2004). Yet Lorkovich et al.'s (2004) research actually found that, in most cases, the birth parents' abusive or neglectful behaviour was the exception within the family of origin. The literature further suggests general skepticism and negative attitudes by caseworkers toward kinship care and government-issued financial support for kinship caregivers (Brisebois, Kernsmith, & Carcone, 2013).

Home Assessment Practice and Policy

O'Brien (2014) suggests that the experience for kinship caregivers is very different from that of adoptive and foster parents; however, assessment practice and policy do not reflect these unique elements—for example, that kinship caregivers tend to be older women, to experience health challenges, and to live in poverty (Berrick, 1997; Shlonsky & Berrick, 2001). They also, however, have an existing emotional connection to the children in their home, and this existing bond contributes to the positive experiences for children placed in kinship care (Messing, 2006). These dynamics contribute to the unique challenges of kinship care home assessment policy and practice.

Most jurisdictions, including Alberta, require a formal kinship home study as part of the approval process. Prospective kinship caregivers typically undergo a home assessment based on tools developed for middle-class adoptive families and based on modernist and empirical approaches (Pitcher, Meakings, & Farmer, 2013). These structured tools do not consider cultural traditions or context and only peripherally consider the opinions of other family members. Modernist home study practices exclude many potential kinship caregivers based on "class bias and are ignorant of the outcomes for children who live in kinship placements" (Calder & Talbot, 2006, p. 31). Furthermore, while families may appreciate the requirement for a formal evaluation of their homes, an extended assessment process can be an "unwelcome, incomprehensible, intrusive and worrying intervention" while they are adjusting to the unexpected provision of child care (O'Brien, 2014, p. 356). These issues become a barrier to many Indigenous family members hoping to provide care to the child.

One tool used extensively in Alberta is the Structured Analysis Family Evaluation (SAFE) home study tool. SAFE was developed in 1989 based on adoption home study practices and, loosely, on the Family Assessment Form (FAF) (Crea, Barth, & Chintapalli, 2007). It was intended to create a uniform home study methodology that would more thoroughly assess adoptive families through uniformity, efficiency, and psychosocial evaluation (Crea et al. 2007; Crea, Barth, Chintapalli, & Buchanan, 2009a). Over time, SAFE has been used not only for adoption but also as an assessment tool for different placement types, such as foster care and then kinship care (Crea et al., 2007). This differential use of home studies has been based on the assumption that "every person caring for a child with special needs should meet the same standards" (Crea et al., 2007, p. 151). However, this differential use does not recognize the difference in motivations or in caregivers' ability to make short- or long-term commitments to children (Crea et al., 2007). As identified earlier, the differences noted in the kinship care experience add a level of complexity in the differential use of a home study. These differences include motivations, demographics, experiences, challenges, structural barriers, and outcomes.

What SAFE does accomplish is to support staff who are inexperienced in home assessment practice. Crea, Barth, Chintapalli, and Buchanan (2009b) found less-experienced staff to be more positive about the use and impact of SAFE than more experienced staff. While this may suggest that inexperienced workers require a structured decision-making tool, or highlight an issue of change-management among senior staff, it also underscores the need for additional practice training in the home study process, including interviewing skills, engagement with clients, and assessment (Crea et al., 2009b).

Concerns have also been raised about the use of SAFE with Indigenous families and caregivers. The Aboriginal Advisor's report on the status of Indigenous child welfare in Ontario suggested that home study programs like SAFE should be removed until they could be modified to reflect Indigenous values and cultures. The report further suggested that home study programs and standards be developed that are specific to Indigenous communities (Beaucage, 2011).

The use of standardized assessment tools has been criticized as a colonizing action. The rise of risk assessment tools was welcomed in the mid-1990s; however, it has since been recognized that these risk assessment tools apply universal truths and assumptions that fail to account for social context and individuality (Swift & Callahan, 2009). The use of a standardized assessment tool for caregivers has been controversial and largely rejected by the Indigenous community (Beaucage, 2011) but welcomed by government agencies and bureaucrats. Standardized assessments are often upheld as beneficial tools aimed at harm reduction (Fairbairn & Strega, 2015). However, these tools have generally been found to be problematic for use with marginalized populations as they neglect the social and political contexts in which individual problems appear to arise. Standardized assessments can reproduce the gendered, classed, and raced constructions and parenting expectations of the dominant culture and impose them on marginalized populations (Choate & McKenzie, 2015; Fairbairn & Strega, 2015). Child welfare assessments become a colonizing process because families are challenged to meet a common dominant standard.

Methodology

In addition to the review of the literature on kinship care, content for this chapter was also generated through a secondary qualitative data analysis and a focus group of kinship care practitioners for discussion.

The secondary data analysis was completed using the comments from a series of community conversations and two summits held in Alberta to examine the Indigenous community's views about Indigenous children in government care. From 2011 to 2013, the Government of Alberta hosted sixteen community conversations in various communities, inviting 782 Indigenous leaders, community members, people with lived experience, and various service providers to speak to what was going well in the child intervention system and what needed to change (Alberta, 2014).

Secondary data analysis is "the use of an existing data set to find answers to a research question that differs from the question asked in the original or primary study" (Hinds, Vogel, & Clarke-Steffen, 1997, p. 408). The secondary use of data in quantitative studies has been common (Gillies & Edwards, 2005; Irwin & Winterton, 2011); however, the secondary analysis of qualitative studies is far less common and has been discussed in the literature more recently (Gillies & Edwards, 2005). Analyzing secondary data sets is a complex approach, yet archived sources of qualitative data have been described as a potential repository of valuable knowledge. Specifically, they are "a rich and unique yet often unexploited source of research material that can be reanalyzed, reworked, and compared with contemporary data" (Corti, Witzel, & Bishop, 2005, p. 1).

Irwin and Winterton (2011) identify areas of investigation that can benefit from a secondary analysis of qualitative data: for example, where further insight on hard-to-reach populations can be gained or sensitive topics can be addressed without further intrusion into vulnerable populations. It is well documented that Indigenous communities have been victimized and oppressed in the name of science (Hart, 2002; Smith, 1999). Decolonizing and anti-oppressive approaches that acknowledge power differences within the history of research with Indigenous populations seek to understand the "truth" for Indigenous populations rather than the "fact" identified by Western knowledge (Smith, 1999). This is also represented in an anti-colonizing approach.

One of the authors was compelled to use secondary data analysis when hearing participants at the community conversations describe their frustration with ongoing consultation and conversation without evidence that the information and comments being shared were used to change or influence practice (Mann-Johnson, 2016). The following comment from the community conversation echoes this frustration:

> *Been to SO MANY of these—this is ANOTHER conversation—where are all the other volumes of reports, all the ideas, all the good things—so frustrating—it's just talk, it's always just talk—nothing has changed.*

Secondary qualitative data analysis provides an opportunity to honour those "ideas" and "good things" shared by the community. In addition to analyzing data from the community conversations, this secondary data set included comments from a number of summits also hosted by the Government of Alberta to discuss home study practice particularly with Indigenous communities.

Challenges exist in secondary data analysis, and the quality of the original data, data "fit," and the nature of the relationship between the research and the data must be considered (Whiteside, Mills, & McCallum, 2012). In a secondary analysis of primary data, consideration must be paid to the quality of the primary data. The quality of secondary data may be problematic if the data is outdated, if some data or information is missing, if there were weaknesses in the original research design, or if there was a poorly documented methodology (Whiteside et al., 2012). Assessing the quality of the primary research design can be challenging, unless the researcher has access to or was involved in the primary research (Hinds et al., 1997). The research question within the secondary data analysis must "fit" with the purpose, context, and time period of the primary research. Furthermore, it is important that the secondary study has a similar theoretical framework to the primary study (Van den Berg cited in Corti et al., 2005) and a similar time frame (Gillies & Edwards cited in Corti et al., 2005).

These limitations were addressed by one of the authors, Mann-Johnson, having had direct contact with or been directly involved in the data gathering and principal investigators of these primary qualitative data collections. Both primary investigations were also grounded in anti-colonialism frameworks. There were, however, instances when the data quality led to comments being unusable. Some comments were ineligible or incomplete, but it is important to note that these were very few (10 of the 13,000) (Mann-Johnson, 2016). Permission was given to use this data for the purposes of an analysis of home assessment practice with the rationale that it had been made clear to participants that the information gathered would be used to enhance child intervention practice.

For both data sets, the direct comments that had been recorded by note takers were reviewed. This included 13,000 comments from the community conversations and flip chart notes from the summit meetings. Comments that related to kin, extended family, caregivers, and the assessment and/or recruitment of caregivers were chosen to be included in the analysis. Thematic analysis was used and specifically approached through thematic network mapping. This approach to analysis provided a means to organize a very large data set. Attride-Stirling (2001) describes the use of thematic networks as an organizational aid to thematic analysis by facilitating the depiction of themes and their interrelationship.

Themes noted from this analysis were then presented to a focus group of ten kinship care practitioners from across Alberta recruited through purposive sampling. The conversation from the focus group was recorded, transcribed, and then analyzed using a similar methodology of thematic analysis and thematic network mapping again.

Listening to the Community-Decolonizing Kinship Care Home Assessment

Comments from the community showed a desire to return to traditional ways of communal caring for children (Mann-Johnson, 2016). This system of communal caring includes involvement from community, Elders, and extended family and is foundational to kinship care. Data findings from Indigenous communities, practitioners, and leaders from child welfare and Indigenous organizations are depicted in terms of an ecological framework that identifies five crucial areas where critical reflection is required: assessor characteristics; important areas to address; home assessment process; safety, policy and legislated requirements; and systemic issues (Mann-Johnson, 2016).

The interconnected themes highlight the complexity of kinship care home assessment. Decolonizing this area of practice cannot be done solely through changes to the process or the practitioner's skill or approach. The complexity comes from a number of systemic, political, and legislative influences, as well as from the practitioner's skill and the process used to complete the assessment. Values, beliefs, worldviews, and personal standards are all influential in the interpretation of an assessment. The interplay of the global themes—assessor characteristics; important areas to address;

home assessment process; safety, policy and legislated requirements; and systemic issues—are crucial elements in understanding this area of home assessment practice. Each of these themes contains subthemes and concepts to further describe elements that are crucial to kinship care home assessment. They all provide depth to understand and critically reflect on practice to ensure an anti-colonizing approach (see Figure 1).

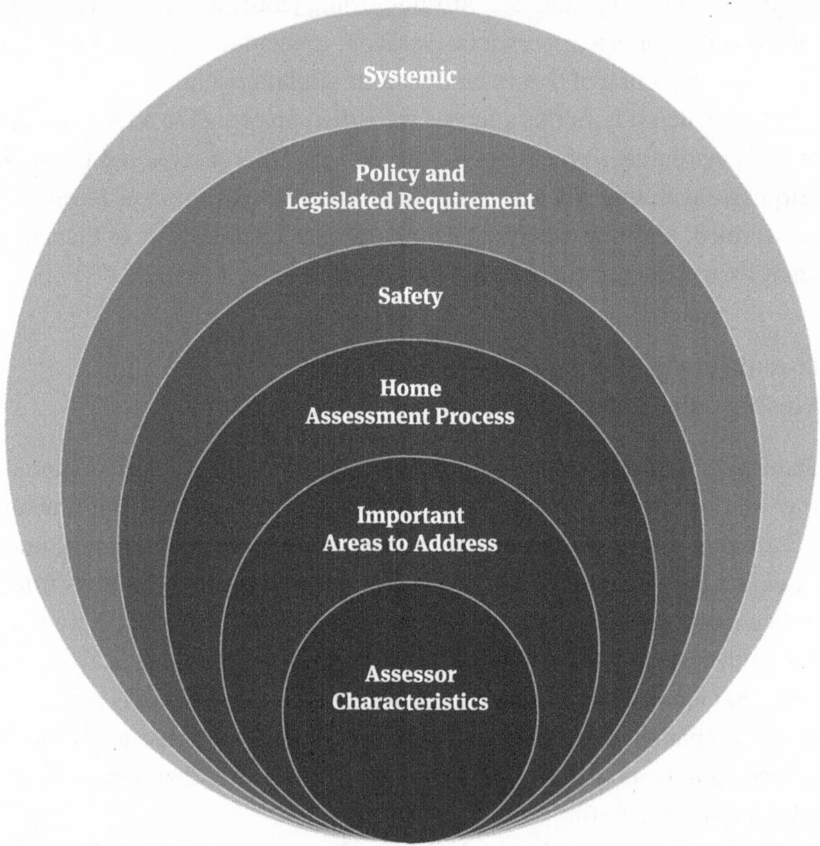

Figure 1. Decolonizing Kinship Care Home Assessment Model

The foundation of the model consists of home assessor characteristics. This describes the social workers completing home assessments with Indigenous families and how they should be supported by child welfare organizations through training, supervision, and mentorship. The characteristics that social workers practising in this area should possess were identified as being collaborative, able to build relationships, skilled in communicating, experienced in home assessment, possessing critical thinking, culturally competent, reflexive, respectful, strengths based, and located in proximity to the community. These should be considerations in the hiring, training, mentoring, and performance management of these staff.

Next in the model is what is referred to as important areas to address. These are the areas that community members identified as being important to a child, the family, and caregivers. Structured assessments in current use might call these important areas to address the "domains" of the assessment. We believe that the following domains suggested by the community be included as part of assessment. These areas include the ability of the caregiver to meet a child's needs, the caregiver's characteristics, and an analysis of the information gathered in the assessment process. A child's needs were identified as love, stability, having special needs met, relationships, and cultural connections. The importance of understanding a caregiver's ability to meet those needs is crucial, but understanding them in a mutually respectful and collaborative manner is paramount.

A compelling example of differing points of view on the crucial elements of kinship care is the concept of love. In this study, a focus group of practitioners saw the concept of love as too complex and difficult to measure or analyze in an assessment, as it is strongly dependent on the practitioner's lens or worldview. It was, however, identified by the community as being very important and relevant. While practitioners agreed that a child being loved and experiencing love was important, they reported in the focus group that love may not get the caregiver through difficult times or through the challenges of caregiving. To the contrary, the community reported that "love can make up for a lack of skills, but skills cannot make up for a lack of love." Experts may not agree that this emotional interaction exceeds the importance of Westernized skill and insight in parenting; however, from an anti-colonizing perspective, the community's position must be respected and honoured as the authority.

Crucial elements identified in the area of the home assessment process included the importance of a user-friendly process, ongoing assessment, being collaborative, and the tool itself. Also of note is addressing the barriers within the current process. One of these barriers is a focus on history and historical concerns. While these findings suggest that the focus on history becomes an unnecessary barrier, the focus group identified the need to address history and potential "legacies" in order to fully assess a potential caregiver's suitability. While many acknowledge the challenges for many kinship caregivers related to their unique demographics, such as poverty, health challenges, or other structural issues, the literature review did not indicate past trauma or legacies for kinship caregivers. In fact, Lorkovich et al. (2004) found that this attitude among caseworkers created barriers and was unfounded. In considering the long-standing impacts of colonizing actions like residential schools and the Sixties Scoop, an inappropriate focus on trauma history and "legacies" immediately places Indigenous families at a disadvantage.

Comments related to the home assessment process also suggest that a "one size fits all" approach to kinship care home assessment is not appropriate in a diverse society. The measurement of what is *good enough* or *safe enough* may not be the same for every population or community. Critics of standardized assessment tools suggest this is the case for standardized assessment. If dominant-culture definitions of parenting are being used, then Indigenous families and parents are again at an immediate disadvantage (Choate & McKenzie, 2015). In this area of practice, standardized assessment should be approached with caution. The dominant culture's notions of parenting, safety, standards, and the "good enough" parent could be irrelevant to marginalized groups, including Indigenous populations. Therefore, it could be further suggested that the elements for assessment that are crucial in one community or population are different from others in terms of values, history, tradition, and social norms. Thus, the crucial elements identified in this research should not be used to create standardized assessment tools. Rather, they can inform practice, process, legislation, policy, and other systemic issues.

Safety is identified as an element in the continuing legacy of colonization and is apparent in the analysis of this element. Assumptions on who gets to decide what is safe enough or good enough for a child strike at the core of colonization, and the institutions, legislation, and other structures that surround each decision suggest structural colonization. For example, the reported difficulties with meeting imposed standards, coupled with a lack of resources, further marginalize these families. Instead, a collaborative approach is suggested where practices such as circle processes, like family group conferencing and collaborative case planning, allow for open discussion and safety planning.

Similarly, the concept of standards is significant. The community comments described standards as colonizing. Particularly in considering that the standards being applied are Western standards, we must accept that they are colonizing. Practitioners using reflexivity recognize the influence of Western standards and their application to marginalized and Indigenous communities as problematic. However, Western standards are entrenched in the practice through environmental checklists and policy requirements. The question of "whose standards" must be addressed. However, in order to address the issue from an anti-colonizing perspective, the community must define these standards. The question remains whether or not the child intervention system will be able to accommodate and accept an external definition and identification of community standards. Some of the tensions regarding standards were in the area of housing. For example, concerns about sharing bedrooms or having a high number of residents in one home are common in Indigenous communities and homes. Yet community members feel these concerns are judged negatively by home assessment practitioners.

Differing worldviews are apparent, and it appears that Indigenous families are being viewed through a Western lens. In the study this is seen in comments relating to role shifts, and the impacts of these shifts on caregivers and children assume a nuclear-family approach to family structure (Mann-Johnson, 2016). Indigenous communities traditionally provide care to their children and Elders communally. The assumption made by some Western practitioners is that a role shift from grandmother to parent may be difficult. However, this may not be the case in an Indigenous family or in other cultures where communal and multi-generational family caregiving is common. This challenge may be an assumption based on the dominant culture's worldview.

An area identified under the theme of policy and legislated requirements was the provision of support to kinship caregivers and implementation of policies enabling this support. Literature suggests that kinship caregivers receive less contact from caseworkers than do non-kin caregivers (Fuentes-Palaez et al., 2015; Keller et al., 2001). Ongoing supports and services were identified as crucial elements in kinship care practice (Mann-Johnson, 2016). This is a worthy consideration in the analysis of kinship care practice in general.

Policy and legislated requirements also identified proceduralism as a barrier, and the data from the community suggested a desire to return to traditional ways of communal caring for children through the involvement of community, Elders, and extended family (Mann-Johnson, 2016). Yet a Western child intervention system demands a level of proceduralism that does not align with the traditional Indigenous ways. Still, it continues to be the priority and drives current practice. A risk-averse system continues to seek risk management in the use of standardized assessments to the detriment of marginalized populations. Proceduralism drives the priorities in practice, but it has also become status quo, making it difficult to entertain the possibility that another approach could be possible. The Mann-Johnson (2016) study identified that, as the participants described what was required in kinship home assessment practice, their description was also heavily influenced by the status quo and a discomforting sense that any deviation from the status quo is not only wrong but potentially dangerous. No one ever wants a child to be at risk in any placement, but does this mean the status quo is the only way to reach a level that is "safe enough"? Critical theorists suggest that there cannot be one universal truth or approach, as there are complex existing realities (Swift & Callahan, 2009).

Systemic issues such as resources, colonization, and the need to preserve families were identified. Social workers practising in the field of home assessments must contemplate the crucial elements and also employ a critical ecological approach to this work. Aligning with the themes identified as crucial elements of home assessment, a critical ecological approach considers a potential caregiver's social context. Assessment from a critical ecological perspective reflects on the "goodness of fit" between the person and the circumstances of the environment (Rothery, 2008). This assessment will inform what the caregiver intends to do in the care of the child and is capable of doing based on a number of influences. This approach would also inform the supports and services required to mitigate any potential challenges in the care of a child with the systemic influences that are important to consider in the assessment. Without this theoretical approach, assessments can be oppressive and continue colonizing legacies.

The findings did not identify one alternative or direction to change in order to decolonize kinship home assessment practice. And as discussed, creating another structured tool is not the answer to meeting the needs of children placed in kinship care or their prospective caregivers. There is no "magic answer" but rather a recognition that to reform kinship home assessment practice changes must occur on many levels. Practice leaders and policy-makers within child welfare organizations must consider the micro and macro elements of this practice and their opportunities to support both areas. These practice leaders and policy-makers may make operational and human resource decisions that support staff to integrate the crucial elements into their practice and to meet community needs. However, they also have opportunities to advocate for systemic or policy and legislative changes that are suggested here to impact kinship caregivers and assessment. Qualitative data suggests potential areas to consider in ensuring that kinship caregivers are appropriately and adequately assessed in considering their roles and experiences. With this data, practitioners could inform their practice by considering what elements they bring with them to a home assessment and its interviews (Mann-Johnson, 2016).

Conclusion

This discussion focused specifically on the impacts of kinship home assessment practices on Indigenous children, caregivers, and families. Completing kinship home assessments that are decolonizing and meet the needs of those children, caregivers, and families is just one area to consider in reforming child welfare practice as called for by the TRC and UNDRIP. Because a great majority of children in the care of child welfare are Indigenous, an Indigenous focus is justified and an anti-colonizing approach is necessary in this field of practice. Without reflecting on the status quo and the policy or legislation that permeates and protects our practice from changing, we are perpetuating colonization in contemporary times.

Positive shifts are occurring. The January 2016 ruling by the Canadian Human Rights Tribunal compelled the Government of Canada to abide by Jordan's Principle, which declares that conflicts over funding and jurisdiction shall not interfere with the receipt of health or social services for First Nations people. The ruling also supported the submission that a discrepancy in funding between First Nations children and non–First Nations children was discriminatory (FNCFCS, 2016). Other policy and practice changes in Alberta—such as the adoption of Family Finding practice and the Child Intervention Practice Framework, which includes an Indigenous experience principle—are promising changes toward decolonizing practice that recognizes the role of kin and the expertise of Indigenous people in caring for their community (Alberta, Ministry of Children's Services, 2017).

There is not one magic answer for decolonizing home assessments or child intervention practice overall. Rather, the community has provided feedback on many ways that practice, process, regulations, and the system can shift toward a decolonized approach that can meet the needs of Indigenous children in government care. And we must listen.

Discussion Questions

1. Discuss some of the ways that kinship care can be utilized to address issues of overrepresentation of Indigenous and racialized children in care.
2. Discuss the importance of social workers' understanding and application of the UNDRIP.
3. How are you incorporating human rights–based approaches into your social work practice?

References

Alberta. (2014). What we heard: *A summary of the community conversations*. Retrieved from http://humanservices.alberta.ca/documents/community-conversations-what-weheard.pdf

Alberta. (2017). *Child intervention information and statistics summary: 2016/17 fourth quarter (March) update*. Retrieved from http://www.humanservices.alberta.ca/documents/child-intervention-info-stats-summary-2016-17-q4.pdf

Alberta Human Services. (2011, October 1). *Enhancement policy manual*. Retrieved from http://www.humanservices.alberta.ca/documents/Enhancement-Act-Policy-Manual.pdf

Alberta. Ministry of Children's Services. (2016). *Children in care*. Retrieved from http://humanservices.alberta.ca/abuse-bullying/17183.html

Alberta. Ministry of Children's Services. (2017). *Child intervention practice framework*. Retrieved from http://www.humanservices.alberta.ca/abuse-bullying/17242.html

Attride-Stirling, J. (2001). Thematic networks: An analytical tool for qualitative research. *Qualitative Research, 1*(3), 385–405.

Ban, P. (2005). Aboriginal child placement principle and family group conferences. *Australian Social Work, 58*(4), 384–394.

Beaucage, J. (2011). *Children first: The Aboriginal Advisor's report on the status of Aboriginal child welfare in Ontario.* Retrieved from http://www.children.gov.on.ca/htdocs/English/professionals/indigenous/child_welfare-2011.aspx

Berrick, J. (1997). Assessing quality of care in kinship and foster family care. *Family Relations, 46*(3), 273–280.

Blackstock, C. (2011) The Canadian Human Rights Tribunal on First Nations Child Welfare: Why if Canada wins, equality and justice lose. *Children and Youth Services Review, 33*(1), 187–194.

Blackstock, C., Clarke, S., Cullen, J., D'Hondt, J., & Formsma, J. (2004). *Keeping the promise: The Convention on the Rights of the Child and the lived experiences of First Nations children and youth.* Ottawa: First Nations Child and Family Caring Society of Canada. Retrieved from https://fncaringsociety.com/sites/default/files/20.KeepingThePromise.pdf

Blackstock, C., Trocmé, N., & Bennett, M. (2004). Child maltreatment investigations among Aboriginal and non-Aboriginal families in Canada. *Violence against Women, 10*(88), 901–916.

Brisebois, K., Kernsmith, P. D., & Carcone, A. I. (2013). The relationship between caseworker attitudes about kinship care and removal decisions. *Journal of Family Social Work, 16*(5), 403–417.

Calder, M. C., & Talbot, C. (2006). Contemporary assessment: A critique. In C. Talbot & M. C. Calder (Eds.), *Assessment in kinship care* (pp. 25–54). Dorset, United Kingdom: Russell House.

Choate, P., & McKenzie, A. (2015). Psychometrics in parenting capacity assessments: A problem for Aboriginal parents. *First People Child and Family Review, 10*(2), 31–43.

Christenson, B., & McMurty, J. (2009). A longitudinal evaluation of the preservice training and retention of kinship and non-kinship foster/adoptive families one and a half years after training. *Child Welfare, 88*(4), 5–22.

Coakley, T. M., Cuddeback, G., Buehler, C., & Cox, M. E. (2007). Kinship foster parents' perceptions of factors that promote or inhibit successful fostering. *Children and Youth Services Review, 29*(1), 92–109.

Corti, L., Witzel, A., & Bishop, L. (2005). On the potentials and problems of secondary analysis: An introduction to the FQS special issue on secondary analysis of qualitative data. *Forum: Qualitative Social Research, 6*(1), Art. 49.

Crea, T. M., Barth, R. P., & Chintapalli, L. K. (2007). Home study methods for evaluating prospective resource families: History, current challenges, and promising approaches. *Child Welfare, 86*(2), 141–159.

Crea, T. M., Barth, R. P., Chintapalli, L. K., & Buchanan, R. L. (2009a). The implementation and expansion of SAFE: Frontline responses and the transfer of technology to practice. *Children and Youth Services Review, 31*(8), 903–910.

Crea, T. M., Barth, R. P., Chintapalli, L. K., & Buchanan, R. L. (2009b). Structured home study evaluations: Perceived benefits of SAFE versus conventional home studies. *Adoption Quarterly, 12*(2), 78–99.

Fairbairn, M., & Strega, S. (2015). Anti-oppressive approaches to child protection: Assessment and file recording. In J. Carriere & S. Strega (Eds.), *Walking this path together: Anti-racist and anti-oppressive child welfare practice* (2nd ed.) (pp. 157–175). Halifax, NS: Fernwood Publishing.

Falconnier, L. A., Tomasello, N. M., Doueck, H. J., Wells, S. J., Luckey, H., & Agathen, J. M. (2010). Indicators of quality in kinship foster care. *Families in Society: The Journal of Contemporary Social Services, 91*(4), 415–420.

Farmer, E. (2009). Making kinship care work. *Adoption and Fostering, 33*(3), 15–27.

Farmer, E. (2010). What factors relate to good placement outcomes in kinship care? *British Journal of Social Work, 40*(2), 426–444.

FNCFCS (First Nations Child and Family Caring Society of Canada). (2016, October 31). *Canadian Human Rights Tribunal decisions on First Nations child welfare and Jordan's Principle* (Information sheet, Case Reference CHRT 1340/7008). Retrieved from https://fncaringsociety.com/sites/default/files/Info%20sheet%20Oct%2031.pdf

Fuentes-Palaez, N., Amoros, P., Pastor, C., Molina, M. C., & Mateo, M. (2015). Assessment in kinship foster care: A new tool to evaluate strengths and weaknesses. *Social Sciences, 4*(1), 1–17. doi:10.3390/socsci4010001

Gillies, V., & Edwards, R. (2005). Secondary analysis in exploring family and social change: Addressing the issue of context. *Forum: Qualitative Social Research, 6*(1).

Greenwood, M., & de Leeuw, S. (2006) Fostering indigeneity: The role of Aboriginal mothers and Aboriginal early child care in response to colonial foster-care interventions. In D. M. Lavell-Harvard & J. Corbiere Lavell (Eds.), *Until our hearts are on the ground: Aboriginal mothering, oppression, resistance, and rebirth* (pp. 173–183). Toronto, ON: Demeter Press.

Hart, M. A. (2002). *Seeking mino-pimatisiwin: An Aboriginal approach to healing.* Halifax, NS: Fernwood Publishing.

Hart, M. A. (2009). Anti-colonial Indigenous social work: Reflections on an Aboriginal approach. In R. Sinclair, M. A. Hart, & G. Bruyere (Eds.), *Wicihitowin Aboriginal social work in Canada* (pp. 25–41). Halifax, NS: Fernwood Publishing.

Hinds, P. S., Vogel, R. J., & Clarke-Steffen, L. (1997). The possibilities and pitfalls of doing a secondary analysis of a qualitative data set. *Qualitative Health Research, 7*(3), 408–424.

Ing, R. (2006). Canada's Indian residential schools and their impacts on mothering. In D. M. Lavell-Harvard & J. Corbiere Lavell (Eds.), *Until our hearts are on the ground: Aboriginal mothering, oppression, resistance, and rebirth* (pp. 157–172). Toronto, ON: Demeter Press.

Irwin, S., & Winterton, M. (2011). *Debates in qualitative analysis: Critical reflections* (Timescapes Working Paper Series No. 4). Retrieved from http://www.timescapes.leeds.ac.uk/assets/files/WP4-March-2011.pdf

Keller, T. E., Wetherbee, K., LeProhn, N. S., Payne, V., Sim, K., & Lamont, E. R. (2001). Competencies and problem behaviours of children in family foster care: Variations by kinship placement status and race. *Children and Youth Services Review, 23*(12), 915–940.

Koh, E. (2010). Permanency outcomes of children in kinship and non-kinship foster care: Testing the external validity of kinship effects. *Children and Youth Services Review, 32*(3), 389–398.

Koh, E., & Testa, M. F. (2011). Children discharged from kin and non-kin foster homes: Do the risks of foster care re-entry differ? *Children and Youth Services Review, 33*(9), 1497–1505.

Kozlowski, A., Sinha, V., & Richard, K. (2012). *First Nations child welfare in Ontario*. Montreal, QC: McGill University, Centre for Research on Children and Families.

Lorkovich, T. W., Piccola, T., Groza, V., Brindo, M., & Marks, J. (2004). Kinship care and permanence: Guiding principles for policy and practice. *Families in Society: The Journal of Contemporary Social Services, 85*(2), 159–164.

Mann-Johnson, J. (2016). *Decolonizing home assessment practice at the kitchen table: A thematic analysis identifying the crucial elements in the assessment of kinship caregivers* (Master's thesis). University of Calgary. Retrieved from http://hdl.handle.net/11023/2938

Messing, J. T. (2006). From the child's perspective: A qualitative analysis of kinship care placements. *Children and Youth Services Review, 28*(12), 1415–1434.

Milloy, J. (1999). *A national crime: The Canadian government and the residential school system, 1879 to 1986*. Winnipeg, MB: University of Manitoba Press.

O'Brien, V. (2012). The benefits and challenges of kinship care. *Child Care in Practice, 18*(2), 127–146.

O'Brien, V. (2014). Responding to the call: A conceptual model for kinship care assessment. *Child & Family Social Work, 19*(3), 355–366.

Perry, G., Daly, D., & Kotler, J. (2012). Placement stability in kinship and non-kin foster care: A Canadian study. *Children and Youth Services Review, 34*(2), 460–465.

Pitcher, D., Meakings, S., & Farmer, E. (2013). Siblings and kinship care. In D. Pitcher (Ed.), *Inside kinship care: Understanding family dynamics and providing effective support* (pp. 47–63). London, United Kingdom: Jessica Kingsley.

Pon, G., Gosine, K., & Phillips, D. (2011). Immediate response: Addressing anti-native and anti-black racism in child welfare. *International Journal of Child, Youth, & Family Studies, 2*(3–4), 385–409.

Rothery, M. (2008). Critical ecological systems theory. In N. Coady & P. Leahmann (Eds.), *Theoretical perspectives for direct social work practice* (pp. 89–118). New York, NY: Springer.

Scannapieco, M., & Hegar, R. L. (1996). A non-traditional assessment framework for formal kinship homes. *Child Welfare, 75*(5), 567–582.

Shlonsky, A. R., & Berrick, J. D. (2001). Assessing and promoting quality in kin and non-kin foster care. *Social Service Review, 75*(1), 60–83.

Smith, L. T. (1999). Decolonizing methodologies: Research and Indigenous peoples. New York, NY: Zed Books.

Statistics Canada. (2011). National Household Survey (NHS)–Analytical products, 2011. Aboriginal people in Canada: First Nations, Métis, and Inuit. Retrieved from http://www12.statcan.gc.ca/nhs-enm/2011/as-sa/99-011-x/99-011-x2011001-eng.cfm

Swift, K., & Callahan, M. (2009). *At risk: Social justice in child welfare and other human services*. Toronto, ON: University of Toronto Press.

Thobani, S. (2007). *Exalted subjects: Studies in the making of race and nation in Canada* (Google Play Books version). Retrieved from https://play.google.com

TRC (Truth and Reconciliation Commission of Canada). (2012). *They came for the children: Canada, Aboriginal peoples, and residential schools*. Retrieved from http://publications.gc.ca/collections/collection_2012/cvrc-trcc/IR4-4-2012-eng.pdf

TRC (Truth and Reconciliation Commission of Canada). (2015). *Honouring the truth, reconciling for the future: Summary of the final report of the Truth and Reconciliation Commission of Canada*. Retrieved from http://nctr.ca/assets/reports/Final%20Reports/Executive_Summary_English_Web.pdf

Trocmé, N., Knoke, D., & Blackstock, C. (2004). Pathways to the overrepresentation of Aboriginal children in Canada's child welfare system. *Social Service Review, 78*(4), 577–600.

UN (United Nations). (2008, March). *United Nations Declaration on the Rights of Indigenous Peoples*. Geneva: UN. Retrieved from http://www.un.org/esa/socdev/unpfii/documents/DRIPS_en.pdf

Whiteside, M., Mills, J., & McCalman, J. (2012). Using secondary data for grounded theory analysis. *Australian Social Work, 65*(4), 504–516.

CHAPTER 4

Aging Out of Care: The Rural Experience

Anne Marie McLaughlin, Richard Enns, and Deena Seaward

Introduction

Between 1992 and 2007, the number of Canadian children in government care is estimated to have increased from 42,000 to 67,000 (Mulcahy & Trocmé, 2010). While these are estimates, exact numbers are difficult to obtain. No system is in place nationally to track children in out-of-home placements. Researchers must rely on aggregating provincial data, recognizing that different jurisdictions may define and count out-of-home care differently. Even when considering this proviso, nearly 1 out of every 100 children will enter the child welfare system at some point in their lives. In Canada, youth typically leave care at eighteen years of age, although extended care agreements and transitional programs enable some youth to receive services past their eighteenth birthday (Lerch & Stein, 2010). For example, in Ontario, services are terminated at the age of twenty-one (OACAS, 2006), while in Alberta services may be provided to the age of twenty-four (Courtney, Piliavin, Grogan-Kaylor, & Nesmith, 2001).

Research in Canada, and internationally, reveals poor outcomes for many of these youth (Courtney et al., 2001; Gough & Fuchs, 2008; Keller,

---

Suggested Citation: McLaughlin, A. M., Enns, R., & Seaward, D. (2018). Aging out of care: The rural experience. In D. Badry, H. Montgomery, D. Kikulwe, M. Bennett, & D. Fuchs, (Eds.), *Imagining child welfare in the spirit of reconciliation* (pp. 69–92). Regina, SK: University of Regina Press.

Cusick, & Courtney, 2007; Stapleton & Tweddle, 2012; Tweddle, 2007). Compared to their peers, a significant number of youth who age out of care have poorer employment and education outcomes (Reid & Dudding, 2006; Rutman, Hubberstey, & Feduniw, 2007), fewer adult supports (Antle, Johnson, Barbee, & Sullivan, 2009; Avery, 2010; Courtney & Dworsky, 2006; Dworsky & Courtney, 2010a; Keller et al., 2007; Samuels, 2009), increased criminal justice involvement (Maschi, Smith Hatcher, Schwalbe, & Scotto Rosato, 2008), higher levels of substance abuse (Brown & Wilderson, 2010; Dworsky & Courtney, 2010a; Rutman et al., 2007), a higher incidence of homelessness (Leslie & Hare, 2000; Serge, Eberle, Goldberg, Sullivan, & Dudding, 2002), and a higher incidence of risky sexual activities that can result in early pregnancies or sexually transmitted infections (Dworsky & Courtney, 2010b; Rutman et al., 2007). Youth leaving care are also more likely to experience mental health issues, including depression (Dworsky, 2005; Dworsky & Courtney, 2010b; Macomber et al., 2008; Reid & Dudding, 2006; Rutman et al., 2007), post-traumatic stress disorder (Dworsky & Courtney, 2010a; McMillen et al., 2004; Rutman et al., 2007; Southerland, Casaneuva, & Ringeisen, 2004), substance abuse, and suicide (Reid & Dudding, 2006). Although they are likely to be at similar risk, less is known about rural youth aging out of care and their outcomes, which is the focus of this chapter.

In collaboration with our community partners (Alberta Child and Family Services and Catholic Social Services, Edmonton), this study endeavoured to explore the transition experiences of youth in care, and the individuals who support them, in order to understand how communities and service providers can better support youth as they age out of government care. The study also builds on prior knowledge to (1) enhance our understanding of the needs of emerging adults who are aging out of government care and (2) increase our understanding of the role of community stakeholders and the factors that influence their participation in the transition process. The following research questions framed our data collection and analysis:

1. What are the experiences of rural youth who are permanent wards of the government as they plan for and prepare to transition out of the care of the government?
2. What are the experiences of caregivers (foster parents, child welfare workers, PGO workers) as they plan for and prepare to transition youth in their care out of the child welfare system?

Procedure and Methodology

Using qualitative research methods, we conducted semi-structured exploratory interviews with research participants to uncover challenges and issues within rural transition experiences for youth leaving the care of the government and their caregivers. Ethical approval was obtained (University of Calgary, Conjoint Faculties Research Ethics Board) prior to our entry into the field. Our research team met with managers in three rural child welfare offices in northern Alberta to better understand transition issues in a rural context and to discuss recruitment strategies. As part of the recruitment process, our research team made presentations to frontline and supervisory staff at each office to explain processes and answer questions. Throughout the study, we met with members of the research team to share and discuss emerging themes.

The sample was recruited from diverse service settings within two separate Child and Family Service Authorities (CFSAs): three rural offices and one urban. Rurality has many definitions, but we adopted the following definition provided by Statistics Canada: towns and municipalities outside the commuting zone of larger urban centres (i.e., outside the commuting zone of centres with population of 10,000 or more) (du Plessis, Beshiri, & Bollman, 2001). Crucial to an exploratory examination, these diverse settings were chosen in order to ensure sample diversity. We were interested in the experiences of rural youth who remained in or near their geographical community, as well as those who had migrated or planned to migrate to an urban community, and the experiences of their caregivers. We interviewed nine youth between the ages of seventeen and twenty-one. In addition, we interviewed foster parents/caregivers (*n*=10) and child welfare workers (*n*=10) who had experience supporting youth as they aged out of care. In total, we conducted twenty-nine qualitative interviews to obtain an in-depth understanding of the challenges of aging out of care in rural Alberta. The initial sample was broadly selected to represent possible variance in the experiences and perspectives of transitions. Included in the initial interviews were participants who varied by stage of transition, age, gender, geographical location, supportive networks, and ethnicity. Once sampling and data analysis of the initial interviews was completed, theoretical sampling around the preliminary and tentative categories guided further sampling and narrowed the research focus (Strauss

& Corbin, 1998). For example, the issue of second chances emerged early as an area of interest.

Potential youth and caregiver participants were identified and informed of the study by our community research partners. If a youth indicated interest in participating in the study, the service providers obtained consent from the participant and his or her legal guardian (where appropriate) to release their names and contact information to the research team. Youth were then contacted by a research team member, who explained the purpose and procedures of the study and inquired about potential participation. Caregiver participants were identified and contacted—also by their service provider—before being contacted by the research team; child welfare workers from the rural offices were recruited on a volunteer basis through the presentations and information provided by the research team. Potential participants were informed that their participation was entirely voluntary, and written consent was obtained from individuals interested in participating in the study. A small stipend was provided to youth (in most cases a twenty-dollar gift card) who were interested and able to participate, in recognition of their contribution to the research.

Interviews were recorded digitally and transcribed verbatim. All identifying information was removed from the transcripts. Computer-assisted qualitative data management and analysis software (NVivo 10) assisted in facilitating data management, coding, and retrieval. Data from each category of participant—caregiver, child welfare worker, and youth—was analyzed separately. Open coding was followed by focused coding as per grounded theory tenets (Charmaz, 2006), and key thematic categories were identified for each of the participant categories. Following individual category analysis, the research team analyzed the main themes in relation to one another in order to identify overarching themes, which best suited a comprehensive understanding of main concerns when considering support of youth aging out of care.

Results

We have used detailed quotations throughout this chapter to reflect the participants' views on the issues and concerns about youth aging out care in rural Alberta. Four central concerns arise from our analysis: extended care, second chances, improved engagement, and coordination and collaboration.

Extended Care

Our results indicate a need for extended government services past the age of eighteen, the currently accepted age of transition in Alberta. Extended care agreements (Supports and Financial Assistance Agreements or SFAAS) are an important element in transitional planning but are not the only tool. In fact, SFAAS appear to be most beneficial to youth who are on track with educational or vocational goals but are struggling and may still fall through the cracks. Still, the need for extended help was recognized by all key stakeholders: youth, caregivers, and social workers. As one caregiver stated,

> *My own kids stayed until eighteen and a little bit older just because it was a safety mechanism for them, and when they were ready to go they went. And I think sometimes the kids in care don't feel they have that option 'cause it's always the magic number sixteen, you might have independent living,...or eighteen you're out.*

The descriptions of the transition process provided by the various stakeholder groups reaffirm the "emerging adult" life stage (Samuels, 2009) during which many youth continue to access familial and parental resources. Unlike many of their peers in the emerging adult stage of development, youth in care are transitioning out of the programs that have previously sustained them; resources available to them are scaled back or eliminated. Highlighting a conflict between the system's emphasis on chronological age and the pursuit of independence, many participants indicated the youth are "not ready" to leave. As one caregiver noted,

> *A lot of people think that at eighteen these kids should go out on their own and live a life. Well, emotionally, you're dealing with a twelve-year-old sometimes. I mean, just because we get them to eighteen in foster homes or adoptive homes, you're still dealing with a child that is two or three years behind.*

While many study participants applauded recent attempts to extend support through changes to the SFAAS, participants revealed numerous policy-to-service gaps within SFAAS and other transitional programming. Among contributing factors, the lack of available resources was highlighted as an area of concern. As one child welfare worker noted,

> *The issue about them changing policies is that change in policy came without resources. There were no added resources. We just simply can keep people, you know, until people turn twenty-four. But it's not like we get any housing for them or that.*

A serious concern expressed was that many youth "fall through the cracks" in what appears to be systemic gaps. For example, current available services are not offered to many youth who would otherwise appear eligible; for instance, one caregiver who was particularly knowledgeable about SFAAS stated, "as soon as she turned eighteen, everything stopped....I asked for [an SFAA], I asked for that, and they said it couldn't happen." The program appears to be interpreted and applied differently in different regions. In some situations, restrictive eligibility requirements or expectations may be used as leverage to control youth, as one youth related: "[My social workers said], 'Well, if you go to counselling and you're stabilizing and what not, like we're not getting any bad reports of you, we will continue to financially support [you].'" Perceived bad behaviour on the part of the adolescent in care was grounds for ending care agreements. In some cases, the most troubled youth, those whose behaviour was seen as difficult, were least able to fully comply with transition plans. In other cases, services may not be offered to the youth in full and comprehensive ways. In addition, the extended care agreements fail to appeal to the basic interests of the youth themselves. A number of youth in the study indicated that they were not interested in signing an extended care agreement. Youth in the study expressed a desire to "make it on my own" and to be independent.

Extended care plans caused some conflict for caregivers as well. After caring for a youth for a number of years, foster parents may be asked to step down their care and convert their arrangement to that of a landlord. Rates of pay and expectations of care would also be stepped down. Caregivers pointed out that this was driven by the system and not by the needs or the abilities of the youth. One participant explained,

> *[Child Welfare] didn't want to keep her in under foster care, they wanted to keep it as room and board, and as a foster family I can't go down to room and board....[I]t's not only the financial piece, it's still you're working very hard with these youth....[I]t's not like*

> *they have a bed and they come and go and you just forget that they're there.*

Foster parents who had a parenting relationship with their youth were often reluctant to change that relationship just because the youth had reached a milestone birthday. For example, one caregiver interpreted the intervention from child welfare as inappropriate for her foster child by indicating that, "when she hit the sixteen mark, the department came to me and said, 'Okay, you know, we're going to put her into independent living,' and they were asking her, you know, did she want to move?" Turning sixteen or eighteen did not always mean that the youth in care required less parental involvement, as the requests to switch from foster care arrangements to room and board seem to imply. The "one size fits all" approach did not appear responsive to the individual needs of the youth.

Second Chances

A second overarching theme in the data was the concept of second chances. This theme relates to opportunities (or a lack thereof) that youth in care have to pursue a path, to fail, and then to be welcomed back. As emerging adults, youth transitioning out of care face significantly more challenges than those youth who have never been in care. Arnett (2014) identifies emerging adults as distinct in the following ways: they are exploring their identity and asking *who am I?*; they experience instability in work, love, and home; they are self-focused; they feel in-between; and they are optimistic and filled with possibilities. Mainstream youth who have a stable home and secure attachments to supportive parents are afforded second chances during this transitioning time if a chosen path ends badly.

While youth who are permanent wards also require the security of second chances, this is not always their experience. Second chances may be blocked by such things as inadequate resources, policies, processes, and even attitudes. One youth summarized his group-care experience this way:

> *Social services to me is a very, very flawed thing and how we go about it. The fact that we're raising kids based on laws and rules written in a book and saying, like, everyone's individual and diverse, but we're going to follow the same rules in the book for everybody.*

This youth was seeking recognition of his individuality but finding his caregivers unable to differentiate him and his needs from those of every other child. He was kicked out of his group home for drinking alcohol but compares his experience to others who get a second chance:

> *I know many parents they tell their kids, like, you can go out and party, and I know that people are going to be drinking, and it's like, whatever, just don't be stupid....[I]f you get so shitfaced and if I need to pick you up at 4 A.M., you know, I need to pick you up at 4 in the morning!*

The consequences for seemingly bad choices for transitioning youth in care can be devastating. Without second chances, youth who prematurely exit the system (either through running away or through the breakdown of placements due to ill-fated choices) and those who choose not to avail themselves of extended care agreements have few opportunities in the future. Leaving home and then returning is increasingly common for children who are not in care as they navigate through the emerging adult stage of the life cycle; however, youth in care are often unable to return after they decide to leave or after halting attempts at independence. The strong desire to find out who they are and to go it alone can have very negative consequences. Rational offers of help fall on deaf ears, as this caregiver explains:

> *As soon as they turn eighteen, well sometimes it starts at sixteen, but it's like "I know I don't have to listen to you anymore," right? "I can do whatever I want."...[T]hey hit eighteen and they're like "I can do whatever I want," and they go and do what they want for a couple years and then realize, "Oh, I need some help 'cause I'm falling apart."*

All three key stakeholder groups were unified in their calls for government to better recognize the unique needs of youth aging out of care by replacing policies and practices that encourage early independent/semi-independent living with those that give youth the time, skills, and resources necessary to achieve outcomes more comparable to those of their peers who have not entered government care. As one child welfare worker stated, "we don't need another model, we need the time and resources to support good work." Investing in youth requires long-term commitment.

Evidence from this study suggests that current child welfare policies and services have been designed with an understanding of the transition out of care as an event, particularly one that is tied to an individual's eighteenth birthday. Consequently, many examples were provided of youth who had exited the system without acquiring the skills necessary to survive, let alone to thrive, independently. Interviews with study participants suggested that the transition out of government care needs to be reconceptualized as a *process*. As one child welfare worker stated, "I think acknowledging that transition is a process....[I]t's not just [an event that happens] when they're eighteen that they're going to be independent and fit to go out on their own." Some youth in this study expressed a level of fearfulness about turning eighteen and transitioning, as they perceived they would no longer be supported by the government. Whether real or perceived, the termination of supports creates increased stress for many youth aging out of care.

Improving Engagement

The results of this study suggest that caregivers and child welfare workers struggle to adjust to the needs of emerging adults. System pressures result in expectations that aging-out youth be treated as competent individuals, or young adults, who have, and ought to have, decision-making power in their transition planning. This poses a dilemma for caregivers and the system of government care. The path from dependency to autonomy and independence (or interdependence) is not a straight line. Youth who are transitioning out of care are at the same time entering the developmental phase of the emerging adult (Arnett, 2014), which is inherently a time of instability and exploration—of striving for independence while at the same time requiring reassurance and security. Further compromising, or at least complicating, the system response is the idea that the child welfare system has been designed primarily to work with children rather than emerging adults (Goodkind, Schelbe, & Shook, 2011). It is difficult to exercise control and support autonomy at the same time.

The challenge of trying to effectively respond to the individual needs of youth in late adolescence, at a time when the system is requiring them to transition into adulthood and out of care, contributes to what one worker identified as a large number of lost youth. The lost youth result from the difficulty of engaging youth in late adolescence, considering their growing desire for independence and autonomy—particularly independence and autonomy from "the system" itself.

> *The youth has to choose, they can decide if they want to continue or not, and most kids that do continue with school post-eighteen do opt for [SFAAS], of course, 'cause that makes life a bit easier. But lots of kids also just want to be done with us. They don't want a caseworker anymore, they don't want anyone calling them or having any control over them, so they just cut their ties and be gone.*

Another worker simply stated, "They don't want a social worker anymore." The growing desire for independence and autonomy is paradoxical because emerging adults long for freedom from institutional control but often do not recognize the employment and educational challenges that lay ahead, inevitably creating a barrier to their self-reliance.

Given the perceived value of extending care, some study participants underscored the importance of enhancing youth buy-in through processes of engagement and empowerment. As one child welfare worker noted,

> *I think catering the plan to what the youth wants and needs and is capable and is willing to do is probably a big one 'cause you set these big goals for education and employment, and if the child's not engaged, they're just being set up for failure.*

Despite this and other ideas being offered by child welfare workers as a means of increasing the youths' interest in maintaining and/or extending care, it is clear that getting the youth to "buy in" remains an immense and ongoing challenge for child welfare professionals. As this worker lamented, "We were able to extend care, [but] she didn't want it, she wanted to be done."

Coordination and Collaboration (or "It Takes a Village")

While caregivers spoke of the immense challenge of supporting youth, many also indicated that this challenge has been reduced recently through changes at the policy level. Transition planning has now become a priority within the Ministry of Children's Services, as this worker states: "I'm finding over the last year or so [the supports have] really increased, and the planning for kids as they transition has really become a priority." A number of participants reported recent and positive changes within the child welfare system, while at the same time recognizing that much more work needs to be done. Addressing this issue specifically within a rural context, one child welfare worker stated, "We can make sure they have youth workers, we can try to ensure that they're getting their medical needs, but in small communities like this we don't have places to place them." Given the immensity of the task, many child welfare workers advocated for a team approach to the transition process. Emphasizing the benefits of more collaborative approaches, one child welfare worker noted that "we are trying to build villages around children now so that we aren't just closing their file at eighteen."

Research participants widely noted that youth transitioning out of government care need dependable and long-term sources of social support. In various ways, this sentiment was expressed by every stakeholder participating in this study. One child welfare worker, reflecting on long-term investment, stated that "we have to do what we do with our own kids, you know, and if you're not a parent, think about what your parents did with you right." Despite unanimity in their belief that long-term and dependable sources of support are a fundamental need for youth transitioning out of care, stakeholders presented as divided with respect to who is best suited and/or situated to fulfill this role. Participants exposed an unsettled debate on whether or not the child welfare workers themselves could appropriately offer such a source of support. Indeed, the data revealed a variety of practice approaches among child welfare workers. On the one hand, some endorsed a more emotionally disengaged, or "hands-off," role—brokering and supporting others, such as the caregivers, community members, and/or biological family, to develop and maintain close networks of social support with the youth, as this worker describes:

> *I didn't come in expecting that was my role, to be nurturing these kinds of relationships, and for me I think that's a good thing because I honestly...I want to put that to their caregivers, I want to focus my energy on having these kids with caregivers that are there for the day to day.*

This was not always in line with what youth leaving care wanted or needed. While some youth described successful, loving relationships with foster parents, others reported that they had been less able to connect. For some, their social worker was the only identified "constant" in their life.

Some workers responded to this need with a more parental, or "hands-on," role, engaging regularly in nurturing behaviours and activities typically associated with the family domain. For instance, one child welfare worker stated,

> *When [the youth in care] was in a tough spot, she would call me, and I would be that consistent person for her, and if she needed a ride to her counselling appointment, then I would get her a ride to her counselling appointment and encourage her to attend.*

Another child welfare worker similarly remarked,

> *I think [the youth] and I had a good relationship, we could pretty much talk about anything, she was really honest, you know, when she got the boyfriend, I had the sex talk with her, I had the, you know, birth control talk, you know, and she was comfortable with that.*

Other workers occupied the more uncomfortable middle ground between "hands-off" or "hands-on" positions. One child welfare worker's comments highlighted the discomfort in this grey zone:

> *That attachment piece between youth and worker is, you know, we try not to allow that to happen because I'm not gonna be her worker for the rest of her life, and so that was a struggle that I found. I knew that she needed that person, I tried to identify that person in her family and friends and teachers....[S]he didn't seem to click with any of them. But she clicked with me, and so that was really what I advocated for.*

Another worker similarly spoke to a sense of role confusion between developing a meaningful relationship with the youth versus brokering meaningful relationships between the youth and others. Acknowledging the difficulty of maintaining what others might call health boundaries, this child welfare worker described the struggle:

> *Technically, I'm the guardian, they need someone else to be their mom, someone else needs to play the role of mom. I find myself...I slip into that because it's very easy to do that. But you can't, and everybody should have somebody that's not a social worker, right?*

Another child welfare worker described an ongoing relationship with a youth who had aged out of care. Although the relationship was initiated by the youth via social media, this worker was conflicted over whether or not an ongoing relationship would be construed as "okay" by others or even permitted in policy.

From a different perspective, in the absence of family or other support, one youth in the study reported having turned to his social worker, feeling comfortable texting with her during times of trouble, day or night. Other youth, describing more engaged relationships with their foster families, suggested that they hardly knew their social workers. Varied practice approaches resulted in child welfare workers adopting communication strategies and interpersonal styles ranging from a more detached style, characterized by information-sharing and advising, to a more relational approach, characterized by attention to affect and personal or intimate communication. A high degree of professional training and insight, including effective communication skills, is necessary to ensure workers can form meaningful relationships with vulnerable youth when appropriate, while also being aware of boundaries and the inherent limits of their role.

While all stakeholder groups reinforced the importance of a coordinated and collaborative approach, many also described feeling as though important stakeholders were working "out of sync." The social workers' expectations of what youth aging out were capable of or ready for were not always in line with the caregivers' impressions. Some caregivers identified concerns with poor organizational communication and inadequate service coordination or accountability as youth age out of care. For instance, one caregiver stated,

> *I'm not so sure I'm happy about [the child welfare worker]...because, like, the guy doesn't seem to be on the same page as everybody*

> *else...like, he encourages [the youth in care] to go into independent living....[This] is a child who will never make it in independent living, ever, you know?*

In another instance, a caregiver described an experience in which communication breakdown resulted in both she and the youth's child welfare worker independently locating a placement. In addition to creating frustrations during an already arduous transition process, the lack of coordination was identified as doing little to support the successful transition of youth out of care.

Skills training and access to resources were identified as specific areas that have been negatively impacted by a lack of organizational collaboration. While there is debate within the literature on the skills and resources that youth need in order to ensure a successful transition out of care (Goodkind et al., 2011; Hook & Courtney, 2011; Mendes, 2011), participants from all stakeholder groups highlighted the importance of skills, resources, and relationship development to the successful transition of youth out of care. Given the many service gaps in rural communities identified by study participants, a key issue is the successful delivery in a sector within which so many work in program silos. Pointing to reduced enrolment limits in a local transvocational program, for instance, one study participant highlighted how a lack of service coordination has even resulted in the loss of valuable resources due to underutilization. Likewise, a number of interview participants shared their hope for changes that would usher in a more coordinated and collaborative approach for youth in care, their caregivers, child welfare workers, and adjunct programs and organizations during the transition process. Successful transitions within this study were often a result of well-coordinated and respectful teamwork.

Coordination and collaboration also relate to the need for openness in maintaining relationships for youth. In general, this related to extended biological families, but other relationships were also identified (siblings, half-siblings, foster relationships, community connections). Many child welfare workers emphasized the importance of foster and biological family support and reinforced the limitations of child welfare workers. As one child welfare worker stated,

> *The role of family is huge....[Youth] need to be connected to family because your worker is only available 8:15 A.M. to 4:30 P.M., Monday to Friday, and when you've had a really shitty day at work, you can't phone them.*

Others highlighted that, upon exiting care, a high number of youth eventually return to their biological families. These workers further argued that family engagement is vital to maintaining the attachments necessary to facilitate a safe and successful reunification.

While all caregivers referenced some level of interaction with the youths' biological families, they also evidenced a degree of variation with respect to how they approached these relationships. Some caregivers embraced a relationship with the biological family, while others appeared to merely tolerate a relationship as a necessary, albeit unfortunate and uncomfortable, aspect of the process. Caregivers who embraced a relationship often described their caregiver role as an extension, rather than a replacement, of a youth's family. For instance, one caregiver stated that "their family is my family....[Y]ou know, it's not about separating family...the good family and the bad family. It's about what's the easiest for the kids." Many of these caregivers described the biological family as an important part of the package. Pursuing connections even in the face of challenges (e.g., addictions, criminal involvement, street life), these caregivers recognize that the youth need connection to, and knowledge of, their biological families. Whether families were described as "healthy" or "unhealthy," connection to one's biological family was viewed as both valuable and necessary. As one caregiver put it, "I think [the youth] all need to know where they came from and what their history is and who they are."

In contrast, others expressed less interest in establishing and maintaining a connection with the youths' biological families. While some of these caregivers described a passive participation in relationship building, others tended to discourage these relationships outright. For many, the perceived severity of dysfunction served as a primary rationale for a lack of engagement with the youths' biological families. One caregiver stated,

> *He was so immature, you know. He shouldn't have been allowed to go back [home], but they gave him a bus ticket and gave him money*

> *to go, you know, so now his [own] children have been adopted out and [are] in care.*

Similarly, another caregiver remarked that "we've tried, and we've had it backfire. Really big problems. So I just said, 'enough is enough, that's it,' you know, 'you're not doing it to these girls anymore.'" Many foster parents felt ill equipped to deal with high levels of family dysfunction.

Supported interventions with biological families during transition planning held promise. From the perspective of some research participants, family group conferencing (FGC) was identified as a particularly helpful strategy for engaging multiple stakeholders, including professionals, caregivers, and the youth themselves. Speaking to the potential benefits of FGC, one child welfare worker stated that

> *that's usually the goal of the family group conferencing, to make those connections so that those kids, once they turn eighteen and we're no longer there,...they know who their aunts and uncles are and have phone numbers.*

Importantly, the ability to collaborate and communicate as a team is vital to assessing the needs of the transitioning youth and meeting these needs in an effective and efficient manner. Taking cues from the youth themselves requires the team providing support to be flexible and to recognize that one size does not fit all.

Implications for Practice and Policy

This study provides some insight into current service delivery issues by identifying perceived strengths as well as gaps and tensions within rural transition services. By speaking with various service providers, who are intimately knowledgeable about the process of transitioning youth out of the care of the government, we were able to glean a more holistic picture of the process of transitioning for rural youth. At the same time, we can identify ways to strengthen system responsiveness within a network of transitioning services and to decrease navigational stressors for youth in care and their caregivers. Permanent wards, as well as those who work with them, are conditioned by the current system to work toward terminating government involvement at a predetermined end point. This goal, when driven by the needs of the system rather than the needs of the youth, may set youth up for future difficulties.

Our results have some implications for policy-makers and decision-makers within government. The notion that government can assume parental responsibilities for youth, on the one hand, but recast its obligations with little or no effect when youth turn eighteen, on the other, needs to be reconsidered. As in other parenting arrangements, governments should be prepared to support youth over the long term, through "good times and bad," and recognize that different youth progress at different rates. Responses from participants suggest that policies should be revised and services delivered along an extended continuum that more adequately addresses the youths' unique short- and long-term needs.

The withdrawal of supports must better coincide with the actual needs and abilities of emerging adults. Governments must recognize that aging out of care is not an "all or nothing" event but a process with numerous starts and stops. In other words, youth who feel as if they are capable of independence today may find out, after time on their own, that they do, in fact, need longer-term supports and services. Research evidence suggests that, from a neurobiological perspective, the prefrontal cortex, responsible for the cognitive regulation of behaviour, continues to develop through adolescence and into emerging and early adulthood (Bennett & Baird, 2006). Policy-makers must design policies that are flexible and sensitive to the individual needs of youth transitioning out of care through such measures as expanding eligibility criteria and creating policies that improve youth engagement. Outreach to those described as lost youth needs to be a priority.

Policy-makers must also recognize that those tasked with supporting permanent wards require specialized training and skills in order to better respond to each child's unique needs. Taking seriously the responsibility to parent wards of the government requires investing in youth, respecting them, listening to them, and celebrating with them as they progress through important milestones such as birthdays, obtaining their driver's licence, landing their first job, and otherwise transitioning through life's challenges. Youth aging out of care have fewer opportunities for continued support once their case files are closed and inactive. At the same time, these youth continue to experience the milestones and losses that in most Canadian families are recognized or celebrated.

It also means being prepared to extend second chances. Rather than relying on rigid guidelines that dictate artificial milestones, child welfare workers must use advanced engagement and assessment skills, as well as relationship-building skills, to respond individually to each youth's needs. This type of practice requires a high level of supervision to ensure that workers maintain boundaries and recognize their limits when working with youth. In addition, child welfare practitioners must work collaboratively with community-based services, caregivers, and extended families. This requires not only the ability to understand delegated responsibility but also the ability to share power. One rural office notably employed the use of FGC as a practice with youth aging out. Anecdotally, this co-operative and non-hierarchical approach has had positive results in one case, reuniting a youth with the paternal side of his family after a prolonged estrangement.

Specialized training and support are required to better equip foster parents in supporting youth as they transition out of care. Perceptions of fostering as an adjunct, rather than an alternative, to biological or pre-existing family relationships may clear the way for a more collaborative approach to caring for children. One perspective suggested by the research is that fostering should resemble the relationships found in extended families. In this model, foster parents would be less likely to be blindsided by the potential of their long-term caregiving role, and children may move between biological and foster families in a more naturalistic fashion, within appropriate limits. Foster parents in our study were not always prepared for the long-term nature of the fostering arrangement. Adopting an extended family model, embracing the involvement of extended family members, and recognizing that foster children should be appropriately connected to their extended families may open more avenues for supporting youth through life transitions. Foster parents caring for youth aging out of care should also be prepared and supported to understand that the transition process may require prolonged engagement, with the possibility of a youth leaving, returning, and leaving again. The need to return to the foster family, after tentative steps toward independence, mirrors the experiences of many youth who have never been in care and is consistent with research into the emerging adult stage of development (Greeson, 2013).

The implications for policy-makers include the need for attention to rural-specific issues and recognition that programs designed for urban centres cannot easily be replicated within rural settings and may not be appropriate. Rural life offers many benefits in terms of belonging, identity, and familiarity; however, for youth with serious intellectual or emotional challenges, and for those who require specialized services, rural life poses increased challenges in terms of appropriateness, availability, and access to services (Bowen, 2000). Specialized services are not readily available. Access to required services comes with increased wait times and additional costs, often including driving long distances in difficult and challenging weather. The findings offer support for a more regular and expansive use of strategies such as FGC, a community development approach to rural child welfare practice, fewer boundaries between service organizations, and flexible mandates and policies within organizations.

Our findings and subsequent changes to policy/supports/resources may bring attention to important issues in rural service delivery for both caregivers and child welfare workers, at a time when there has been a significant reduction in the number of caregivers, particularly within rural settings (Belanger, Price-Mayo, & Espinosa, 2008). There has been a notable and high turnover rate in child welfare workers within rural settings (Fulcher & Smith, 2010). It is important that this resource be protected. Decreasing "burnout" through specialized and supported caseloads may help to reduce this turnover rate and provide more consistency to youth and their caregivers.

Further Research

Youth who are able to extend their care agreements and to continue to enjoy the supports available through government and community resources ultimately fare better. This research points to the need to explore why and how many youth have left care without accessing opportunities or available resources. What are the reasons that youth refuse extended services, and under what conditions would they be willing to accept them? In addition, policy-makers need to develop pathways for lost youth to be reunited with services.

Among the lost youth, and many youth in care, a significant percentage have disabilities that either are undiagnosed or are borderline on measures used to establish eligibility for services. This vulnerable group of youth may be the least prepared to manage successfully on their own and also the most likely to reject services. Without additional supports, their futures look bleak. Research is needed that examines the gaps created by overly rigid entrance and exit criteria based on unidimensional tools such as intelligence tests, as compared to criteria based on assessments of individual functionality and social supports.

In a related vein, services for youth with challenges are hard to locate and hard to access in rural and remote communities. As a result, many children in need simply do not receive adequate care, for either mental health needs or developmental needs. This impacts the foster experience and the ability of foster families to provide support. During the course of this research, we heard of the closure of important programs that thereby increased the challenges of successful transitions in rural communities. Rural individuals and families cope with resource disparities and encounter many obstacles to service access. It is worth exploring how feasible it would be to develop a dedicated position within government to assist with system-level transition issues: to provide advice on how to navigate the system, to identify resources (and gaps in resources), to lobby for increased access and availability, to remove barriers, and to provide support not just to youth but also to foster families and child welfare workers—much like patient navigators used in the healthcare system (Natale-Pereira, Enard, Nevarez, & Jones, 2011).

Our research suggests that many policies and programs are driven by system issues and are perceived by service users to arrive in a top-down fashion. These policies and programs do not adequately meet the needs of some of the most vulnerable youth. Researchers must be willing and able to engage youth in care in ways that contribute meaningfully to the development of policy/resources/programs that address their concerns and unique perspectives. Unless youth are engaged and willing to consent to extended care, it simply will not happen. Future research that involves youth in a meaningful way should examine how the system can more effectively accommodate the voices and experiences and expressed needs of youth. The increase in the number of children and youth in care, and the increased likelihood of negative outcomes across a number of health and psychosocial domains, highlight the importance of creating services that are more responsive to the needs of youth aging out of care and their caregivers.

Discussion Questions

1. Participants described problems accessing SSFA benefits. Based on your experience, do you think these problems are an exception or fairly common? If problems like this are common, how can they be addressed, and what barriers may arise in trying to resolve them?
2. What are the potential tensions that child welfare workers might experience in their role supporting youth who age out of care? What about foster parents?
3. Youth who age out of care are also entering a newly described developmental stage, emerging adulthood. How do these two processes conflict?

References

Antle, B., Johnson, L., Barbee, A., & Sullivan, D. (2009). Fostering interdependent versus independent living in youth aging out of care through healthy relationships. *Families in Society, 90*(3), 309–315.

Arnett, J. J. (2014). *Emerging adulthood: The winding road from the late teens to the twenties* (2nd ed.). Oxford, United Kingdom: Oxford University Press.

Avery, R. J. (2010). An examination of theory and promising practice for achieving permanency for teens before they age out of foster care. *Children and Youth Services Review, 32*(3), 399–408.

Belanger, K., Price-Mayo, B., & Espinosa, D. (2008). The plight of rural child welfare: Meeting standards without services. *Journal of Public Child Welfare, 1*(4), 1–19.

Bennett, C., & Baird, A. (2006). Anatomical changes in the emerging adult brain: A voxel-based morphometry study. *Human Brain Mapping, 27*(9), 766–777.

Bowen, S. (2000). Access to health services for underserved populations in Canada. In *"Certain circumstances": Issues in equity and responsiveness in access to health care in Canada* (A collection of papers and reports prepared for Health Canada) (pp. 1–60). Ottawa, ON: Health Canada.

Brown, S., & Wilderson, D. (2010). Homelessness prevention for former foster youth: Utilization of transitional housing programs. *Children and Youth Services Review, 32*(10), 1464–1472.

Charmaz, C. (2006). *Constructing grounded theory: A practical guide through qualitative analysis*. London, United Kingdom: Sage.

Courtney, M. E., & Dworsky, A. (2006). Early outcomes for young adults transitioning from out-of-home care in the USA. *Child & Family Social Work, 11*(3), 209–219.

Courtney, M., Piliavin, I., Grogan-Kaylor, A., & Nesmith, A. (2001). Foster youth transitions to adulthood: A longitudinal view of youth leaving care. *Child Welfare, 80*(6), 685–715.

du Plessis, V., Beshiri, R., Bollman, R. D., & Clemenson, H. (2001). Definitions of rural. *Rural & Small Town Canada Analysis Bulletin, 3*(3), 1–16.

Dworsky, A. (2005). The economic self-sufficiency of Wisconsin's former youth. *Children and Youth Services Review, 27*(10), 1085–1118.

Dworsky, A., & Courtney, M. E. (2010a). *Assessing the benefits of extending foster care beyond age 18 on post-secondary education: Emerging findings from the Midwest study*. Chicago, IL: Chapin Hall, University of Chicago.

Dworsky, A., & Courtney, M. E. (2010b). The risk of teenage pregnancy among transitioning foster youth: Implications for extending state care beyond age 18. *Children and Youth Services Review, 32*(10), 1351–1356.

Fulcher, G. M., & Smith, R. (2010). Environmental correlates to public child welfare worker turnover. *Administration in Social Work, 34*(5), 442–457.

Goodkind, S., Schelbe, L., & Shook, J. (2011). Why youth leave care: Understandings of adulthood and transition successes and challenges among youth aging out of child welfare. *Children and Youth Services Review, 33*(6), 1039–1048.

Gough, P., & Fuchs, D. (2008) *Transitions out-of-care: Youth with FASD in Manitoba* (CECW Information Sheet #67). Centre of Excellence for Child Welfare. Retrieved from http://cwrp.ca/sites/default/files/publications/en/FASDTransitions67E.pdf

Greeson, J. K. (2013). Foster youth and the transition to adulthood: The theoretical and conceptual basis for natural mentoring. *Emerging Adulthood, 1*(1), 40–51.

Hook, J. L., & Courtney, M. E. (2011). Employment outcomes of foster youth as young adults: The importance of human, personal, and social capital. *Children and Youth Services Review, 33*(10), 1855–1865.

Keller, T. E., Cusick, G. R., & Courtney, M. E. (2007). Approaching the transition to adulthood: Distinctive profiles of adolescents aging out of the child welfare system. *Social Service Review, 81*(3), 453–484.

Lerch, V., & Stein, M. (2010). *Aging out of care: From care to adulthood in European and Central Asian societies*. Innsbruck, Austria: SOS Children's Villages International.

Leslie, B., & Hare, F. G. (2000). Improving the outcomes for youth in transition from care. *Ontario Association of Children' Aid Societies Journal, 44*(3), 19–25.

Macomber, J., Kuehn, D., McDaniel, M., Vericker, T., Pergamit, M., Cuccaro-Alamin, S.,...Barth, R. (2008). *Coming of age: Employment outcomes for youth who age out of foster care through their middle twenties*. Washington, DC: Urban Institute. Retrieved from http://www.urban.org/research/publication/coming-age-employment-outcomes-youth-who-age-out-foster-care-through-their-middle-twenties/view/full_report

Maschi, T., Smith Hatcher, S., Schwalbe, C. S., & Scotto Rosato, N. (2008). Mapping the social service pathways of youth to and through the juvenile justice system: A comprehensive review. *Children and Youth Services Review, 30*(12), 1376–1385.

McMillen, J., Scott, L. D., Zima, B. T., Ollie, M. T., Munson, M. R., & Spitznagel, E. (2004). Use of mental health services among older youths in foster care. *Psychiatric Services, 55*(7), 811–817.

Mendes, P. (2011). Towards a community development support model for young people transitioning from state out-of-home care: A case study of St. Luke's Anglicare in Victoria, Australia. *Practice: Social Work in Action, 23*(2), 69–81.

Mulcahy, M., & Trocmé, N. (2010). *Children and youth in out-of-home care in Canada* (CECW Information Sheet #78). Centre for Research on Children and Families. Retrieved from http://cwrp.ca/sites/default/files/publications/en/ChildrenInCare78E.pdf

Natale-Pereira, A., Enard, K., Nevarez, L., & Jones, L. (2011). The role of patient navigators in eliminating health disparities. *Cancer, 117*(15), 3541–3550.

OACAS (Ontario Association of Children's Aid Societies). (2006, April). *Youth leaving care: An OACAS survey of youth and CAS staff.* Retrieved from http://cwrp.ca/sites/default/files/publications/en/ON-YouthLeavingCare_OACASReport.pdf

Reid, C., & Dudding, P. (2006). *Building a future together: Issues and outcomes for transition-aged youth.* Ottawa, ON: Centre of Excellence for Child Welfare. Retrieved from http://cwrp.ca/sites/default/files/publications/en/BuildingAFutureTogether.pdf

Rutman, D., Hubberstey, C., & Feduniw, A. (2007). *When youth age out of care—Where to from there?* Victoria, BC: University of Victoria. Retrieved from https://www.uvic.ca/hsd/socialwork/assets/docs/research/WhenYouthAge2007.pdf

Samuels, G. M. (2009). Ambiguous loss of home: The experience of familial (im) permanence among young adults with foster care backgrounds. *Children and Youth Services Review, 31*(12), 1229–1239.

Serge, L., Eberle, M., Goldberg, M., Sullivan, S., & Dudding, P. (2002, December). *Pilot study: The child welfare system and homelessness among Canadian youth.* Ottawa, ON: National Homelessness Initiative. Retrieved from http://cwrp.ca/sites/default/files/publications/en/HomelessnessAndCW.pdf

Southerland, D., Casaneuva, C. E., & Ringeisen, H. (2004). Young adult outcomes and mental health problems among transition age youth investigated for maltreatment during adolescence. *Children and Youth Services Review, 31*(9), 947–956.

Stapleton, J., & Tweddle, A. (2012). *Not so easy to navigate: A report on the complex array of income security programs and educational planning for children in care in Ontario*. Toronto, ON: The Laidlaw Foundation. Retrieved from http://cwrp.ca/sites/default/files/publications/en/ON_SocialAssistance_2012.pdf

Strauss, A., & Corbin, J. (1998). *Basics of qualitative research techniques and procedures for grounded theory* (2nd ed.). London, United Kingdom: Sage.

Tweddle, A. (2007). Youth leaving care: How do they fare? *New Directions for Youth Development, 113*, 15–31. doi:10.1002/yd.199

CHAPTER 5

Inappropriate Application of Parenting Capacity Assessments in the Child Protection System

Peter W. Choate and Gabrielle Lindstrom

We would like to acknowledge the contributions of the Blackfoot Elders who, in sharing their knowledge and wisdom, became instrumental in guiding the conceptual framework of our study and truly demonstrated how the voices of the ancestors act as cultural signposts for generations to come. This chapter honours those voices.

Introduction

In this chapter, we draw on the results of our study that examined the deficiencies in current parenting capacity assessment (PCA) tools used by the child intervention system (CIS) in Alberta. Our approach included an in-depth review of the literature on definitions of family and parenting from an Indigenous perspective as well as the use of data gleaned from an expert consultation with Blackfoot Elders in Alberta.[1] Specifically, we were interested in addressing (1) a significant gap in the research and

---

1 The terms "Indigenous" and "Aboriginal" are used throughout this chapter to refer to First Nations, Métis, and Inuit peoples in Canada (INAC, n.d.).

Suggested Citation: Choate, P., & Lindstrom, G. (2018). Inappropriate application of parenting capacity assessments in the child protection system. In D. Badry, H. Montgomery, D. Kikulwe, M. Bennett, & D. Fuchs, (Eds.), *Imagining child welfare in the spirit of reconciliation* (pp. 93–115). Regina, SK: University of Regina Press.

clinical literature on Indigenous perspectives on parenting and family and (2) how the reliance on Eurocentric definitions remains insufficient in informing appropriate assessment of the parenting capacity of Indigenous caregivers. The expert consultation with the Blackfoot Elders provided a more nuanced perspective on how traditional Indigenous understandings of family and caregiving remain as relevant today as they did in the past.

Within this context, we contribute to the argument that assessing Aboriginal families within the CIS cannot be done in the absence of understanding the roots of the present practices. Further, there is a lineage of disregard that runs from the colonial settlers no longer accepting partnership with Aboriginal peoples to a rapid and oppressive movement toward the desire for a country—Canada—which would become a dominion in 1867. Roberta Jamieson (2017) notes that Canada's first prime minister, Sir John A. Macdonald, stated, "Providence has been pleased to provide us with one nation, unbroken from sea to sea, populated by one people with one common heritage and a common religion." As Jamieson goes on to say, Macdonald was describing a Canada without Aboriginal people—indeed, without anyone who differed from the settlers. This then becomes the heritage for the development of legislation and policy, including that which would impact the administration of child intervention in Canada.

In this chapter, we historically trace an oppressive and overbearing government presence in the lives of Indigenous peoples and how the role of the CIS has evolved as an equally overbearing presence. We expand upon the social constructions of key definitions drawn from our literature review that are useful in conceptualizing how oppression becomes operationalized within the CIS. We do this in the context of conceptualizing a new approach to assessment that may draw upon the approach used in the criminal justice system with Gladue reports.[2] Finally, we discuss the implications for social work practice and advocate for an increased awareness

2 Gladue reports and plans—named for *R. v. Gladue* ([1999] 1 SCR 688)—contain information on the unique circumstances of Aboriginal people accused of an offence or Aboriginal offenders. The court can consider these reports during sentencing. Sentencing in a Gladue court focuses on restorative justice and community justice programs, while also making sure that offenders receive fair sentences (Legal Aid Ontario, n.d.).

of personal biases and judgments by individuals working within the CIS. First, we begin with the key themes drawn from the consultation with Elders, as their voices are paramount in validating our arguments. These voices are woven within and throughout our discussion.

Elder Teachings

The consultation with six Blackfoot Elders from the Kainaiwa, Pikuni, and Siksika First Nations was recorded, with permission, and later transcribed. Notably, this consultation process offers one view of how Indigenous people conceptualize the role of family within the broader contexts of community, how traditional caregiving was/is practised, and how the child is seen as a central figure in the worldview of the Blackfoot people. We caution against generalizing the results of our consultation across Indigenous culture as a whole, since great diversity constitutes Indigeneity. Indeed, one Elder participant stated, "You have to be careful not to use a pan-Indian approach because there is very specific teachings that Blackfeet have, that Lakota people have, that Anishnaabe people have, and I think we have to respect those instead of saying you all do this" (Lindstrom & Choate, 2016, p. 51).

We identified six key themes that, taken together, make up a network of domains that are connected to the development of a healthy child. These themes include Creator; culture; Knowledge Keepers; community; family; and child. Emerging from these themes were central practices, beliefs, and values that, from the Elders' perspectives, were essential components of a traditional approach to caregiving. First and foremost is the notion that the child is seen as a gift from the Creator and is given to the entire community. The concepts of "family" and "parenting" are broadly defined. Indeed, "Aboriginal families are seen as part of a larger network....Primacy of parenting does not necessarily rest with the biological parents....This means that cousins, for example, may be seen more as siblings" (Lindstrom & Choate, 2016, p. 52). Notably, according to the Elders, the notion of the nuclear family is a foreign concept. Significantly, healthy child development occurs within a network of relational alliances and is a process grounded in the worldview of traditional culture: the strength of a child originates from his/her connection—or, in many cases, reconnection—to traditional culture. To be sure, the Elders emphasized the importance of providing opportunities for children to reconnect with their culture as an integral factor of caregiving.

In conclusion, the Elders stressed that successful parenting practices existed in the past and continue to exist today. These success stories act as counternarratives to those that focus on the perceived deficiencies of Indigenous parents that are commonly held by mainstream society (Lindstrom & Choate, 2016). Importantly, it is these successes that should act as the foundation for developing CIS assessment and intervention strategies. In the following section, we expand on the place of government in the lives of Indigenous peoples from a historical perspective beginning with the dissolution of Indigenous and Euro-settler partnerships during the era known as the Fur Trade.

Historical Perspectives on the Place of Government in the Lives of Indigenous Peoples

The impacts of colonization have left a lasting legacy on Indigenous peoples' reality and ensured that the evolution of the colonial government into what is now Canada would be a permanently oppressive fixture controlling nearly every aspect of Indigenous peoples' lives. The following discussion on the Fur Trade is important because, as Vibert (2016) states, records kept during this time "have profoundly shaped subsequent understandings of Indigenous societies" (p. 123). Indeed, these records reflect a general consensus among the European fur traders that Indigenous cultures were primitive and inferior (Vibert, 2016).

During the heyday of the Fur Trade, which lasted from the early sixteenth century to the turn of the nineteenth century (Dickason, 2006), the relationship between Indigenous nations and early colonial settlers was rooted in mutually beneficial socioeconomic partnerships. Indeed, these partnerships were often formalized through intercultural marriage arrangements and treaty-making processes. Very often early settlers would also adopt the cultural traditions of their Indigenous trade partners in reciprocated efforts to maintain peaceful relations. It is important to keep in mind that, in the early days of the Fur Trade, Indigenous nations greatly outnumbered early settlers, which explains the settlers' willingness to forge alliances with their Indigenous counterparts. Conversely, Vibert (2016) argues that, regardless of these alliances, early fur traders organized First Nations according to a hierarchy through which they favoured some First Nations tribes over others in terms of their primary subsistence pursuits—for example, the hunting tribes were seen as more valuable allies than those who fished.

However, with the increasing migration of European settlers to Indigenous territories, the relational framework that emerged out of the Fur Trade was gradually replaced with one based less in mutually beneficial and balanced partnerships and more in settler self-interest. Two key factors led to the disruption of the relational balance: (1) the depletion of resources and (2) a growing interest in creating an agricultural economy. Instead of partners, Indigenous nations were seen as impediments to progress since they occupied the most treasured resource: land for settlement and farming. These early settlers not only advanced the colonial interests of their homeland but also brought with them an ethnocentric worldview within which cultural difference was seen as degenerate and deficient (Dickason, 2006).

In 1857, the Canadian Parliament passed the Act to Encourage the Gradual Civilization of Indian Tribes in this Province, and to Amend the Laws Relating to Indians. The intent of this Act was essentially assimilation, in that any "Indian" male (as they were then referred to) twenty-one years of age or older would be enfranchised if he could read or write English or French; thus, the person would become a British subject and not an Indian (Binnema, 2014). In section 91(24) of the Constitution Act, 1867, which was the divisive factor in determining federal and provincial powers over state and civil matters, power was given to Parliament to govern and make laws in regard to Indigenous peoples and lands reserved for their use (Devlin, DeForrest, & Mason, 2012). The Constitution Act of 1867 was followed in 1869 by An Act for the Gradual Enfranchisement of Indians, the Better Management of Indian Affairs, and to Extend the Provisions of the Act 31st Victoria, Chapter 42. The former legislation had sought voluntary enfranchisement, which failed, leading to the latter legislation, which sought more active efforts toward assimilation (Canada, RCAP, 1996b). These would be consolidated in the Indian Act of 1876. It is important to note that a 1951 amendment to the Indian Act would rupture this legislative arrangement and, later, create jurisdictional tensions within the CIS as to which governmental powers have responsibility over Indigenous children.

The Royal Commission on Aboriginal Peoples (Canada, RCAP, 1996a) noted that these legislative processes had as their goal full assimilation, limitation of the rights and freedoms of Native peoples, and the removal of self-government and self-direction. The approach was highly paternalistic and clearly diminished the worth of Indigenous peoples. The Indian Act of 1876 was, and is, a particularly oppressive piece of legislation. It granted the early federal government the power to ban and outlaw Indigenous ceremony, spirituality, and cultural and healing traditions of family. Cultural practices, traditions, and the community and family structures would become ruptured. Many of these practices went underground as a means for nations to preserve them. As our Elders noted, this acted as the link that permitted the practices to be known and brought forward for open use today.

It must also be mentioned that, during the earliest times of colonization, some of the first settlers to arrive in what is now Canada were missionaries. Intent on saving the souls of the Indigenous peoples, whom they deemed as heathens bereft of humanity, the missionaries, and particularly the religious organizations they served, would become central in carrying out the colonial government's assimilationist agenda, primarily through the implementation of the so-called Indian residential schools (Kirmayer, Simpson, & Cargo, 2003). These church-run schools were essentially institutes of government-sanctioned child abuse that served to solidify the loss of family and cultural influence. This is evident in the words of Prime Minister Macdonald: "When the school is on the reserve the child lives with his parents, who are savages; he is surrounded by savages. Indian children should be withdrawn as much as possible from the parental influence" (TRC, 2015, p. 164). The schools also functioned as alternative homes for Indigenous children who were thought to be experiencing maltreatment or neglect (Sinha & Kozlowski, 2013).

Clearly, a pattern of disregard for Indigenous peoples can be traced from the early missionary and fur trading times to the evolution of colonial legislative policies that legally authorized the destruction of Indigenous culture. This disregard would advance an oppressively paternalistic approach on the part of the colonial government toward Indigenous parents—one that considered them incompetent and deficient. It was an approach that would eventually be adopted by social systems such as the CIS.

Role and Presence of Child Protection

Sinha and Kozlowski (2013), in their article outlining the development of CIS policy as it applies to Indigenous families, argue that the pattern of legislated removal of Indigenous children that began with the residential schools was continued through the policy structure of the CIS. Indeed, Devlin, DeForrest, and Mason (2012) also affirm that "the lasting legacy of Canada's assimilation policies is one of the factors that contributes to the fact that First Nations children are five times more likely to be taken into the child welfare system than non-Aboriginal children" (p. 6). An aforementioned amendment made to the Indian Act in the 1950s allowed for provincial and territorial power over Indigenous peoples.

This change in legislation happened during an era when residential schools were also being phased out—the latter half of the twentieth century. Thus, responsibility for Indigenous children was transferred to the provincial child welfare authorities. Sinha and Kozlowski (2013) provide further insight, stating, "For the first time, provincial or territorial child welfare legislation applied on-reserve. Provinces and territories initially provided on-reserve services only in extreme emergencies, but expanded their efforts upon allocation of federal funds to support provincial and territorial delivery of on-reserve services in the mid-1950s" (p. 4). McKenzie, Varcoe, Browne, and Day (2016), in their study examining the neocolonial discourses in child welfare, suggest that the shift in jurisdictional control over child welfare service delivery often resulted in a provincial scramble for funding that failed to consider the realities of Indigenous family structures and instead interpreted and translated services based on Eurocentric ideals of childrearing.

This legislative arrangement signalled the beginning of an era of rapid removal of Indigenous children from their families and communities known as the Sixties Scoop—an era that is reflective of the continuation of the belief that Aboriginal families were unfit for raising children. It is worth noting that the federal government sustained responsibility for funding CIS on-reserve, which continues today. Evidence before the Canadian Human Rights Tribunal shows that on-reserve children receive about one-third less financial backing for services than do children off-reserve served by provincial authorities (*First Nations Child & Family Caring Society of Canada et al.*, 2017).

During the Sixties Scoop period, large numbers of children were removed from Aboriginal families across Canada. The vast majority were adopted into white families in Canada, the United States, Europe, and elsewhere outside Canada. Today studies such as those conducted by Blackstock, Trocmé, & Bennett (2004) point us to the fact that Indigenous children in the care of the CIS now outnumber those who were in residential schools during the peak of their operations by as much as four times (McKenzie et al., 2016). Figure 1 provides a visual representation of how government legislation has impacted the lives of Indigenous peoples as well as how CIS policy involving Indigenous children has evolved. These events compound upon and intersect with each other to create a narrative that moves from generation to generation. This occurs within Indigenous family systems as well as in non-Indigenous communities—the difference being the power dynamics.

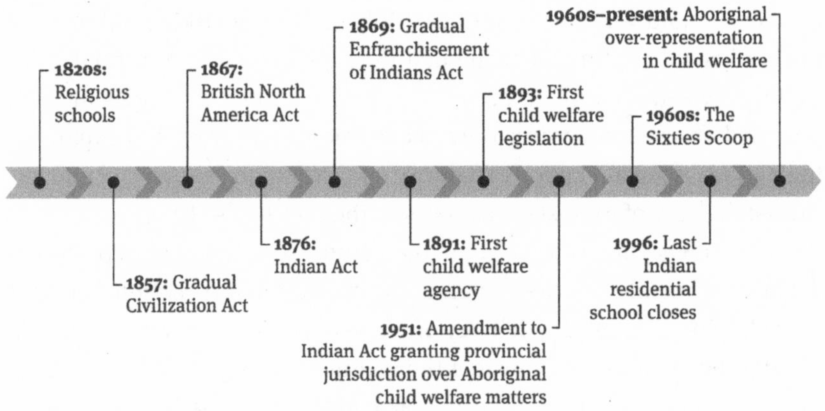

Figure 1. Impact of Government Legislation over Time

Social Construction of Key CIS Meanings and Definitions

As the above discussion illustrates, child protection matters in Canada take place in the context of both the colonial legacy and current practices that can be framed as ongoing colonial practices in an environment where the majority of clients in several provinces are Indigenous. In this section, we look at the application of child welfare methodology in this context. Specifically, we look at the assessments of parents that determine whether they are "good enough" to care for their children.

Child welfare operates within the tension of determining the safety of the child while, at the same time, trying to be as unintrusive as possible and finding ways to preserve family connection. The media commonly focus on high-profile cases of death or serious injury, framing them as clear evidence of systemic failure, often suggesting that workers had leaned too far toward family preservation at the expense of the child. Another common theme in the media is a general sense of incompetence. At the Alberta Ministerial Panel on Child Intervention, which focused on the province's child death review process and system improvement, senior system managers presented evidence that 85 per cent of cases are related not to imminent harms of physical or sexual abuse but rather to issues such as poverty, untreated or poorly treated mental health, and substance abuse. This means it is not a forensic response to child intervention that was needed for that group but mechanisms to support and enhance family functioning and resiliency. It also means there is a group—the other 15 per cent—for whom a forensic approach is required (J. Reeves, personal communication, Panel on Child Intervention, June 2017).

Within the 85 per cent, the majority of cases will involve Indigenous families. Using the assessment of families as a foundation, we have several concerns about the utility of assessment definitions and methodology in this population. We start this discussion with key definitions and the associated implications as contextualized with the CIS.

Family

As the Elders in our project made clear, as does other literature (Cajete, 2000; Castellano, 2002; McCaslin & Boyer, 2009), the notion of family in Indigenous cultures is not defined by biology, nor does it fit the "nuclear" definition seen in the dominant culture of Canada. Rather, Indigenous cultures are communal. This means that biological connections are included in the definition of "family," as are a variety of other people in the community who serve in roles that might be seen as belonging to parents when Eurocentric definitions are used. For example, a close family friend might be referred to as "auntie" or "uncle" and serve in roles that may periodically look familiar to the Eurocentric definition of that position and at other times do not.

Parent Functioning

In the Eurocentric approach, parents act in the dominant leadership role within the nuclear-family system. They would be responsible for leadership, mentoring, modelling, rule setting, discipline, opportunity development, and nurturing functions. In Indigenous parenting, these roles can belong to a variety of people and not be exclusive to the mother or father. An example given by our Elders is that an uncle may perform certain discipline in order to keep that function from interfering with the nurturing function. Community members and Elders may also act in a variety of parenting/ leadership roles with a child and do so without the express permission of the parent. Rather, the Elder, for example, is seen as occupying a role within the culture and community that affords certain opportunities.

Parenting within an Indigenous community is also less focused on managing risk and keeping the child under parental direction. Instead, the growth of autonomy, which allows children to try things out and learn their own ways, is a common practice.

Attachment Theory

At the Panel on Child Intervention, Indigenous representatives presented a great deal of oral evidence that attachment theory (Bretherton, 1992) is being used to keep children separated from their culture and family connections. Essentially, the argument begins when a child is in the temporary care of CIS, during which time the child is placed in a non-Indigenous home. For whatever reason, the child cannot be returned to parental care. Foster parents make application for private guardianship of the child using attachment theory as the basis for it, suggesting that the child has now become attached to the foster family. Thus, removal of the child would break the attachment bonds, and the child would be forever harmed.

The argument fails to consider the cultural connections and the supportive role of extended and community family support systems. It also fails to acknowledge the work of Deklyen and Greenberg (2008), which outlines the need to consider not only attachment but also the needs of the child, the role of the parent, and contextual factors, which, in this type of case, would include cultural connection. In essence, there are other mediators that impact a successful trajectory for development. Questions remain as to the universality of attachment theory (LeVine, 2014).

Rottger-Rossler (2014) raises three core questions about the cross-cultural application of attachment theory. She wonders about the persistence of a mother bias in attachment research, which does not take into consideration local attachment patterns that might have quite different roles for fathers, grandparents, or other caretakers who are meaningful to the child. Second, she asks about the role of local practices and meanings about what constitutes safe and appropriate handling of babies and young children. Third, she notes a complete neglect of the agency of the child, which would be relevant given the greater presence of autonomy in Indigenous family systems.

Parenting

There is a paucity of literature on what constitutes "good enough" parenting (Choate & Engstrom, 2014). However, a much larger literature base exists on parenting in general, which outlines acceptable or preferable behaviours. This literature is often drawn from a Eurocentric understanding of successful parenting, child development, and outcomes. Traditional parenting practices of Indigenous groups are represented much less in the literature. Yet what is a successful parenting practice is a core question in assessing parenting competence.

The literature on best practices for assessing parents is rooted in Eurocentric definitions of family (Budd, Clark, & Connell, 2011; Choate & Engstrom, 2014; Choate & Hudson, 2014; Pezzot-Pearce & Pearce, 2004; Reder, Duncan, & Lucey, 2003). These authors recommend focusing on the primary parent(s), following steps that include interviews, assessment measures, observations, and collateral interviews, as well as reviewing records. Choate and McKenzie (2015) have examined the norming of the major assessment measures used in parenting capacity assessments, noting they have not been normed on Indigenous populations. Thus, their irrelevance to the formulation of parenting questions is concerning. When non-Indigenous researchers develop questions for an Indigenous population, they do so without knowing the cultural meaning of either the questions or the possible answers (Walter & Anderson, 2013).

Shepherd (2008) looked at a comparison of determinants of parenting between Canadian Western mothers and Indigenous mothers. She considered the effects of psychological adjustment, parenting readiness, and environmental protectiveness on the parenting of these mothers. She found that these factors could be predictive for the Western mothers but not for the Indigenous mothers. This serves as a single example of the larger problem of the transferability of studies done in parenting as the foundations for both assessment and intervention.

If the observation uses Eurocentric understandings of parent-child interactions, then the roles of extended support systems and cultural practices may well be misunderstood or missed. In contrast, assessors can be trained in a cultural practice and be guided by Elders, which would improve their understanding of what is going on for the child. The subtleties of parenting behaviours deeply rooted in culture may then not be missed.

It is worthwhile noting that much of the research has not included non-Western peoples or cultures, thus limiting its application to an Indigenous context. Henrich, Heine, and Norenzaya (2010) led a series of articles outlining what they referred to as WEIRD research: research on Western, Educated, Industrialized, Rich, and Democratic populations. Our review of PCA assessment literature suggests that this acronym would characterize that data as well. For example, the definitions of family tend toward the notion of nuclear families or those in which parenting is related to bloodline or legal orders such as adoption or foster care. The definitions do not consider the notion of community systems or clans (Lindstrom & Choate, 2016).

Legislation and Policy

The assessor determines capacity within the definitions laid out in policy and legislation. Using Alberta as an example, while "family" is not specifically defined, section 2(a) of the Child, Youth and Family Enhancement Act (CYFEA) states that "the family is the basic unit of society and its well-being should be supported and preserved." The Act does not help the assessor determine what a family unit is, which, as Elders told us, is quite different in Indigenous cultures than in Eurocentric cultures. Thus, what is the assessor meant to determine should be preserved? The assessor is also faced with coming to understand what is to be assessed. There have been high-profile cases in which that has not been clear, which has led to narrow interpretations of the assessment focus (for example, Baby Annie in Alberta and Baby Peter and Victoria Climbie in the United Kingdom, discussed in Choate, 2016).

Under the CYFEA, an Indian is defined as such in reference to the Indian Act of Canada—in other words, as a person who has status under that federal statute. The CYFEA does not offer further definition, leaving to policy and practice who is to be treated as an Indigenous person. We argue that the narrowness of this definition is a reflection of policy and legislation, both nationally and provincially, that continues to reinforce colonial approaches (see Figure 1). Blackstock (2007) has made a compelling case that the child welfare system has in fact morphed into the stepchild of the residential school system.

Intergenerational Trauma (IGT)

The Truth and Reconciliation Commission of Canada (TRC) has profoundly illustrated the trauma that has occurred across generations in the Indigenous communities across Canada. Marginalization, isolation, family fragmentation, and direct violence-based traumas and betrayal represent the overarching themes of the Indigenous experience in Canada. This is seen in the residential schools, failure to honour treaties, isolation on reserves, legislation disempowering self-government, and efforts at forced assimilation. The TRC (2015) has documented this history in detail.

PCAs have not been developed to consider the impact of such racially based trauma across multiple generations, now being expressed through family, community, and cultural experiences that connect to the overrepresentation of Indigenous children in CIS. IGT has been understood to have long-lasting impacts and should be taken into consideration. The criminal justice system of Canada has come to some level of understanding about the unique needs of Indigenous offenders. In what is known as the Gladue decision (*R. v. Gladue*, 1999), the Supreme Court of Canada determined that criminal courts have an obligation to consider the special circumstances of Indigenous offenders as a result of the systematic influences on behaviours. The decision applies to all self-identified First Nations, Inuit, and Métis offenders. The SCC indicated that courts must

> *consider unique circumstances arising from or specific to Indigenous heritage (e.g., marginalization, residential school, overt racism, chronic substance abuse in his or her community, family or community background, isolation, community relocation, dislocation from Indigenous community given adoption and/or product of child welfare system, etc.), and to consider other sanctions specific to Indigenous heritage (e.g., sentencing circles, Indigenous healing lodges, etc.). (Ministry of Correctional Services, 2007b: 3).* (cited in Hannah-Moffat & Maurutto, 2010, p. 267)

It is our position that the same position should apply with PCAs. Parenting does not exist in a vacuum but rather is influenced by the full context of experiences that have come to frame the parent as a person. That context will include his or her own individual journey through life, but an Indigenous parent will also be impacted by the cultural genocide that occurred in Canada. The typical intergenerational modelling of parenting has been severely damaged, and thus utilizing approaches based on that will yield negatively prejudicial results.

An example of how care must be taken with assessment data is the use of the Adverse Childhood Experiences (ACE) questionnaire, which has been validated, broadly, in a general population (Fellitti et al., 1998). It has also been used to affirm that adverse childhood effects are more prominent in Indigenous populations (Aguiar & Halseth, 2015; Bombay, Matheson, & Anisman, 2009). When applied to a CIS Indigenous population, we suggest, the results will yield high scores. This is problematic if not considered alongside safety and resilience factors. The presence of assimilation, residential schools, and the Sixties Scoop alone would create higher scores. Our Elders spoke, however, of the ways in which Indigenous peoples have been resilient and are using cultural practices such as ceremony to begin overcoming the intergenerational traumas and heal within their culture. Thus, a practice such as using an ACE score when not balanced with recovery, resiliency, and healing would act prejudicially against an Aboriginal parent.

Mohatt, Thompson, Thai, and Tebes (2014) accept that trauma creates public stories that are transmitted across and within generations. They go on to ask how peoples and communities respond to these narratives and then build resilience. They also posit that the focus on present-day meanings for the health and well-being of persons may not be accurately reflected when trauma histories are present. The IGT needs to be understood in its historical place but then also within community efforts to build strength from the narrative utilizing cultural and spiritual connections. Brown-Rice (2013) adds that the trauma was collective and systematic and continues to occur, which acts as a context within which to understand individual and collective functioning. We are presently lacking both a literature of and a methodology for assessing parents for child protection in a manner that is inclusive of these factors. In the following section, we provide examples of oppression as operationalized within the CIS.

The Operationalization of Oppression

A hypothetical case study will illustrate how oppression becomes functionally operationalized and incorporated into routine practice.

Clarence is a three-year-old child who is believed to be First Nations. He was apprehended in Red Deer from his mother, Juliette, who is a member of a Cree nation in Saskatchewan. Clarence is not registered with the band. His father is unknown. Juliette suffers from significant mental health concerns that are difficult to manage. Clarence has been in care since the age of eight months and has been with the same foster family. The director of child welfare has now applied for permanent guardianship of Clarence. As a result of the application, the social worker has successfully found family: an aunt and uncle living in northern Saskatchewan. These relatives have been visiting Clarence for three months and building a relationship. The foster parents also make an application for private guardianship of Clarence, on the basis that he has formed a secure attachment to them. The foster parents have provided some connection with culture by taking Clarence to a few powwows. The director of child welfare opposes the foster parent application, but the foster parents have arranged for the completion of an attachment assessment. This report strongly favours the foster parents.

The CYFEA addresses private guardianship of an Indigenous child by a non-Indigenous person as follows, in section 57.01:

> *If a private guardianship order is made under section 56 appointing a guardian of an aboriginal child, that guardian shall*
> *(a) take reasonable steps to comply with the cultural connection plan included in the application in respect of that child under section 52(1.3), and*
> *(b) if the aboriginal child is an Indian,*
> *(i) take reasonable steps on behalf of the child necessary for the child to exercise any rights the child may have as an Indian, and*
> *(ii) inform the child of the child's status as an Indian as soon as, in the opinion of that guardian, the child is capable of understanding the child's status as an Indian.*

This language is repeated in section 71.1 in respect to adoption. Section 67(1) of the CYFEA makes consultation with a band mandatory if an adoption agency "has reason to believe that a child who is being placed for adoption is an Indian and a member of a band...." It is unclear whether any authority would monitor the compliance with such an order.

These are cited as examples of how legislation reinforces a colonial view and sets up the context for the assessment of parenting. The Act also continually references the "guardians" of a child, as that is the legal status of a person charged with caring for the child. A collectivistic culture will see guardianship in a different manner.

We raise this to help illustrate the context of PCAs. They must comply with legislative direction while at the same time serving the needs of the CIS to make judgments about children's safety and best interests. They may be best suited to the forensic aspect of child protection, where courts are more involved and the risks arising from the parents more pronounced. Given the 85/15 experience of Alberta, PCAs may not be the most effective approach to understanding the majority of cases. Alberta, along with a number of jurisdictions in various parts of the world, has been adopting alternative approaches, such as Signs of Safety (SOS) (Turnell & Murphy, 2017), Family Finding (Vandivere & Malm, 2015), and Structured Decision Making (SDM) (NCCD Children's Research Center, 2015), which are designed to be more flexible. SOS in particular seeks to consider support systems, not just biological systems. The SOS approach has been used with Indigenous populations in Canada and Australia, yet this approach, according to a recent research report from the UK, has not yet undergone rigorous outcome research that is available in the peer-reviewed literature (Molloy, Barton, & Brims, 2017). In our view, there is a core question to ask about the importation of methodology from other cultures: Why could it not be developed with the Aboriginal cultures in the jurisdiction being served?

Equally, a careful review of the literature on PCAs indicates a similar lack of outcome research in this field. To date, there has been no follow-up research to determine the accuracy, impact, or longitudinal benefits of PCAs. This is of particular relevance to Indigenous families where the PCA foundational base is not developed with Indigenous culture and may run counter to it. In the following section, we offer some critical recommendations that are informed by our discussions above and the Elder teachings through consultation and describe how these are relevant to CIS practice with Indigenous families.

Implications for Practice (Be Aware of What You Are Walking in With)

As noted above, SOS is a methodology that has been widely adopted in Alberta and is being used in other Canadian and international jurisdictions, often replacing the need for a PCA. Presentations at the Panel on Child Intervention indicated that some First Nations in Alberta see this as a step forward, while others have wondered why an approach developed in Australia is being imposed on Indigenous people in Alberta. As the Elders in our consultation noted, success has occurred and continues to occur in Indigenous communities of Canada, and these successes should act as the foundation for developing assessment and intervention strategies. Moreover, the Elders described how historical trauma has alienated child protection from Indigenous people. In concert with the TRC (2015), that relationship also needs to be healed. As the TRC is a call to action for the CIS to alter that relationship, the need for action is vital. The Elders also noted that, no matter how effective a program from elsewhere might be, it still represents the imposition of a solution by the colonizing peoples onto Aboriginal peoples.

We wonder if the implementation of approaches that are developed with Aboriginal peoples could not better serve all parties. This could begin with a functional view of how the child is being raised and within which systems. This would require an understanding of who is in that system and may require a broader assessment, which is conducted in the Signs of Safety. In functional assessment, the needs of the child are identified as supporting the child, but it also takes into consideration that in many Aboriginal cultures caregiving can be fluid, involving many natural and informal agreements. For example, a child may be with a grandmother for several months while the mother is unable to care for the child; the grandmother intends that the child will return to the mother but accepts that this may or may not occur. The child stays within the culture, community, and family and may well have a relationship with the mother, even though not in her care.

Such an arrangement follows the pattern described by Elders: that tradition supports what the child needs and does so without the courts or CIS. The community, Elders, and ceremony combine to ensure the development and well-being of the child. There can be reasons why this may not work, but which is to be the primary response?

In the context of this query, we suggest several points of entry to consider and/or act upon that would both be culturally appropriate and align with many of the calls for CIS mandate reform. By approaching CIS issues related to a child in these ways, the Eurocentric PCA method may well be avoided or at least approached from a culturally sensitive lens. These entry points include the following:

- Establishing funding for CIS services on-reserve at the same rate as for services offered to children off-reserve;
- Addressing the assessment of Aboriginal families by introducing a model that may be built upon the Gladue precedent but ensures cultural, historical, and contextual factors are addressed;
- Applying Jordan's Principle in accordance with the CHRT decision (FNCFCS et al., 2017);
- Ensuring culturally appropriate placements so that children do remain connected;
- Extending aging out of care to twenty-five or twenty-six (Ontario just moved to twenty-five), better reflecting the longer-term needs of children involved in CIS transitioning to adulthood;
- Addressing the colonization in legislation, which would require a consultative approach to redrafting legal frameworks;
- Increasing services across jurisdictions for addictions and mental health;
- Ensuring greater inter-agency/inter-ministerial supports of CIS children and families;
- Focusing on reconciliation—as identified by the TRC.

In addition to the above, we advocate for building in reflective practice that is premised on a relational framework with Indigenous peoples in the context of Elder teachings. Crawford (2011) reminds us that social "certainties" couched in positivist conceptualizations of progress as being innovative and better often force us to reject the possibility that ancient Indigenous knowledges could provide alternative, and equally valid, ways of approaching social work practice. Notably, Crawford further states that Western culture's privileging of these social certainties

> *can blind us to the importance of reflective thinking and dialogue, which examines how we frame issues as well as how we assess and measure them. In terms of social work with Indigenous people, this can result in (a) an assumption that the category of Aboriginal presumes a homogeneity of all those so labelled and (b) a "deafness" by central policy makers to the voices of frontline practitioner, both Indigenous and non Indigenous.* (p. 199)

The above quotation holds significance for our argument in that it not only reminds us of the Elders in our study, who cautioned against approaching Indigenous cultures from a position that assumes cultural homogeneity, but also emphasizes that individuals working with Indigenous families must be aware of the biases and assumptions they hold when walking into these interactional relationships. Moreover, reflective practice offers a starting point from which frontline practitioners can begin tracing their professional growth, chronicling the dynamics involved in putting theory into action, and, if practised at a department level, it can be used as a source of documentation in appealing for changes to policy. As is clearly evidenced by our discussions and recommendations above, active participants in CIS reform should include Indigenous peoples, CIS policy-makers, and individual CIS workers, to work toward identifying and understanding opportunities for collaborative partnerships to develop appropriate parenting assessment tools, changing or amending existing CIS policies where necessary, and advocating for reflective practices that empower individual CIS practitioners.

Conclusion (What This All Tells Us Is You Are an Active Player in This Field)

As this chapter has indicated, the assessment of parents continues colonization by imposing standards of parenting practices upon Indigenous cultures that do not accurately reflect the parenting practices of those cultures. Discontinuing the use of a Eurocentric methodology would be a move in the right direction—a move that would demonstrate good faith. It would also be an opportunity to enter into dialogue with Indigenous peoples on how assessments might be developed in a culturally appropriate way, recognizing that Indigenous peoples, their cultures, and their ways of knowing are not homogeneous.

Discussion Questions

1. How do parenting capacity assessments present challenges when applied to Indigenous families?
2. Do you see a way to include Indigenous ways of knowing in assessment approaches?
3. What three key questions are identified regarding cross-cultural application of attachment theory?
4. What is your understanding of intergenerational trauma as it applies to Indigenous peoples in Canada?
5. What is your understanding of the "operationalization of oppression" based on the case study presented in the chapter?
6. What are some of the practices that are considered in assessments that reflect dominant Eurocentric belief systems?

References

Aguiar, W., & Halseth, R. (2015). *Aboriginal peoples and historic trauma: The processes of intergenerational transmission.* Prince George, BC: National Collaborating Centre for Aboriginal Health.

Binnema, T. (2014). Protecting Indian lands by defining *Indian*: 1850–76. *Journal of Canadian Studies, 48*(2), 5–39.

Blackstock, C., Trocmé, N., & Bennett, M. (2004). Child maltreatment investigations among Indigenous and non-Indigenous families in Canada. *Violence against Women, 10*(8), 901–916. doi:10.1177/1077801204266312

Bombay, A., Matheson, K., & Anisman, H. (2009). Intergenerational trauma: Convergence of multiple processes among First Nations peoples in Canada. *Journal of Aboriginal Health, 5*(3), 6–47.

Bretherton, I. (1992). The origins of attachment theory: John Bowlby and Mary Ainsworth. *Developmental Psychology, 28*(5), 759–775.

Brown-Rice, K. (2013). Examining the theory of historical trauma among Native Americans. *The Professional Counsellor, 3*(3), 117–130.

Budd, K. S., Clark, J. R., & Connell, M. A. (2011). *Parenting capacity assessment in child protection.* New York, NY: Oxford University Press.

Cajete, G. (2000). *Native science: Natural laws of interdependence.* Santa Fe, NM: Clear Light Publishers.

Canada. RCAP (Royal Commission on Aboriginal Peoples). (1996a). *Report of the Royal Commission on Aboriginal Peoples.* 5 vols. Retrieved from http://data2.archives.ca/e/e448/e011188230-01.pdf

Canada. RCAP (Royal Commission on Aboriginal Peoples). (1996b). *Report of the*

Royal Commission on Aboriginal Peoples. Vol. 1: *Looking forward, looking back*. Retrieved from http://caid.ca/RRCAP1.6.pdf

Castellano, M. B. (2002). *Aboriginal family trends: Extended families, nuclear families, families of the heart*. Contemporary Family Trends. Ottawa, ON: Vanier Institute of the Family.

Child, Youth and Family Enhancement Act, RSA 2000, c C-12 (Alberta).

Choate, P. (2016). Child protection inquiries: What are they teaching us? A Canadian perspective. In H. Montgomery, D. Badry, D. Fuchs, & D. Kikulwe (Eds.), *Transforming child welfare: Interdisciplinary practices, field education, and research* (pp. 61–85). Regina, SK: University of Regina Press.

Choate, P. W., & Engstrom, S. (2014). The "good enough" parent: Implications for child protection. *Child Care in Practice*, *20*(4), 368–382. doi:10.1080/13575279.2014.915794

Choate, P. W., & Hudson, K. (2014). Parenting capacity assessments: When they serve and when they detract in child protection matters. *Canadian Family Law Quarterly*, *33*(1), 33–48.

Choate, P. W., & McKenzie, A. (2015). Psychometrics in parenting capacity assessments – A problem for First Nations parents. *First Peoples Child & Family Review*, *10*(2), 31–43.

Crawford. F. (2011). Local regeneration in social work with Indigenous peoples: The Kimberley across 40 years. *Australian Social Work*, *64*(2), 198–214. doi:10.1080/0312407X.2011.575169

Deklyen, M., & Greenberg, M. T. (2008). Attachment and psychopathology in childhood. In J. Cassidy & P. R. Shaver (Eds.), *Handbook of attachment: Theory, research, and clinical application* (2nd ed.) (pp. 637–665). New York, NY: Guilford Press.

Devlin, C., DeForrest, L., & Mason, C. (2012). *Jurisdictional quagmire: First Nation child welfare as a human right*. Retrieved from http://www.dgwlaw.ca/wp-content/uploads/2014/12/Child_Welfare_Human_Rights_Paper.pdf

Dickason, O. (2006). *A concise history of Canada's First Nations*. Don Mills, ON: Oxford University Press.

Fellitti, V. J., Anda, R. F., Nordenberg, D., Williamson, D. F., Spitz, A. M., Edwards, V., Koss, M. P., & Marks, J. S. (1998). Relationship of childhood abuse and household dysfunction to many of the leading causes of death in adults: The Adverse Childhood Experiences (ACE) Study. *American Journal of Preventive Medicine*, *14*(4), 245–258.

First Nations Child & Family Caring Society of Canada et al. v. Attorney General of Canada (representing the Minister of Indigenous and Northern Affairs Canada), 2017 CHRT 14.

Hannah-Moffat, K., & Maurutto, P. (2010) Restructuring pre-sentence reports: Race, risk, and the PSR. *Punishment & Society*, *12*(3), 262–286. doi:10.1177/1462474510369442

Henrich, J., Heine, S. J., & Norenzayan, A. (2010). Most people are not WEIRD. *Nature*, *466*(7302), 29.

INAC (Indigenous and Northern Affairs Canada). (n.d.). *Indigenous peoples and communities*. Retrieved from http://www.aadnc-aandc.gc.ca/eng/1100100013785/1304467449155

Jamieson, R. (2017, June 30). Canada's original promise: Still waiting to be realized. *CBC Ideas*. Retrieved from http://www.cbc.ca/radio/ideas/canada-s-original-promise-still-waiting-to-be-realized-1.4185851

Kirmayer, L., Simpson, C., & Cargo, M. (2003). Healing traditions: Culture, community, and mental health promotion with Canadian Indigenous peoples. *Australasian Psychiatry*, *11*(Suppl. 1), S15–S23. doi:10.1046/j.1038-5282.2003.02010.x

Legal Aid Ontario. (n.d.). What are Gladue reports? *LawFacts*. Retrieved from http://lawfacts.ca/node/460

LeVine, R. A. (2014). Attachment theory as cultural ideology. In O. Hiltrud & H. Keller (Eds.), *Different faces of attachment: Cultural variations on a universal human need* (pp. 50–65). Cambridge, United Kingdom: Cambridge University Press.

Lindstrom, G., & Choate, P. (2016). Nistawatsiman: Rethinking assessment of Aboriginal parents for child welfare. *First Peoples Child & Family Review*, *11*(2), 45–59.

McCaslin, W. D., & Boyer, Y. (2009). First Nations communities at risk and in crisis: Justice and security. *Journal of Aboriginal Health*, *5*(2), 61–87.

McKenzie, H. A., Varcoe, C., Browne, A. J., & Day, L. (2016). Disrupting the continuities among residential schools, the Sixties Scoop, and child welfare: An analysis of colonial and neocolonial discourses. *International Indigenous Policy Journal*, *7*(2), Art. 4. Retrieved from http://ir.lib.uwo.ca/iipj/vol7/iss2/4

Mohatt, N. V., Thompson, A. B., Thai, N. D., & Tebes, J. K. (2014). Historical traumas as public narrative: A conceptual review of how history impacts present-day health. *Social Science & Medicine*, *106*(April), 128–136. doi:10.1016/j.socscimed.2014.01.043

Molloy, D., Barton, S., & Brims, L. (2017). *Improving the effectiveness of the child protection system: Overview*. London, United Kingdom: Early Intervention Foundation.

NCCD Children's Research Center. (2015). *The Structured Decision-Making system for Child Protective Services: Policy and procedures manual: Saskatchewan* (Updated ed.). Madison, WI: National Council on Crime and Delinquency.

Pezzot-Pearce, T. D., & Pearce, J. (2004). *Parenting assessments in child welfare cases: A practical guide*. Toronto, ON: University of Toronto Press.

Reder, P., Duncan, S., & Lucey, C. (2003). *Studies in the assessment of parenting*. London, United Kingdom: Routledge.

Rottger-Rossler, B. (2014). Bonding and belonging beyond WEIRD worlds: Rethinking attachment theory on the basis of cross-cultural anthropological data. In O. Hiltrud & H. Keller (Eds.), *Different faces of attachment: Cultural variations on a universal human need* (pp. 141–168). Cambridge, United Kingdom: Cambridge University Press.

R. v. Gladue, [1999] 1 SCR 688.

Shepherd, K. A. (2008). *Determinants of parenting among Aboriginal and European Canadian young mothers* (Master's thesis). University of Maryland, Baltimore County, MD. Retrieved from ProQuest Dissertations and Theses database (UMI No. 1456440).

Sinha, V., & Kozlowski, A. (2013). The structure of Indigenous child welfare in Canada. *International Indigenous Policy Journal*, *4*(2), Art. 2. Retrieved from http://ir.lib.uwo.ca/iipj/vol4/iss2/2

Truth and Reconciliation Commission of Canada. (2015). *Honouring the truth, reconciling for the future: Summary of the final report of the Truth and Reconciliation Commission of Canada*. Winnipeg, MB: TRC.

Turnell, A., & Murphy, T. (2017). *Signs of safety: Comprehensive briefing paper* (4th ed.). East Perth, Western Australia: Resolutions Consultancy.

Vandivere, S., & Malm, K. (2015). *Family Finding evaluations: A summary of recent findings* (Child Trends Publication #2015-01). Bethesda, MD: Child Trends.

Vibert, E. (2016). Wretched fishers and manly men: The meaning of food in the plateau fur trade. In K. Burnett & G. Read (Eds.), *Aboriginal history: A reader* (pp. 122–134). Don Mills, ON: Oxford University Press.

Walter, M., & Anderson, C. (2013). *Indigenous statistics: A quantitative research methodology*. Walnut Creek, CA: Left Coast Press.

CHAPTER 6

Listening in a Settler State: (Birth) Mothers as Paraprofessionals in Response to FASD

Michelle Stewart, Lisa Lawley, Rachel Tambour, and Alexandra Johnson

Introduction

The Truth and Reconciliation Commission of Canada (TRC), in its *Calls to Action* (TRC, 2015), outlines the need for a fundamental reordering of how child welfare policy is enacted in Canada. More specifically, the TRC draws into sharp focus the ways in which Indigenous children have been, and continue to be, impacted by settler colonialism through child welfare practices that aggressively displace children by stripping them from their birth families and communities. The TRC links the practices of the residential schools to contemporary manifestations of settler colonialism as child welfare continues to justify the forced separation of families and children, including recommendation 5, which calls for the development of culturally appropriate programs for Indigenous parents.

For well over a decade it has been the case that more children are in state "care" in Canada currently than during the height of residential

Suggested Citation: Stewart, M., Lawley, L., Tambour, R., & Johnson, A. (2018). Listening in a settler state: (Birth) mothers as paraprofessionals in response to FASD. In D. Badry, H. Montgomery, D. Kikulwe, M. Bennett, & D. Fuchs, (Eds.), *Imagining child welfare in the spirit of reconciliation* (pp. 117–136). Regina, SK: University of Regina Press.

schools (Assembly of First Nations, 2006)—indeed, "by a factor of three" (Blackstock, 2007, p. 74). This phenomenon has been labelled the "Millennium Scoop"—a term and practice extending from the ideologies that facilitated the residential schools and the Sixties Scoop (Fraser, Vachon, Hassan, & Parent, 2016; McKenzie, Varcoe, Brown, & Day, 2016; R. Sinclair, 2007). From residential school programs to the Sixties and Millennium Scoops, a cluster of programs and practices continues to be actively and continuously decentring Indigenous parents and their perspectives. In conversation with the work of the TRC, and informed by qualitative research, this chapter calls for the re-centring of Indigenous parents, calling for parents to be understood to have capacity as paraprofessionals (someone without formal training but nevertheless an expert) in child welfare. Placing the perspectives of parents at the centre of this analysis, this chapter focuses on the lived experiences of two mothers and their strategies to counter structural racism and to retain their role as parents—a role that is actively displaced and negated through contemporary child welfare practices in Canada.

Fetal alcohol spectrum disorder (FASD) is a diagnostic term that describes a range of conditions that can result from prenatal exposure to alcohol (Cook et al., 2016). It is a disability often framed negatively, according to families, who find through discussions with professionals that the focus is often on the limits of individuals (and families) and less so on their strengths. Grounded in qualitative research, this chapter focuses on the resiliency of two families who are raising children with FASD and offers the perspectives of mothers in particular, as they discuss the challenges of identifying culturally safe(r) programs/practices and identify the strategies they deploy to protect themselves and their community from unsafe practices. Feeling unsafe is understood to mean facing a direct threat of child apprehension. Included in the analysis is the racialization of the disability via programs and practices that often further stigmatize the condition through isolation and ambivalence.

Drawing from a broader cross-Canada research project focused on FASD, this chapter argues that parents can be viewed as potential paraprofessionals, as their lived experiences of raising a child with a complex disability should be recognized and respected when identifying and accessing appropriate supports and services (across the child's lifespan). Further, we argue that the lived experiences of Indigenous moms must be recognized as particularly unique and honoured; in addition to raising children with complex needs, they must also navigate a racialized disability while facing ongoing microaggressions and structural inequality that is laced with the real threat of child apprehension. The mothers who shared their stories recognize the powerful role they play in their children's lives; we argue that they also offer insights into child welfare practices by identifying micro- and macroaggressions that make for culturally unsafe programs/practices. We write this chapter as non-Indigenous researchers who endeavour to speak about a racialized disability with the intent of illustrating some of the micro- and macroaggressions that fuel racism and child apprehension in Canada. We do so in collaboration with two Indigenous mothers who are experts in the experiences of their children, and in conversation with the TRC, which begins its ninety-four recommendations by focusing on child welfare—as well as a national conversation that joins many voices in calling for a paradigm shift in how Indigenous parents and children are treated in a settler state.

Fraser et al. (2016) argue that contemporary child welfare practices use surveillance and social control in the name of "'child protection' in a context where parents and communities are perceived and assessed as being unable to care for the children" (p. 68; drawing from Kirmayer, Simpson, & Cargo, 2003). Sarah de Leeuw (2014) argues that, to decolonize state practices, a rupture in the hegemonic nature of commonsensical practices is required. She writes,

> *Undoing contemporary colonial power, manifest in the ongoing disruption of Indigenous families and communities, requires destabilizing commonsense ideas about what constitutes good child-welfare practices and in whose best interests those practices are being undertaken....If child-welfare policies and practices are seen as powerfully grounded examples of colonial incursions into Indigenous spaces, destabilizing them can be understood as holding remarkable potential for destabilizing neo settler-colonial power.* (p. 73)

Decolonizing social work and child welfare practices (Cross et al., 2015; Libesman, 2013; Reid, 2005; R. Sinclair, 2004) will be central to reconciliation. Accordingly, this chapter draws on the perspectives of parents and communities who are subject to state surveillance and practices of "contemporary colonial power" to focus on their experiences and strategies to address the systemic racism (and stigma) they face. As paraprofessionals, these individuals offer much-needed insight on how to provide supports and services for parents and children; they do so by actively pushing back against colonial sensibilities that implicitly and explicitly facilitate the effacement of Indigenous families through the displacement of Indigenous children.

Methods, Co-authorship, and Language

Prior to turning to the interviews, we will offer a few words about methods, the choice to focus on these stories, and the process by which the research team came to co-author this chapter with key interviewees. This chapter is the product of an ongoing cross-Canada research trip using mixed methods that have included an environmental scan completed in November 2015 and cross-country interviews conducted in 2016 and 2017. The environmental scan informed the qualitative data collection that was approved by the research ethics board in 2016. To date, data collection has taken place in all territories and provinces with the exception of Nunavut, where data collection is forthcoming in 2018. The research team has focused on interviews in regional hubs (placing an emphasis on non-southern locations, as a disproportionate number of resources are located in the southern parts of most provinces). To date, the team has undertaken interviews with over seventy individuals, including six individuals with FASD and nearly twenty parents/caregivers. This project has employed semi-structured interview methods; interviewees were asked to choose a location where they felt most comfortable meeting, and these meetings ranged in duration from approximately thirty minutes to three hours. Selection was based on a review of relevant agencies in each community, key contacts in the FASD support community, and snowball sampling from these initial contacts.

While the project focal point was on how FASD is experienced by families and individuals more broadly, this chapter focuses specifically on the lived experiences of two Indigenous mothers. These mothers were originally enrolled in the project as participants who had initially signed consents as participants with the understanding that their interview material was confidential. However, in the months following the research data collection, these mothers were independently approached to speak at a national symposium on FASD, justice, and reconciliation. In hearing the two mothers (Lisa and Rachel) share their stories with the audience, it was clear to the research team that it was time to revisit the question of authorship in this chapter. Following consultation with the research ethics board about the appropriate process by which to transform informants into co-authors, the researcher approached each woman individually to explain the interest in co-authorship and to ascertain if she was interested in co-authoring the chapter, which would require that she waive the confidentiality that was originally promised. Both women agreed separately, and at that time we opened a direct communication line among all authors: the principal investigator (Michelle), a student researcher (Alexandra), Lisa, and Rachel. This chapter is grounded in their stories. Lisa and Rachel shared their stories with us in the hopes that practices and policies might change to better serve the needs of both those with FASD and their families. All authors are hoping this chapter might reshape child welfare and the practices of frontline social workers and others.

The process of sharing authorship also involved reviewing some of the language that is commonly used to describe parenting or "types" of parents. Initially, this chapter deployed the language of "birth parents" to describe the mothers we focused on. As we moved toward co-authorship, language has been modified to reflect the language preferred by all. We will not be using this term, as, for some, classifying moms as "birth mothers" versus adoptive or foster mothers is a contentious issue. The women who have provided their perspectives in this chapter identify, first and foremost, as mothers to children with FASD. When specification was needed, one of the mothers said that she prefers the term "maternal mother." Accordingly, we will use the terms "parent" and "mother." However, in a few spots, the delineation is necessary, and we will adopt the term "maternal mother" as used by one of the co-authors.

At the centre of Lisa's and Rachel's stories are the ongoing acts of racism and structural inequality that serve as the foundation for settler colonialism. The stories of mothers, in encounters from clinical settings to FASD conferences, serve as stark reminders of the need to bring about change as they share their lived experiences of racism and trauma as well as the strategies they have developed to counter microaggressions (at the hands of other parents) and macroaggressions (at the hands of the medical industry). Parents have differing capacities, but this chapter argues that many can hold expert-level understandings of their child's disability. Their stories highlight the particularly racialized experience of Indigenous parents raising children with this disability.

Parents as Paraprofessionals

A paraprofessional is an individual who provides services without formalized training through an external agency (Peacock, Konrad, Watson, Nickel, & Muhajarine, 2013). Although paraprofessionals gain outcomes that are comparable to those of the professional workforce (Durlak, 1979), they may lack access to relevant education and training (Ghere & York-Barr, 2007; Giangreco, Edelman, Broer, & Doyle, 2001). Certain sectors have made efforts to increase access to professional development for paraprofessionals, and, while many parents have become accustomed to accessing paraprofessionals in the classroom (Russell, Allday, & Duhon, 2015), this chapter makes the case for parents of children with FASD to be able to take on a similar role in clinical and non-clinical settings.

It does so, however, with a stipulation that training is required for paraprofessionals to be taken seriously as experts in any field and to combat professional skepticism toward collaboration with paraprofessionals (Carter, O'Rourke, Sisco, & Pelsue, 2008; French & Pickett, 1997). Maintaining collaborative relationships between paraprofessionals and professionals is contingent upon fostering recognition of the value and role of paraprofessionals in professional spaces, and training acts to elevate the perceived status of paraprofessionals among professionals (Biggs, Gilson, & Carter, 2016; Carter et al., 2008; McCulloch & Noonan, 2013). Parents of children with a disability are often placed in a default role of advocate (Brennan, 2014; Mead & Paige, 2008). This chapter recognizes the challenge of that work and argues for an explicit role for these parents as paraprofessionals—allowing them to move beyond the framework of advocate—and for paraprofessionals to be recognized in these settings.

Although multiple sectors have reconceptualized paraprofessionals by increasing their access to professional development and making explicit the value and skills that they bring to the sector as a whole, parents of individuals with FASD have not been afforded these opportunities or recognition. Parents possess a wealth of experience, which informs the ways in which they fill in the gaps in services that are present in the lives of their children. Parents may be required to navigate medical, educational, and financial systems. Although this experience is undoubtedly valuable, our research indicates that parents are denied the opportunity for further professional development. Education is aimed at frontline workers and service providers, often with limited scope, focusing on the ways in which individuals may interact with various sectors. Educational opportunities then tend to be limited for those individuals, i.e., the parents, who are filling the gaps in existing service provision. Thinking collectively as researchers, workers, and community members, we need to be actively facilitating spaces that include parents not only as participants but also as educators, so that they can share their experiences and help to shape understandings of FASD both in research and in the areas of prevention and intervention.

Research indicates that individuals with FASD can have disproportionate contact with social services (Brintnell, 2009), justice (Douglas, Hammill, Russell, & Hall, 2012; Fast & Conry, 2009; B. Sinclair, 2004), and youth and child welfare (see, for example, Burnside & Fuchs, 2013; Muhajarine, McHenry, Cheng, Popham, & Smith, 2013). FASD is stigmatized and follows a "racialized script" (Oldani, 2009). It requires careful interventions (Pei, Job, Poth, & Atkinson, 2013) and prevention practices (Stewart, 2016), including culturally specific prevention and intervention (Elliot, Latimer, Fitzpatrick, Oscar, & Carter, 2012; Salmon, 2011; Salmon & Clarren, 2011). This chapter highlights the roles of Indigenous women in reshaping how we think about FASD and their strategies for navigating this highly racialized disability at a time in which racialization comes with the ongoing threat of child welfare engagement.

When Safe Spaces Are Not Safe

We met Lisa in a small community in Western Canada where she is a mother and support worker. A strong community advocate, Lisa shared her experience of raising children living with FASD who have faced a lifetime of struggles and successes. As a mother of children living with FASD, Lisa identifies a lack of safe spaces for maternal moms. She highlighted the need for community programs that provide "a safe space for women to come forward and ask for help," programs void of the judgment and stigma that are overwhelmingly present in our discussions with parents—especially maternal mothers. She discussed the various ways that FASD is racialized and the broader context(s) of FASD in lives of Indigenous women and families. "FASD and residential schools are interconnected," she explained. While residential schools were not part of her own immediate background, she recognizes the legacies of the residential school and the Sixties Scoop and the role they might have in the lives of Indigenous women and families.

Lisa is forthright in how she addresses the stigma facing Indigenous mothers and families—she always has been. She recalled that, many years back when she was living in her home community, the health nurse would make rounds, but the pregnant women in the community would not answer the door. Lisa had been one of those women; she did not trust the health nurse and avoided contact with her. She told us about having recently run into the community nurse in the grocery store and the nurse telling her about a conversation they had had many decades prior. Lisa laughed, in part because she was taken aback by how candid she had been in that conversation when she had told the community nurse, "People don't want to see you because of the way you are"—because that young nurse didn't understand where people were in their lives and what backgrounds they were coming from. Lisa had spoken so candidly to that new nurse so many years ago to impress on her that the "relationship is a key piece." In their chance encounter in the grocery store years later, the nurse told Lisa that her comments had fundamentally changed how she conducted her work as a nurse in the years that followed. Lisa laughed at that, because she eventually took on that job of knocking on women's doors. This is a challenging job, because so many women are afraid to open their doors—afraid to open themselves up to scrutiny, to sanction, and to judgment. In that exchange years ago between a young nurse and a community member, one could argue that the nurse had treated Lisa as a paraprofessional in taking direction from her and engaging her feedback. In the years that followed, Lisa became the paraprofessional as she visited the homes of young mothers.

The philosophy that Lisa had introduced to the young community nurse was about building relationships. Lisa explained, "Just because you have some education means nothing—can you create a relationship with this person?" She emphasized the importance of relationships as they relate to the work at hand: "[When] you've created a relationship with this person, you can have these difficult conversations...[because] you're coming from a place of safety but also...a relationship." She was pointing out that workers can easily forget the importance of relationships—that they are a key piece in community work. Lisa's approach to support for mothers is not about scrutiny, sanction, or judgment but about support: "You're on her team, on her side; you're her cheerleader." She spoke about the immense challenges women face when they are pregnant and seeking support, and she cultivates a space of support, asking, "Who are we to dictate to women...telling them what to do?" She asks these questions as an intervention into practices that might otherwise put women on edge or make them feel judged. She does so because, she says, if women do not feel safe, "they never come back to us." Much of the work Lisa undertakes in her community is focused on making women feel safe and supported—to make sure they keep coming back and do not feel judged or alone. While she holds a paraprofessional role as community worker, being seen as a paraprofessional who is also a mother might support having her perspectives better recognized and appreciated as she intervenes on micro- and macroaggressions that make her feel unsafe.

Lisa spoke of the microaggressions she would face as a maternal mom of children living with FASD. Turning to the literature, Sue et al. (2007) state,

> *Racial microaggressions are brief and commonplace daily verbal, behavioral, or environmental indignities, whether intentional or unintentional, that communicate hostile, derogatory, or negative racial slights and insults toward people of color. Perpetrators of microaggressions are often unaware that they engage in such communications when they interact with racial/ethnic minorities.* (p. 271)

Lisa indicated that, immediately, there were "the judgments, that automatically I'm an alcoholic, that I don't take care of my kids....I've raised all of my kids." The assumptions that Lisa's family had contact with social services and that Lisa was an alcoholic were pervasive. Like so many other women, "the drinking happened before I knew I was pregnant." Moreover, while prevention discourses about FASD indicate that many women might not know they are pregnant, and that supports should recognize that

(Thurmeier, Deshpande, Lavack, Agrey, & Cismaru, 2011), Lisa identified the racism that surrounds the disability—and specifically mothers: "I knew the stereotype, that they were stereotyping us as Aboriginal women." Lisa discussed facing racism in both clinical and non-clinical settings. While one might expect that Lisa would encounter this when dealing with larger systems (social services, medicine), she also described microaggressions that occurred between parents.

Lisa has attended national conferences on FASD. These events bring together researchers, parents, policy-makers, and frontline professionals. As researchers who have attended such conferences, we understood these to be explicitly collaborative spaces—we also, falsely, understood them to be accepting spaces. Lisa told us about her experience attending a conference (the last one she went to) and how the space she assumed would be safe and supportive was instead studded with judgment—judgment about maternal moms that fuels the isolation they already experience.

Riding the escalators, Lisa would overhear participants discussing maternal moms. She later explained, "I'm so sick of them saying, 'those women, those women.'...It's frustrating." She wondered aloud if these individuals were working with families and maternal parents—"because they shouldn't be." She worried that, as workers, they would bring prejudice and judgment to families already struggling with the challenges of raising a child with a disability. While conference participants perhaps inadvertently marginalized maternal mothers within earshot, with conversations about "those women" who drink and give birth to children with FASD, a whole other cluster of conference-goers made the space feel exceedingly unsafe for Lisa.

Lisa described an immediate feeling of discomfort upon walking into a pancake breakfast that was advertised as a space for parents and caregivers. She said that, as one of the few Indigenous women in the room, she felt that she was immediately understood to be a maternal parent. "They should have a breakfast thing for foster parents and a breakfast for birth parents, because, when you walk in there and once they realize you're a birth parent, those foster parents give you an attitude....I felt unwelcome and unsafe."[1] Much to Lisa's surprise, her experience was not isolated.

1 The term "birth parent" is included here because it was employed specifically to draw attention to the distinction experienced by parents in these spaces.

She was able to connect with another mother who had had similar negative experiences. "There's a judgment that these foster parents have of us," Lisa explained, and "we weren't feeling welcome." She felt a certain naiveté about events that bring biological and foster/adoptive families together. The pancake breakfast becomes a microcosm; Lisa noted that "the idea to not separate [the events that bring parents together] make[s] people think that it's inclusive, but it doesn't mean that it's safe." For Indigenous women who are parents, she explained, there is a group at the "margins of what is considered the norm in the room." This experience of marginalization is an outcome of the microaggressions that Lisa faced at the conference.

The individuals on the escalator likely did not know that Lisa was a maternal mother as they voiced their perspectives on *those* women; similarly, foster and adoptive parents likely did not know that they were *acting* in such a way that Lisa could pick up on their judgment. Nevertheless, these attitudes and behaviours persist, with real-world impacts on women like Lisa—and she has strategies that she must then deploy to protect herself.

Similar to the strategies that she used in her own community, Lisa steps back when needed to spend time with other mothers. Reflecting the discussion about effective supports in her community, Lisa turns to other moms who can understand the unique challenges she faces. In her own community, Lisa indicated, the best support she has is from a friend—instead of reaching out to community organizations, Lisa reached out to her friend who was also raising a child with FASD. Through shared experience, the women supported each other and eventually became a support for other women going through similar experiences in their community. Lisa believes that the efficacy of these supports goes unrecognized in professional settings. She suggests that, while professionals often acknowledge that individuals living with FASD are the experts on FASD, they neglect to recognize that "the experts in prevention of FASD are the birth mothers." The expertise of birth/maternal mothers that is grounded in their own lived experiences would greatly affect how professionals learn about and work with FASD. Instead, whether talking about prevention or just general supports, parents are positioned as the receivers of information from other professionals. This can serve to silence rather than elicit the informed perspectives of parents. This was further evidenced when the researchers spoke to parents across Canada, who indicated an explicit interest in attending conferences and receiving direct training. Instead, as one parent explained, "all the workers get the training," while the parents who are raising children need similar training opportunities.

While some training exists for parents, it is limited compared with the training that frontline professionals receive. Similarly, there are spaces for parents at conferences, but these are limited and largely focus on them being passive recipients of expert knowledge. Instead, events that facilitate "families coming together" at training and conferences could focus on awareness, talking circles, and support circles. Through the sharing of stories, parents would then have an opportunity to increase their knowledge of FASD while simultaneously having an outlet to share their own experiences. These could be generative spaces where workers are invited to listen and learn. This would be a reordering of how mothers are imagined in most community and agency settings—transforming them into active agents and partners. Whether seen as paraprofessionals or not, they must be seen and respected as partners in this work. As a result, mothers like Lisa would be given the space to share these critical perspectives because, as she pointed out, just because a place or activity is identified as "'inclusive' it doesn't mean that it's safe."

"It About Broke Me"

While conducting research in northern Canada, the researchers met Rachel. Rachel is a maternal mother who agreed to sit down and talk to us about her experiences raising a son living with FASD. Rachel was trained in social work and has a long history of working in the community with individuals who have complex disabilities. She shared the challenges of being an Indigenous woman raising a child with a highly racialized disability—she also shared an experience that is common among mothers who have a child with FASD: that she did not realize she was pregnant when she was drinking.

We sat in a quiet hotel as Rachel patiently and generously shared her story—and her tears. She revisited the pain of finding out she was pregnant and realizing that she had been drinking. She talked about the guilt of knowing she had been drinking during her pregnancy and the grief and trauma it caused when she found out she was pregnant. "I cried because I drank and I knew I drank. At that moment I stopped everything." Although her son was born at a healthy weight and she thought he might be fine, she was cautious. "I kept my eye on him because my mom, she always told me, 'Don't drink when you're pregnant,' and this woman didn't speak English, but she knew it wasn't safe," she recalled. "She didn't see it on TV or anything, she just knew it wasn't safe to drink alcohol during pregnancy." While Rachel was optimistic after her son's birth, when he started school she could see some potential concerns, such as developmental lags and delays.

Proactive about the issues she could see arising, she sought medical assistance, but seeking a diagnosis came with its own challenges. She indicated that discussing FASD with her son was difficult and that the tests themselves were challenging. Her son would quiz her: "Why are you taking me to these brain tests? Is there something wrong with my brain?" In retrospect, Rachel believes that he started to do increasingly poorly on the tests not only because they were challenging but also, in part, because he was tired of the tests themselves. After a battery of tests, the doctor rendered the verdict—coldly and matter-of-factly—about the FASD diagnosis: "I'm sorry to tell you this, but your son is never going to read past a grade three level, your son is not going to make it further than grade seven, and he will never obtain his driver's licence."

Rachel was devastated. When asked if the doctor was compassionate in delivering the diagnosis, she indicated that he was not. As with any difficult diagnosis, medical practitioners need to be equipped, and compassionate, when delivering challenging news:

> *The delivery of sad, bad, and difficult news will always be an unpleasant but necessary part of medicine. In the past decade recognition has grown of the need to integrate appropriate communication skills teaching into undergraduate and postgraduate education....Training health-care professionals how to do the task more effectively will produce benefits for them as well as their patients, but this training needs to be based on sound educational principles, informed by evidence, and assessed and monitored adequately.* (Fallowfield & Jenkins, 2004, pp. 317–318)

While the medical establishment might frame this necessity in terms of the "task [being done] more effectively," there is a need to include the role of compassion when discussing diagnoses of complex disabilities like

FASD, because FASD is "in fact a diagnosis for two: an affected child and a vulnerable birth mother" (Berube, 2011, p. 342). Thinking about the challenges of receiving an FASD diagnosis, Badry and Choate (2015) offer an overview of key literatures and argue that evidence indicates that birth moms face a range of challenges, including but not limited to poverty and trauma. They argue,

> *These are complex families....The diagnosis of a child with a FASD should represent the need to trace back into a mother's history the roots of the problem. It is this beginning place in which a compassionate response to FASD is found.* (Badry & Choate, 2015, p. 23)

Thinking back to Rachel's experience, and layering it with Lisa's approach to building relationships, a "beginning place" would be to see the complexity of the disability and reach out to Rachel with compassion. While Rachel may or may not agree with the characterization that a root problem can be found in her own background, she would likely have welcomed a medical diagnosis that sought to build a relationship in order to assist her and her son. Instead, Rachel was given a diagnosis that cut like a knife. She was left alone to navigate the experience of raising a child with a disability and to navigate the shame of the diagnosis.

Rachel described her experience of leaving the doctor's office after the diagnosis, alone and vulnerable. "At that time I was two years sober, and that just about broke me right there, you know, I just felt like such a loser. It took a lot for me to drive by that liquor store that day; I didn't know what to do." She did not go into the liquor store but instead anchored in and helped her son. Despite the cold clinical experience in which a challenging diagnosis had come with limited additional assistance, Rachel raised a little boy who struggled but who persevered to become a young man and a loving father.

Yet the challenges facing her as a mother persisted as her son would raise difficult questions. While telling us that her son's girlfriend got pregnant when they were teens, Rachel noted what a great father he is. Her voice shone when she spoke about her son, who is now a father of two; he has successfully navigated an amicable separation agreement outside of courts to be a co-parent in raising two young children. Then her voice cracked as she described the questions he would ask during his girlfriend's pregnancies, relative to his own disability: "Are my babies going to be smart? Is my baby going to be smart?" Rachel's voice cracked and faded as she repeated one of his comments in a near whisper: "I hope my baby's not going to be dumb like me." Her son, who is careful and cautious with his own children, inadvertently reminds his mother of her role in his disability as it continues to be a diagnosis for two. Rachel would respond that his baby would be fine because the mother was not drinking. She both affirms the choice of their young family to abstain from drinking and asserts that she did not purposely inflict FASD on him. She wonders about how other women handle the diagnosis. "This is why I think other women are sweeping it under the rug, because it is tough to deal with." Mothers like Rachel and Lisa are not sweeping FASD under the rug; they are tackling it head-on, and in so doing they have many lessons and perspectives to share. The question is, who is listening?

Rachel's and Lisa's stories are about being active and ongoing supports in the lives of their children. In that way, they join all other parents raising children with a complex disability: it is a challenging job. The diagnosis of FASD is delivered with a focus on limitations and strengths. For some this feels like a list of limitations that is very challenging to look at and, we were told, is often not an accurate reflection of their experiences. In the case of Rachel, the limitations that underlined her son's diagnosis were stunning, but her son persevered. Not only did he exceed the educational forecast, but he also attained a driver's licence and established a well-paying career. When we spoke, Rachel's son was threatening to move back home so he could pursue a post-secondary degree—she laughed that this was a threat she welcomed. The resilience in Rachel's story might appear to lie with her son and his achievements, but as with all parents the researchers spoke to, resilience is at the core of the families that are supporting children with FASD.

Parents and children work, and struggle, together for most successes. Many of the successes are the result of advocacy; all the parents we spoke to, Indigenous and non-Indigenous alike, were thrown into a default role of advocate to secure much-needed resources throughout their children's lives. In this chapter, we make the case that parents must be listened to and should be seen as potential paraprofessionals, or experts, in the lives of their children. In so doing, we highlight the particular experience of Indigenous maternal moms as they occupy a deeply challenging space because of the micro- and macroaggressions they face. However, we must also recognize that not all parents are in a position to act as paraprofessionals. That being said, we must find new ways to engage with all parents, because parents are frequently not listened to, and this experience often only compounds their experiences of racism and colonialism.

"We Have the Stories"

When developing this chapter, we discussed the role of maternal mothers as it relates to frontline programs and practices. Rachel noted that maternal moms are a source of knowledge and wisdom especially in relation to prevention practices, and it is important to recognize that they also have a unique role when it comes to education, outreach, and training. "We have the stories," she explained, adding that there is more value in these stories than in having workers parachute into communities to do training. These stories can help all parents better understand FASD and how to prevent it.

By way of example, Rachel shared a story about abstract thought—a known challenge for individuals with FASD. She explained how her husband had once asked her son "what shape the game was in," as a way of asking if a video game disc was damaged, and her son responded, "A circle," referring to the physical shape of the disc itself. Rachel suggests that stories about experiences such as this hold meaning and insight and can be shared with others. So, in taking these personal experiences and using the stories to educate others on the more challenging aspects of FASD as a racialized disability, mothers have an opportunity to "hit them in the heart" in ways that reading books or watching professional development presentations cannot. Rachel has lived the stories of opening the doors, asking for help, and being met with both positive and negative responses. She can communicate the emotions behind the experience of FASD both as a mother and as somebody who hears and understands the experiences of her children.

Despite seeing the benefits to professionals and community members of hearing her stories, Rachel also recognizes that work must be done to make spaces (community, clinical, and professional) safe for mothers to share their stories. The safety of these spaces is contingent upon respect and value for mothers—mothers of children with complex disabilities and mothers who are Indigenous women. As Rachel states, these ideas "come along with what I've experienced—not feeling important, not feeling valued for what my thoughts are." However, when she feels valued, feels respected, she also feels empowered to share her story powerfully and in certain terms. People need to take these stories seriously, to listen to and hear these mothers, because these stories provide us with direction in terms of supports and services, and listening can serve to support and confront the micro- and macroaggressions these mothers face.

Conclusion—Hearing versus Listening

This chapter brought together empirical research to discuss the ways in which programs and practices can be unsafe for parents. Its aim was to influence the delivery of frontline services including child welfare practices. The chapter addressed how FASD is taken up in various settings to demonstrate the ways in which parents could serve as paraprofessionals—and could be engaged as collaborators in finding the best ways to meet the needs of their children (and their families). Child welfare practices need to shift in Canada, and health collaborations between families and social workers could change the current practices. With that in mind, we have highlighted the perspectives of two Indigenous mothers to share their experiences of micro- and macroaggressions alongside their shared strategies to address practices that feel culturally unsafe.

The intention of this chapter is to highlight the perspectives of families and workers as a step in facilitating collaborative discussions and collective action meant to expand our shared capacity to take up the TRC's calls to action. Further, it is important to honour Lisa's and Rachel's stories by seeing the ways in which they can help bring about changes in how Indigenous mothers and families are constructed through child welfare practices. This chapter offers but one small intervention: it asks that the voices of mothers and families be heard by frontline workers as well as researchers. There is a politics to hearing *and* listening in the settler state. To hear. To listen. These are verbs, and verbs are action words. We hope that is what this chapter inspires: action.

Discussion Questions

1. What has the Truth and Reconciliation Commission identified in response to FASD?
2. Why is it important to hear the voices of families in this work?

3. What can be done to make training and conferences more inclusive and safer spaces for mothers who work in the area of FASD prevention as allies and paraprofessionals?
4. What will you take forward in your practice in response to the TRC's calls to action? What can you do to make a difference in shifting practice to promote social justice?

References

Assembly of First Nations. (2006). *Leadership action plan on First Nations child welfare*. Ottawa, ON: AFN.

Badry, D., & Choate, P. (2015). Fetal alcohol spectrum disorder: A disability in need of social work education, knowledge, and practice. *Social Work & Social Sciences Review, 17*(3), 20–32.

Berube, M. D. (2011). A social work perspective on policies to prevent alcohol consumption during pregnancy. In E. P. Riley, S. Clarence, J. Weinberg, & E. Jonsson (Eds.), *Fetal alcohol spectrum disorder: Management and policy perspectives on FASD* (pp. 339–351). Weinheim, Germany: Wiley-VCH Verlag.

Biggs, E. E., Gilson, C. B., & Carter, E. W. (2016). Accomplishing more together: Influences to the quality of professional relationships between special educators and paraprofessionals. *Research & Practice for Persons with Severe Disabilities, 41*(4), 256–272.

Blackstock, C. (2007). Residential schools: Did they really close or just morph into child welfare? *Indigenous Law Journal, 6*(1), 71–78.

Brennan, S. (2014). The goods of childhood, children's rights, and the role of parents as advocates and interpreters. In F. Baylis & C. McLeod (Eds.), *Family-making: Contemporary ethical challenges*. New York, NY: Oxford University Press.

Brintnell, S. (2009, October). *Social service needs of adults with FASD in the correctional system*. Paper presented at the IHE Consensus Development Conference on Fetal Alcohol Spectrum Disorder – Across the Lifespan, Edmonton, AB.

Burnside, L., & Fuchs, D. (2013). Bound by the clock: The experiences of youth with FASD transitioning to adulthood from child welfare care. *First Peoples Child & Family Review 8*(1), 41–62.

Carter, E., O'Rourke, L., Sisco, L. G., & Pelsue, D. (2008). Knowledge, responsibilities, and training needs of paraprofessionals in elementary and secondary schools. *Remedial and Special Education, 30*(6), 344–359.

Cook, J. L., Green, C. R., Lilley, C. M., Anderson, S. M., Baldwin, M. E., Chudley, A. E., & Mallon, B. F. (2016). Fetal alcohol spectrum disorder: A guideline for diagnosis across the lifespan. *Canadian Medical Association Journal, 188*(3), 191–197.

Cross, T., Blackstock, C., Formsma, J., George, J., & Brown, I. (2015). Editorial: Touchstones of hope: Still the best guide for Indigenous child welfare. *First Peoples Child & Family Review, 10*(2), 6–11.

de Leeuw, S. (2014). State of care: The ontologies of child welfare in British Columbia. *Cultural Geographies, 21*(1), 59-78.

Douglas, H., Hammill, J., Russell, E., & Hall, W. (2012). Judicial views of foetal alcohol spectrum disorder in Queensland's criminal justice system. *Journal of Judicial Administration 21*(3), 178–188.

Durlak, J. A. (1979). Comparative effectiveness of paraprofessional and professional helpers. *Psychological Bulletin, 86*(1), 80–92.

Elliot, E., Latimer, J., Fitzpatrick, J., Oscar, J., & Carter, M. (2012). There's hope in the valley. *Journal of Paediatrics & Child Health, 48*(3), 190–192.

Fallowfield, L., & Jenkins, V. (2004). Communicating sad, bad, and difficult news in medicine. *The Lancet, 363*(9405), 312–319.

Fast, D., & Conry, J. (2009). Fetal alcohol spectrum disorders and the criminal justice system. *Developmental Disabilities Research Reviews, 15*(3), 250–257.

Fraser, S., Vachon, M., Hassan, G., & Parent, V. (2016). Communicating power and resistance: Exploring interactions between Aboriginal youth and non-Aboriginal staff members in a residential child welfare facility. *Qualitative Research in Psychology, 13*(1), 67–91.

French, N. K., & Pickett, A. L. (1997). Paraprofessionals in special education: Issues for teacher educators. *Teacher Education & Special Education: The Journal of the Teacher Education Division of the Council for Exceptional Children, 20*(1), 61–73.

Ghere, G., & York-Barr, J. (2007). Paraprofessional turnover and retention in inclusive programs: Hidden costs and promising practices. *Remedial & Special Education, 28*(1), 21–32.

Giangreco, M. F., Edelman, S. W., Broer, S. M., & Doyle, M. B. (2001). Paraprofessional support of students with disabilities: Literature from the past decade. *Exceptional Children, 68*(1), 45–63.

Kirmayer, L., Simpson, C., & Cargo, M. (2003). Healing traditions: Culture, community, and mental health promotion with Canadian Aboriginal peoples. *Australasian Psychiatry, 11*(Suppl. 1), S15–S23.

Libesman, T. (2013). *Decolonising Indigenous child welfare: Comparative perspectives*. New York, NY: Routledge.

McCulloch, E. B., & Noonan, M. J. (2013). Impact of online training videos on the implementation of and training by three elementary school paraprofessionals. *Education & Training in Autism & Developmental Disabilities, 48*(1), 132–141.

McKenzie, H. A., Varcoe, C., Browne, A. J., & Day, L. (2016). Disrupting the continuities among residential schools, the Sixties Scoop, and child welfare: An analysis of colonial and neocolonial discourses. *International Indigenous Policy Journal, 7*(2), Art. 4. Retrieved from http://ir.lib.uwo.ca/iipj/vol7/iss2/4

Mead, J. F., & Paige, M. A. (2008). Parents as advocates: Examining the history and evolution of parents' rights to advocate for children with disabilities under the IDEA. *Journal of Legislation, 34*(2), 123–167.

Muhajarine, N., McHenry, S., Cheng, J., Popham, J., & Smith, F. M. (2013). *Phase one evaluation: Improving outcomes for children with FASD in foster care: Final report*. Saskatoon, SK: FASD Support Network.

Oldani, M. (2009). Uncanny scripts: Understanding pharmaceutical emplotment in the Aboriginal context. *Transcultural Psychiatry, 46*(1), 131–156.

Peacock, S., Konrad, S., Watson, E., Nickel, D., & Muhajarine, N. (2013). Effectiveness of home visiting programs on child outcomes: A systematic review. *BMC Public Health, 13*(1), 17.

Pei, J., Job, J. M., Poth, C., & Atkinson, E. (2013). Assessment for intervention of children with fetal alcohol spectrum disorders: Perspectives of classroom teachers, administrators, caregivers, and allied professionals. *Psychology, 4*(3A), 325–334.

Reid, M. (2005). First Nations women workers' speak, write, and research back: Child welfare and decolonizing stories. *First Peoples Child & Family Review, 2*(1), 21–40.

Russell, C. S., Allday, R. A., & Duhon, G. J. (2015). Effects of increasing distance of a one-on-one paraprofessional on student engagement. *Education & Treatment of Children, 38*(2), 193–210.

Salmon, A. (2011). Aboriginal mothering, FASD prevention, and the contestation of neoliberal citizenship. *Critical Public Health, 21*(2), 165–178.

Salmon, A., & Clarren, S. (2011). Developing effective, culturally appropriate avenues to FASD diagnosis and prevention in northern Canada. *International Journal of Circumpolar Health, 70*(4), 428–433.

Sinclair, B. (2004). Commentary on "The challenge of fetal alcohol syndrome in the criminal legal system" by D. K. Fast & J. Conry. *Addiction Biology, 9*(2), 167–168.

Sinclair, R. (2004). Aboriginal social work education in Canada: Decolonizing pedagogy for the seventh generation. *First Peoples Child & Family Review, 1*(1), 49–62.

Sinclair, R. (2007). Identity lost and found: Lessons from the Sixties Scoop. *First Peoples Child & Family Review, 3*(1), 65–82.

Stewart, M. (2016). Fictions of prevention: Fetal alcohol spectrum disorder and narratives of responsibility. *North American Dialogue, 19*(1), 55–66.

Sue, D. W., Capodilupo, C. M., Torino, G. C., Bucceri, J. M., Holder, A., Nadal, K. L., & Esquilin, M. (2007). Racial microaggressions in everyday life: Implications for clinical practice. *American Psychologist, 62*(4), 271–286.

Thurmeier, R., Deshpande, S., Lavack, A., Agrey, N., & Cismaru, M. (2011). Next steps in FASD primary prevention. In E. P. Riley, S. Clarence, J. Weinberg, & E. Jonsson (Eds.), *Fetal alcohol spectrum disorder: Management and policy perspectives on FASD* (pp. 175–192). Weinheim, Germany: Wiley-VCH Verlag.

TRC (Truth and Reconciliation Commission of Canada). (2015). *Truth and Reconciliation Commission of Canada: Calls to Action*. Winnipeg, MB: TRC. Retrieved from http://www.trc.ca/websites/trcinstitution/File/2015/Findings/Calls_to_Action_English2.pdf

PART III

Research

CHAPTER 7

A Summary: On the Edge between Two Worlds: Community Narratives on the Vulnerability of Marginalized Indigenous Girls

Marlyn Bennett and Ainsley Krone

Introduction

In recent years, high-profile assaults and homicides of young Indigenous girls in Manitoba have underlined a growing tragedy. The racist and gendered violence, vulnerability, and oppression that Indigenous girls and women have faced for well over 250 years unite the victims of recent local tragedies with many others who have died as a result of the ongoing violence perpetrated against Indigenous girls and women.

In its widely publicized report, *Stolen Sisters*, Amnesty International (2004) concluded that myriad oppressive forces—or *intersecting sites of violence*—culminate to create untenable living conditions for the majority of Indigenous women and girls in Canada today. One of those sites of violence, where high-profile tragedies have captured the attention of the public locally and beyond, is the child welfare system. A significant number of Indigenous girls are in care through the Indigenous and non-Indigenous

Suggested Citation: Bennett, M., & Krone, A. (2018). A summary: On the edge between two worlds: Community narratives on the vulnerability of marginalized Indigenous girls. In D. Badry, H. Montgomery, D. Kikulwe, M. Bennett, & D. Fuchs, (Eds.), *Imagining child welfare in the spirit of reconciliation* (pp. 139–162). Regina, SK: University of Regina Press.

child welfare systems both within Manitoba and across Canada. During their time in care, some Indigenous girls become increasingly vulnerable and are at risk of being exploited, trafficked, and possibly murdered. While this research began with exploring narratives about the overall experiences of Indigenous girls in care, it expanded to look at an understanding of the unique factors that can increase vulnerability of Indigenous girls when they become involved in an array of public services.

This chapter is based on research conducted for the Office of the Children's Advocate in Manitoba. Thirteen questions were created to explore the experiences of Indigenous girls. Community members were asked to share their wisdom and learning about what is happening and what is needed to repair relationships and build up young women and girls so they can once again become the anchors and influencers of a healthy and healed society. This chapter is a collection of narratives stitched together to create a choir of voices that at times is empowering and gentle and at other times roils with understandable anger and passion.

Ultimately, what we learned is that the key lies in the strength of relationships—between nations, between members of a community, within partnerships, and inside ourselves. The health of our communities is tightly tied to the strength and tenacity of those bonds. We have focused this chapter on the experiences of young Indigenous women, because this issue is both racialized and gendered; however, there are just as many lessons applicable to all youth and to all Manitobans who want our province to be repaired and renewed.

Literature Review

The literature review for this project focuses on the history of colonization and the oppression of Indigenous people—primarily women—including the impacts of residential schools and the Sixties Scoop, as well as the continued overrepresentation of Indigenous children in the child welfare systems. It looks at resources where government policies and international human rights legislation each fall short of protecting children and women. It discusses a perceived apathy and indifference in the media to the plight of Indigenous women and girls, and it concludes with a brief discussion of the federal government's earlier resistance to the implementation of a national inquiry into missing and murdered Indigenous women and girls.

The long and contentious history of contact between Indigenous and settler populations has led to situations today in which Indigenous girls are placed in precarious and marginalized positions. Colonization of Indigenous populations was perpetrated through Christianity and residential schools that were designed to ensure that the "Indian problem"—a quote famously said by Duncan Campbell Scott—was eradicated. The enactment of overreaching legislation designed to control every aspect of Indigenous lives resulted in the eventual devaluation and marginalization of Indigenous populations but has specifically been detrimental to Indigenous girls and women. Indigenous women were stripped of honoured roles and responsibilities and further disadvantaged through land surrenders, wills, band elections, Indian status, band membership, and enfranchisement (Anderson, 2000; Walmsley, 2005). Indigenous girls and women continue to be undervalued. This devaluation manifests itself in the current state of affairs in which Indigenous children are overrepresented in the child welfare system, and Indigenous girls and women are among those who are the most likely to be missing or murdered across this country.

Smith (2005) argues that the main objective of residential schools for girls "was to inculcate patriarchal norms into Aboriginal communities so that women would lose their place of leadership in Aboriginal communities" (p. 37). The subjugation of Indigenous women's bodies, the victimization of women, the domination by men, hierarchical categories, and violence against women were imposed as norms. These Eurocentric values and belief systems were in direct contrast to the traditional roles, responsibilities, and values placed on Indigenous women. Indigenous women traditionally played a central role within the tribal community. Women are also central to almost all Turtle Island creation legends. For the Anishinabe, it was a woman who came to earth through a hole in the sky to care for the earth; it was a woman who taught the original man about the medicines of the earth; and it was a woman who brought the pipe to the people that is used in the most sacred of ceremonies. In most Indigenous communities, the women play the leading role in child education and food gathering, but both sexes share the roles of healers, lawmakers, performers, and custodians over traditional ways of life (Buffalohead, 1983).

Residential schools can be considered one of colonial Canada's first child welfare institutions geared toward Indigenous persons (Mandell, Clouston, Fine, & Blackstock, 2003). Usually church-owned and government-funded, these residential schools were designed to eradicate Indigenous cultures and replace them with Christian and Euro-Canadian values instead (Milloy, 1999). The last of these residential schools closed in 1996 (Blackstock, 2007). However, even with the dismantling of residential schools, there has been a long and lasting legacy of social, psychological, and economic problems among Indigenous peoples as a direct result of their forced attendance at these schools. Residential schools became the first level of oppression that attacked the spirit of most Indigenous children. In these schools, both boys and girls came to understand the power of violence (TRC, 2015). The intergenerational trauma from the experience of residential schools produced generations of individuals who did not have an opportunity to heal from the psychological, physical, and sexual abuses inflicted upon them (Wesley-Esquimaux & Smolewski, 2004).

When Canada's child and family services system began to expand in the late 1960s, many Indigenous children were taken from their homes and communities and placed off-reserve, in non-Indigenous homes as adopted or fostered children (Heinrichs & Hiebert, 2009). This practice became ubiquitous throughout the 1960s and 1970s and was thus famously labelled the Sixties Scoop. Essentially, this new form of child welfare supplanted the residential schools as a means of colonizing Indigenous children. Much as in the residential school era, researchers have pointed to the fact that child welfare has been used as a tool to continue the colonization of Indigenous peoples (Blackstock, 2007; McKenzie & Hudson, 1985). While the Sixties Scoop is now well known, there were also seventies, eighties, and nineties scoops. In fact, many have argued that the scoop of children from First Nations and other Indigenous communities has not stopped. Children continue to be removed from their homes in such high numbers that the term "Millennium Scoop" (Sinclair, 2007) has been increasingly used to emphasize the extent of the problem.

According to the Assembly of First Nations, the overrepresentation of Indigenous children within child welfare systems is an extension of the historical pattern of removal of children from their homes. The number of children in care continues to rise even though Indigenous children are increasingly serviced by Indigenous agencies. As of March 2017, Manitoba had 11,352 children in care, 89 per cent of whom were Indigenous (First Nations and Métis) children (Manitoba, Department of Families, 2017, p. 89). According to information supplied on request to the Office of the

Children's Advocate by the Department of Families, exactly 50 per cent of the children in care are female (Child and Family Services Division, personal communication, January 28, 2016).

Female children in care face the greatest risk of negative effects, responses, and outcomes because female children face the highest risk of sexual abuse (Allnock, 2010). Indigenous girls are particularly vulnerable when placed in underresourced foster care and alternative placements without adequate supervision. When the task of supervising marginalized Indigenous girls is delegated to untrained caregivers, it increases the girls' vulnerability to sexual violation, exploitation, and exposure to drug and alcohol addictions (Manitoba, FSH, 2008).

Parallels have been drawn between the overrepresentation of Indigenous children in the child welfare system with their overrepresentation among those involved in the commercial sex industry. As Sikka (2009) notes, Indigenous children are pushed into the child welfare system at three times the rate of other Canadian children, and consequently their involvement in commercial sexual exploitation increases. As a result, Indigenous girls in the child welfare system are vulnerable to the violence that is inherent in the very systems intended to protect them. Research by the Native Women's Association of Canada (2010) suggests that "the intergenerational impact and resulting vulnerabilities of colonization and state policies—such as residential schools, the Sixties Scoop, and the child welfare system—are underlying factors in the outcomes of violence experienced by Indigenous women and girls" (p. 9).

Many Indigenous women have experienced racist responses from the law when they report incidences of violence (NWAC, 2010). For example, Indigenous women who call police after being assaulted by an intimate partner are more likely to be accused of engaging in the violence and more likely to be arrested when police intervene than are non-Indigenous women (Richardson & Wade, 2009). Such circumstances lead Indigenous women to believe that it is unsafe for them to call police to report such violence (McGillivray & Comaskey, 1999). Furthermore, Indigenous women tend to blame themselves for the abuse (Richardson & Wade, 2009).

Allnock (2010) addresses reasons why children do not report sexualized violence. The leading factor noted is that children think that they will not be believed if they disclose. Where one is not believed, the tendency is to self-blame. Women who, as girls, received negative social responses to early disclosures of abuse are less likely to report abuse as adults and more likely to avoid authorities (Andrews, Brewin, & Rose, 2003; Richardson & Wade, 2009). Clark (2012) has noted that policies designed to protect children can often further victimize them. Indigenous girls who have disclosed instances of sexual abuse have been labelled and pathologized, diagnosed as having mental health issues, accused of using drugs and drinking, and questioned about the ulterior motives behind making such disclosures rather than being protected like non-Indigenous girls who disclose similar abuses (Clark, 2012).

Periodic reviews of international laws—specifically, the UN Convention on the Elimination of Discrimination against Women; the UN Convention on the Rights of the Child; the International Convention on the Elimination of All Forms of Racial Discrimination; and the International Covenant on Economic, Social, and Cultural Rights—have found Canada to be lacking and failing in its ability to uphold these laws as they pertain to Indigenous populations, particularly in relation to the circumstances that lead to violence against Indigenous girls (Aleem, 2009). As it stands, Indigenous girls do not receive distinct consideration under either domestic or international law. Broader issues of concern to Indigenous peoples—including land rights, self-government, and political representation—obscure the situation of Indigenous girls. As long as the rights of Indigenous girls are subsumed under the collective rights of Indigenous peoples, their human rights will continue to be marginalized under international law.

Apathy is also reflected in the media's failure to report on high-profile cases. For instance, the trial of John Martin Crawford in Saskatchewan for the murders of three Indigenous girls and young women (ages sixteen, twenty-two, and thirty) can be compared to that of Paul Bernardo in the deaths of two non-Indigenous girls (ages fourteen and fifteen)—except for the media circus that followed (Clark, 2012, p. 144). Media coverage was virtually non-existent in the Crawford matter, which should have been front-page news. Warren Goulding (2001), one of the few journalists to cover the trial of Crawford, noted, "I don't get the sense the general public cares much about missing or murdered Aboriginal women. It's all part of this indifference to the lives of Aboriginal people. They don't seem to matter as much as white people" (quoted in Purdy, 2003).

Along with the violence against and devaluing of Indigenous women and girls was the long-time resistance by the federal government to the implementation of a national inquiry into the issue of missing and murdered Indigenous women and girls. With the federal election in October 2015, the new Liberal government proceeded immediately with the creation of the National Inquiry into Missing and Murdered Indigenous Women and Girls. This ongoing inquiry has been dogged by mounting criticism that it has, so far, been a dismal failure (Macdonald & Campbell, 2017).

The Methods

A qualitative approach to conducting this study was identified as the most appropriate means of getting at the heart of understanding the vulnerability of marginalized Indigenous girls in Manitoba. Narrative inquiry was applied, as it is closely compatible with Indigenous values related to oral traditions. Oral traditions have been central and foundational in transmitting and preserving Indigenous knowledge, heritage, and ways of being, knowing, and doing (Hulan & Eigenbrod, 2008; Ormiston, 2010). A narrative research methodology was selected primarily for its function of including the participant in the research process. Andrews (2007) explains that, although there is the possibility of creating harm with a narrative research approach, there can also be an opportunity for beneficial and positive outcomes for the participants. Benham (2007), an Indigenous scholar, addresses the issue of engagement in narrative research:

> *Depending on the intention of the researcher, narrative can lead to illumination—activity that makes a just difference in the lives of people—or it can lead to parochialism. The challenge is to develop complementary approaches to indigenous narrative so that it is neither exclusive nor insular but instead inclusive and dynamic. The goal, then, of indigenous narrative is to invite participation of native people and their communities in the narrative process. This participation engages the researcher/scholar and native/indigenous people in building relationships that bring to the surface stories of experienced phenomena—concrete evidence—around pressing issues (e.g., historic hurt and pain). Making visible and loud what has been silent and invisible—transcending the concrete—has the power to promote a generative learning process... that might lead to community transformation.* (p. 517)

This research project had a small sample size to meet the criterion of depth versus breadth, which aligns with narrative research methodology (Clandinin, 2007). As such, the study relied upon a sample size of eleven Indigenous individuals in order to capture in-depth and rich narrative data in response to thirteen questions (see next section). This narrative inquiry centres on conversations with eleven community leaders and advocates primarily from the Indigenous community within and outside Winnipeg. Interviews were conducted during the summer months of 2015. The length of interviews ranged from 45 to 120 minutes. All interviews were audio-recorded. Participants were asked to formally consent to being interviewed for this report prior to the start of the interview. The Elders reminded the researcher that consent to participate is done orally because "that's the way it is with our people." Copies of the interview questions were provided to all participants at the beginning of the interviews so that they could anticipate how to respond to the questions asked as the interview proceeded.

In keeping with Indigenous traditions, all of the participants were gifted with tobacco and presented with a small gift such as a painted or unpainted rock. Interviews were held at various locations: in private homes, at outdoor coffee shops, in parks, at offices, and, in one case, in a parking lot. Interviews were conducted with Indigenous women, with young adults, and with well-respected Knowledge Holders (one grandfather and a number of grandmothers) recognized by the Indigenous communities in and around Winnipeg.

The transcripts from the interviews yielded over 300 pages of narrative content. Textual analyses of the narrative data from the responses to each question involved multiple readings and interpretations that were generally inductive in nature. Inductive analysis is an approach that uses detailed readings of raw data to derive concepts, themes, or a model of interpretation made from the raw data by the researcher (Thomas, 2006). Organization of the data that emerged from the interviews with community was conducted using NVivo, a software program for organizing qualitative data.

Questions and Findings

The responses gathered from the thirteen questions are set out below. For the purposes of this chapter, the questions have been organized according to the order in which they were asked. As the discussions were quite in-depth, the responses have been generalized and edited for brevity.[1] In this section of the chapter, the voices of community members are privileged over the voice of the researcher. These voices represent community authenticity, authority, love, and expertise on the fundamental understanding of why Indigenous women and girls are so vulnerable in society. The narratives reflected in this report represent a culturally nuanced way of knowing and are a form of intergenerational knowledge transfer (Cruickshank, 1998), reflect ancestral ways of knowing (Kovach, 2009), and privilege relationship building as part of the way in which to inquire and conduct this kind of research in Indigenous communities (Wilson, 2008).

Question 1: Why are girls so vulnerable when they come into care?

This question yielded a number of responses that pointed to the process of colonization, the oppression of traditional values, and the outlawing of cultural practices. All participants recognized that the vulnerability of Indigenous girls today is tied to the history of settler societies enforcing racist ideologies of religion and patriarchy. Over time, Indigenous men took on a patriarchal ideology. The teachings that had guided men and women have been lost; religion and the Bible have replaced these teachings. In some communities in the province, Christianity has displaced traditional Indigenous knowledge. The mindset that Indigenous culture and traditional practices are considered evil and based on "witchcraft" is still evidenced in many First Nations communities. When traditional cultural strengths were lost, traditional abilities to keep vulnerable individuals safe were then also undermined. As a result, Indigenous men have been indoctrinated to live by and promote male dominance over Indigenous women and girls.

Question 2: Why are young women and girls mistreated and exploited?

Mistreatment of Indigenous women and girls is a result of a barrage of continuous violations against their human rights as Indigenous women. Indigenous girls begin life at a disadvantage. The Indian Act is the root of mistreatment and exploitation of Indigenous females. This Act is one

1 Readers can access and read the complete report online; see Bennett, 2016.

of the major elements introduced by settler society that allowed for the violations, mistreatments, and exploitation of Indigenous women and girls that is ongoing, even today. The Indian Act set the stage for other violations that allowed for Indigenous women to be sterilized against their will, to be denied the right to vote, and to lose their status after marrying non-Indigenous men, among many others.

Stereotypical perceptions have taught men they can get away with mistreating and exploiting Indigenous girls and women. The mistreatment and exploitation of Indigenous girls and women has been normalized by society historically and continues today—in, for instance, the terminology that labels Indigenous girls and women as "prostitutes" and describes them as willingly involved in the sex trade. As one participant shared,

> *When you continue to use the mainstream language and identify someone as a prostitute or involved in prostitution or the sex trade, everybody knows what it is. So it is normalized because of that. It's normalized in the behaviour of the perpetrators, as well, because they are not seeing that what they are doing is they are victimizing a child or a young woman.*

Question 3: What messages do we need to communicate to other people about the roles of young girls and women?

The primary perspective is that other people need to understand that Indigenous peoples and communities traditionally valued girls and women. Indigenous girls and women are sacred because they are life givers. The ability to produce and sustain life puts them at the centre of their families and communities because they are responsible for the transmission of culture. Community members noted that it is incumbent on us to ensure that young girls understand that they are sacred, as this is the seed from which self-respect grows. Learning about this sacredness must start early.

As noted by the individuals interviewed for this study, the recent recommendations by the Truth and Reconciliation Commission of Canada (TRC) provide an excellent and safe opportunity for this learning to begin, because, as one participant told us, it "created a unique opportunity for people that didn't know anything but were too uneasy to ask or learn." Young men in particular need to understand the sacredness of Indigenous girls, as these girls will become life givers in the future. As one participant said, "I would like to see that these roles are taught to groups of young Indigenous men, teenage boys, and all young boys."

The individuals interviewed for this report felt there was a need to start sharing messages that celebrate Indigenous girls and women for being Indigenous girls and women. Just as we celebrate the academic achievements of others, we should celebrate Indigenous girls and women who are following their traditional ways. It was also shared that we need to celebrate not just academic and work achievements but any kind of achievements, no matter how small, of those who are living marginalized lives. As one participant put it,

> *No one celebrates the girl who just got off crack. No one celebrates the girl who tried so many times not to get pregnant but ended up getting pregnant. We don't celebrate those things, but these are the types of things that some of our girls and women are facing, and they are shamed for it.*

Question 4: If Indigenous girls cannot live with their birth families and there are limited safe options for these girls to live with extended family or trusted community members, where else can they find support, development, and teachings?

Many of the individuals we spoke to believe that the best place for Indigenous girls to obtain and receive support, development, and teachings is in the existing community-based organizations in the province that rely on Indigenous knowledge and teachings. It was noted that these organizations need stable funding, and many felt that it would be important to build up these community-based organizations where deep relationships are already happening. Governments need to boldly embrace new funding structures. Participants noted that there are many Indigenous organizations that could take up the responsibility of working with vulnerable Indigenous girls and youth if they were funded substantially to do that work.

With better funding, Indigenous organizations feel that they could hire more Elders and Knowledge Keepers to work with and bring more teachings to Indigenous girls. It was said that girls as well as women need "Indigenous spaces" where they feel safe, where they will feel comfortable, and Indigenous organizations can play an important role in creating such spaces. Furthermore, participants stated that the government needs to take courageous steps forward in re-allocating and redirecting funds to better support Indigenous girls so they are able to access "independent, stand-alone support drop-in centres." If girls and women are experiencing vulnerability and are stuck on the streets, they should have access to Indigenous spaces where they can sleep, be fed, do laundry, or take a shower. These safe spaces must be available day and night and must be welcoming, with access to Elders, Knowledge Keepers, and other supports. However, this solution can only be realized with the redirecting of what Indigenous advocates believe are "millions and millions of dollars" that currently flow into non-Indigenous organizations—funding that has not successfully affected the key drivers of the vulnerability experienced by Indigenous girls and women.

Question 5: What is missing in how we teach boys to interact with girls?

Those interviewed said Indigenous boys and men need to become healthier because they are one-half of the balance that is necessary in life, according to the Indigenous worldview. More role models for young boys and men are necessary. Young men, it was acknowledged, "need to have an equal opportunity, a sacred responsibility to be caregivers, to be protectors, to be providers, fathers, and grandfathers. They are just as important in a family." Indigenous boys and men have lost their way and need access to traditional teachings as much as Indigenous girls.

Question 6: How can public systems be improved so outcomes for young girls get better?

Participants stated that there is a need to end the way systems within the province operate. Services are seen to be predicated on protectionism and silos. Participants described a yearning for more meaningful collaboration where reciprocity is crucial to the way that services are rolled out, and the province must play a key role in addressing some of the power imbalances that currently exist.

Participants also believed that service providers need to be aware of their own beliefs and ideas and of how these influence the ways they see and interact with Indigenous youth. The ways in which Indigenous girls are viewed by various systems were highlighted as problematic among the individuals we interviewed. One community advocate shared that the people working in many public systems need to stop saying that Indigenous girls "exploit themselves" or "are prostituting themselves." Some have even heard it said that "Indigenous girls enjoy that kind of lifestyle." Such attitudes demonstrate a lack of understanding of root issues while amplifying levels of risk.

Question 7: What elements of traditional parenting/family structures would help improve the situation for young girls and women?

Most of the responses reflected on the need to bring back elements of Indigenous knowledge, traditions, and teachings. As one young interviewee said, "Ceremonies are just like learning our roles." Participants also stated that working with one member of the family and not others would not create lasting change. Healing and self-discovery are critical for girls who come into care but also must extend to their parents and extended family members. Land-based teaching was identified as an important healing tool and can be developed and built on the natural curiosity of young people. Extended family members need to be a part of this experience as well, and participants indicated that it is just as important to have mentors in the community guiding youth to know their role in the family.

Participants indicated the need for more positive role models—grandmothers, Elders, Knowledge Keepers, and others—for young women as well as for young men. Extended families are also a part of traditional family structures and need to be utilized more than they currently are when Indigenous girls interact with systems outside their family structures. This was strongly emphasized in the following response:

> *I think extended family is so important. In the Indigenous ways, our second and third cousins, they are our cousins, and in the clanship with Anishinabe people, if you are in the bear clan, you would be my sister. We would be relatives. So our family units are much closer than the European structures of family....So you would have that sense of belonging, and you would have that sense of care. To instill that in the young people is important.*

Question 8: What do communities need to be able to provide more safe and nurturing homes for young girls?

Participants noted that Indigenous organizations need access to funding that is equitable in order to be able to provide more culturally safe and nurturing homes for Indigenous girls. Also fundamental is the need to ensure better education among those who foster Indigenous girls. Ideally, Indigenous girls need safe and nurturing homes where Indigenous people who are familiar with Indigenous traditions can support them. When those arrangements cannot be secured because of a shortage of placements, then non-Indigenous people who provide care for Indigenous youth must be trained and supported to provide culturally safe environments where youth are encouraged to access their culture.

The licensing requirements and standards set by the provincial child welfare system were highlighted as being particularly problematic for ensuring safe homes for Indigenous girls, as these standards do not take into consideration the housing realities among Indigenous populations. One participant shared that she "would rather have a child sleeping on a couch surrounded by his aunties, and his uncles, and his loved ones, with no bedroom to sleep in but still part of that family, rather than disconnecting him."

Question 9: What can be done to keep Indigenous girls safe when they come into care?

Participants indicated that Indigenous girls need to be surrounded by the grandmothers to feel safe. Many Indigenous girls are in a state of shock when they come into care, and they often feel overwhelmed by the change, by the legal system, by new homes, schools, and routines. Even when Indigenous girls come into care, they need to maintain a connection to family. When relationships to family are severed, the chances that Indigenous girls may go missing are increased. Interviewees expressed that the more control is placed on young people, the more it destabilizes them. The child welfare system is frequently criticized for not including young people in the decisions that impact them when they come into care.

One participant strongly stated that the most important way to keep Indigenous girls safe when they come into care is to make sure they are not "assimilated." She further explained:

> *Don't assimilate these children—they are not your children. You are there to be able to provide them with a safe space, hopefully it is temporary....I know that there are foster parents to do that, but there are those foster parents who wouldn't participate in those things, and they should, they should be mandatory.*

Question 10: Are there any programs that need to be developed to address the vulnerability of Indigenous girls in care?

It was noted by many of those interviewed for this report that everyone has a role in ensuring Indigenous girls are safe, but non-Indigenous peoples and their organizations need to pause, listen, take advice, and let Indigenous peoples take the lead. Instead of looking to invent new solutions, participants said, many of the answers already exist within families and communities, while numerous programs are being delivered by Indigenous community-based organizations.

Question 11: What do young girls need to thrive in life?

Participants stated that Indigenous girls need access to their culture: they need to be able to access that culture when they want and as often as they need. Indigenous girls need to be taught how to love themselves, and they must be engaged to learn this from Indigenous people, Elders, and Knowledge Keepers through cultural teachings and connections to the land. There are women in Indigenous communities who can make this happen, provided the appropriate resources are in place.

Indigenous girls are incredibly resilient, and this fact is often overlooked. When an Indigenous girl is in a safe place, she may exercise resiliency and feel confident about just being herself; Indigenous girls need to have a sense of belonging in order to thrive. This sense of belonging comes from family, community, and various cultural practices and teachings. These girls need to be part of a community system. If they cannot be with their families and in their communities, then "we need to be able to provide them with a home away from home with Indigenous peoples and communities and/or with non-Indigenous people who care and understand the history of Indigenous people and the Indigenous way."

The ability to build relationships is an important part of sustaining relationships. One thing that was noted by a number of the people interviewed is that, when you are working with Indigenous youth, you "have to go into these relationships with love." Participants shared that some Indigenous girls in care have been threatened with having access to cultural teachings cut off as a form of punishment when they are not conforming to the rules of being in care. Young people need not only to be a part of a community but also to *feel* that they belong, and adults have a clear role to play in actively demonstrating the strength of the community fabric. Access to culture should never be denied as a form of behaviour modification. When young people experience positive reinforcement, they can build strong identities that will carry them into adulthood.

Indigenous girls need to know who they are in order to thrive in mainstream society. The message reiterated by all of the men and women interviewed for this report was clear: Indigenous girls need to learn their culture in order to grow and thrive. They need to know how to get their spiritual names, participate in ceremonies like the Sundance, and sing the songs. They need to learn about the rites of passage that will take them from being a girl to a woman. They need to participate in ceremonies like "the full moon ceremony, get involved in the rites of passage for both young men and women, so that they know their respective roles and responsibilities and their purpose on this earth." As one interviewee noted, "so many girls don't even know about being on their time, how sacred that is, and that's a ceremony. They need to relax and honour themselves at that time." In particular, girls need to be on the land and to connect with it, as land is part of ceremony.

Question 12: What suggestions do you have that would make all Indigenous girls safer?

Participants said that the voices of Indigenous girls need to be heard, community organizations need to be supported in providing Indigenous girls with access to cultural teachings and ceremony, and all people and organizations have a responsibility to aggressively target those who exploit Indigenous girls. More public pressure is needed to ensure that predators are not empowered to continue exploiting girls' vulnerabilities; maintaining apathy about ending the violence is akin to encouraging it. More support in this area needs to come from the general public and the mainstream political leadership, both Indigenous and non-Indigenous.

Question 13: If you could pass a message on to young girls, what would you tell them?

The messages from the people interviewed for this report consistently focused on the fact that Indigenous girls are loved despite the fact that many of them might not know whom or where this love comes from. Participants want young girls to know that they are loved; shouldn't give up; are smart, kind, and important; are sacred and deserve respect; can heal; and are beautiful. Indigenous girls need to be reminded that they are not just vulnerable but powerful and resilient too.

Recommendations Generated from the Findings

There is widespread agreement that the Manitoba child welfare system is struggling to meet the needs of children, youth, and families. Many interventions continue to prioritize short-term, crisis-oriented fixes at the expense of strong, coordinated planning for improved future outcomes. The scope of challenges that many Indigenous families face is broad and reflects deeply rooted manifestations of the racist and discriminatory policies and practices of historical governments. Generations of lived experience where Indigenous children were forcibly torn from their families and communities, and then subjected to calculated efforts to kill all traces of culture in those children, stand as a horrible and shared legacy that all Canadians are today being called to acknowledge, understand, and heal. At local, provincial, and national levels, there is a growing call that public services need to be responsive to and reflective of the populations they serve. In the case of Manitoba's child welfare system, nearly 90 per cent of the 11,352 children in care are Indigenous, and Manitoba has an opportunity to become a leader in how meaningful restructuring and root-cause investments can reshape and redress the abuses of the past.

As an advocate for children and youth, the Office of the Children's Advocate sees young people every day who are living the legacies of residential schools, the Sixties Scoop, and other examples of systemic racism. This study has looked specifically at the experiences of Indigenous girls in the community as a way to examine one of the groups of youth most impacted *today* by the experiences of their parents, grandparents, and great-grandparents. As a society, we have heard the voices and experiences of survivors through the incredible efforts of the TRC (2015). We also have access to a growing body of social research that identifies a clear correlation between what happened to Indigenous families in the past and the incredible disadvantages many are experiencing today. Support needs are complex for many families, and in broad terms the provincial child welfare system has been largely ineffective at improving outcomes for Indigenous children and youth. Apprehensions, removals from community, government-controlled programs, "one size fits all" policies, funding formulas that reflect government priorities instead of community realities—the increasing pressure on agencies and individual workers to deliver results without the requisite resourcing has left far too many children and youth unsupported to meet their potential. This is due partly to ineffective policies and practices and partly to the child welfare system being expected to patch service gaps when other public systems fall short or walk away. Nevertheless, readers should be encouraged that in Manitoba we have many opportunities to make meaningful changes that can bring about significant improvements to end the trauma and create tangible reconciliation.

Community voices, from the Indigenous leaders who participated in this project, were clear. Collectively, they described the perception among many families and communities that the government has not positioned itself as an ally to Indigenous youth and their families. The participants in this research—respected leaders in their community and profession—told us that the government still exerts rigid control over the care and protection of children to the unfortunate exclusion of the families and communities who want to be a bigger part of the solution. They also told us that the structure and policies of Manitoba's child welfare system too often ignore the critical importance of culture as a pathway to healing trauma and protecting children. What is lacking, they shared, is a system built on principles of fairness, hope, and inclusion. Regardless of background, all humans desire to be valued and needed members of a larger whole. Perhaps most critically, the participants in this study emphasized that there is a vast wealth of knowledge in the Indigenous communities that can help reverse the trend of the unacceptably high apprehension and in-care rates in this province. They shared many ideas about policies, programs, and values that could improve the lives of some of the most vulnerable individuals in our province. Many of the ideas shared with us during the course of this research echoed many of the calls to action released in the final report of the TRC (2015). As such, the recommendations that follow focus on three main themes that, as advocates for children and youth, we believe can reverse the trend of overwhelmed systems of government care: improving broken areas of the current structure; ensuring children can remain as close to home as possible when help is needed; and vastly improving the system's ability to ensure that all children and youth have access to their culture.

Four Key Recommendations

Four recommendations emerged from these narratives and were issued as formal recommendations by the Office of the Children's Advocate (Bennett, 2016).

The first recommendation is for a cultural audit and overhaul of foster care licensing standards and regulations. Safe, temporary caregivers exist in communities throughout the province, but many do not qualify as foster care providers under the current regulations, which do not reflect an understanding of cultural diversity and community norms. Safety must never be compromised, but much more can be done to develop safe foster homes around Manitoba so that children and youth in care have more options for staying close to home while services are being delivered to the family.

The second recommendation is for the Manitoba government to develop resources and tools for foster parents who are caring for children who are not of their own culture. While nearly 90 per cent of the children and youth in care are Indigenous, foster families reflect a broader diversity of the general public, and cross-cultural placements of children in care are common. To ensure that children in care have open and supported access to their own culture and traditions, it is important that the child welfare system ensures that families who foster have access to those resources that can best equip them to ensure children placed in their home are able to understand and explore their own cultural identity. This connection to culture is not only a protected right under international law; research strongly supports the view that the best outcomes for children in out-of-home care are correlated with strong cultural identity.

The third recommendation calls on the Manitoba government to provide a significant new investment in hiring cultural workers who can be utilized by the child welfare system and who can work primarily with children and youth but also with their families. As part of the recommendation, we noted that it is important these investments be made in organizations outside mandated child welfare agencies, where strong and trusting relationships with youth and their families already exist. The messages we heard throughout the development of this report have been that cultural exploration and the building of cultural knowledge are the pathways that can lead to stronger individuals and stronger communities and ultimately will improve the outcomes for children and youth involved with child welfare. As noted, wide bodies of social research reinforce these community views of the importance of cultural training.

The final recommendation focuses on acknowledging that, when community values are reflected in the structures of public services, service quality and accessibility for marginalized populations are improved. To that goal, we recommend that the government (1) look to people who have long held positions of influence and wisdom within Indigenous culture and (2) work with Indigenous leaders and cultural advisors to establish a Grandmothers' Council that can provide guidance at this time of incredibly important social reconstruction. The council would provide guidance and wisdom to government as it creates and improves services that respond to the needs of communities. The advisory council, or *Ganawenamig* (an Oji-Cree word meaning "looking after the children"), would be a resource and asset to any government department, but most specifically it would guide the departments that deliver services that impact the lives of children and youth across Manitoba.

Our province and our country face an incredible opportunity. This is the time when we must honestly acknowledge the disgrace of how Canada's Indigenous peoples were treated at the hands of those who came here from away. We have heard the stories of racism, abuse, and genocide. We see the effects of that collective history every day across our province, and we all have a responsibility to do our part to heal relationships and build up those who have been hurt. This is the most basic form of humanity—to be kind to others simply because we are all humans.

Conclusion

The backbone of this chapter is the narrative testimony obtained from a select number of community members, who expressed deep concern for Indigenous women and girls. The perspectives are based on community knowledge that is deeply rooted in the oral testimony and narrative of Indigenous communities, which represents a culturally nuanced way of knowing and is itself a form of intergenerational knowledge transfer. We asked thirteen questions of eleven individuals from the Indigenous community within and outside Winnipeg. The responses to these questions reflect the Debwewin journey (Gehl, 2012) that each participant has taken in travelling from the mind to the heart in coming to understand the truth about the vulnerability of Indigenous girls involved in the child welfare system. The truth is that it all comes down to the strength of relationships. The health of our communities is integrally tied to the strength and tenacity of those bonds. The voices of the community that resonate within these pages have offered many ideas for how the child welfare system can ensure healing, which is needed to arrive at a vision of a safe and healthy society that hears, includes, values, and protects all children and youth, particularly those who are Indigenous.

The issues may seem complex and heavily intertwined, and yet the solutions cover the spectrum from the simple to the more detailed, and there are valuable roles for all Manitobans. There is reason to believe that, by investing in organizations and approaches that promote healthy relationship building and actively facilitate outreach activities within communities where vulnerable Indigenous girls live, outcomes will improve. On a systemic level, there is also a critical need to audit and aggressively address areas of the public systems that remain tethered to outdated approaches, which have clearly not improved the lives of Indigenous girls and youth. These issues can be solved when each of us commits to actively creating compassionate and reciprocal relationships, which should be of comfort and serve as motivation to anyone who can see the trauma and no longer wishes to see it continue.

Discussion Questions

1. Why are Indigenous girls so vulnerable when they come into care?
2. Why are so many young Indigenous women mistreated and exploited?
3. What messages do we need to communicate to other people about the roles of Indigenous girls and women?
4. If Indigenous girls cannot live with their birth families, and there are limited safe options for these girls to live with extended family

or trusted community members, where else can they find support, development, and teachings?

5. What is missing in how we teach boys to interact with girls?
6. How can public systems (such as child welfare, justice, health, education) be changed to improve outcomes for Indigenous girls?
7. Are there elements of traditional parenting or traditional family structures that would help improve the situation for young women who are vulnerable?
8. What do communities need in order to be able to provide more safe and nurturing homes for Indigenous girls?
9. What are some of the things that can be done to keep Indigenous girls safe when they come into the care of child welfare?
10. Are there any programs that need to be developed to address the vulnerability of Indigenous girls in care?
11. What do you believe young girls need to thrive in life?
12. What suggestions do you have that would make all Indigenous girls safer?
13. If you could pass a message to young girls, what would you want to tell them?

References

Aleem, R. (2009). *International human rights law and Aboriginal girls in Canada: Never the twain shall meet*. Justice for Girls International. Retrieved from http://www.justiceforgirls.org/uploads/2/4/5/0/24509463/international_human_rights_of_indigenous_girls.pdf

Allnock, D. (2010, April). *Children and young people disclosing sexual abuse: An introduction to the research* (Research Briefing, NSPCC Fresh Start). Retrieved from http://www.childmatters.org.nz/file/Diploma-Readings/Block-2/Sexual-Abuse/3.4-children-and-young-people-disclosing-sexual-abuse-updated.pdf

Amnesty International. (2004). Stolen sisters: A human rights response to discrimination and violence against Indigenous women in Canada. *Canadian Woman Studies, 26*(3–4), 105–121. Retrieved from http://cws.journals.yorku.ca/index.php/cws/article/viewFile/22119/20773

Anderson, K. (2000). The dismantling of gender equality. In K. Anderson (Ed.), *A recognition of being: Reconstructing Native womanhood* (pp. 57–78). Toronto, ON: Second Story Press.

Andrews, B., Brewin, C. R., & Rose, S. (2003). Gender, social support, and PTSD in victims of violent crime. *Journal of Traumatic Stress, 16*(4), 421–427.

Andrews, M. (2007). Exploring cross-cultural boundaries. In J. D. Clandinin (Ed.), *Handbook of narrative inquiry: Mapping a methodology* (pp. 489–511). Thousand Oaks, CA: Sage.

Benham, M. K. P. (2007). On culturally relevant story making from an Indigenous perspective. In J. D. Clandinin (Ed.), *Handbook of narrative inquiry: Mapping a methodology* (pp. 512–534). Thousand Oaks, CA: Sage.

Bennett, M. (2016). *On the edge between two worlds: Community narratives on the vulnerability of marginalized Indigenous girls*. Winnipeg, MB: Office of the Children's Advocate. Retrieved from http://www.childrensadvocate.mb.ca/wp-content/uploads/FINAL-Indigenous-Girls.pdf

Blackstock, C. (2007). Residential schools: Did they really close or just morph into child welfare? *Indigenous Law Journal, 6*(1), 71–78.

Buffalohead, P. K. (1983). Farmers warriors traders: A fresh look at Ojibway women. *Minnesota History: The Quarterly of the Minnesota Historical Society, 48*(6), 236–244.

Clandinin, D. J. (Ed.). (2007). *Handbook of narrative inquiry: Mapping a methodology*. Thousand Oaks, CA: Sage.

Clark, N. (2012). Perseverance, determination and resistance: An Indigenous intersectional policy analysis of violence in the lives of Indigenous girls. In O. Hankivsky (Ed.), *An intersectionality-based policy analysis framework* (pp. 133–158). Vancouver, BC: Institute for Intersectionality Research and Policy, Simon Fraser University. Retrieved from http://learningcircle.ubc.ca/files/2013/10/7_Indigenous-Girls_Clark-2012.pdf

Cruickshank, J. (1998). *The social life of stories: Narrative and knowledge in the Yukon Territory*. Vancouver, BC: UBC Press.

Gehl, L. (2012). Debwewin journey: A methodology and model of knowing. *AlterNative: An International Journal of Indigenous Peoples, 8*(1), 53–65.

Goulding, W. (2001). *Just another Indian: A serial killer and Canada's indifference*. Calgary, AB: Fifth House.

Heinrichs, M., & Hiebert, D. (2009). *Taking care of our own: Dakota Ojibway Child and Family Services*. Brandon, MB: Rosetta Projects.

Hulan, R., & Eigenbrod, R. (2008). Introduction: A layering of voices: Aboriginal oral traditions. In R. Hulan & R. Eigenbrod (Eds.), *Aboriginal oral traditions: Theory, practice, ethics* (pp. 7–12). Halifax, NS: Fernwood Publishing.

Kovach, M. (2009). *Indigenous methodologies: Characteristics, conversations, and contexts*. Toronto, ON: University of Toronto Press.

Macdonald, N., & Campbell, M. (2017, September 13). Lost and broken. *Maclean's*. Retrieved from http://www.macleans.ca/lost-and-broken

Mandell, D., Clouston Carlson, C., Fine, M., & Blackstock, C. (2003). Aboriginal child welfare. In G. Cameron, N. Coady, & G. R. Adams (Eds.), *Moving toward positive systems of child and family welfare: Current issues and future directions* (pp. 115–160). Waterloo, ON: Wilfrid Laurier University Press.

Manitoba. Department of Families. (2017). *Manitoba families: 2016–2017 annual report*. Winnipeg, MB: Department of Families. Retrieved from https://www.gov.mb.ca/fs/about/annual_reports.html

Manitoba. FSH (Family Services and Housing). (2008). *Tracia's trust—Front line voices: Manitobans working together to end child sexual exploitation*. Retrieved from http://www.gov.mb.ca/fs/childfam/pubs/tracias_trust_en.pdf

McGillivray, A., & Comaskey. B. (1999). *Black eyes all the time: Intimate violence, Aboriginal women, and the justice system*. Toronto, ON: University of Toronto Press.

McKenzie, B., & Hudson, P. (1985). Native children, child welfare, and the colonization of Native people. In K. Levett & B. Wharf (Eds.), *The challenge of child welfare* (pp. 125–141). Vancouver, BC: UBC Press.

Milloy, J. S. (1999). *A national crime: The Canadian government and the residential school system, 1879 to 1986*. Winnipeg, MB: University of Manitoba Press.

NWAC (Native Women's Association of Canada). (2010). *What their stories tell us: Research findings from the Sisters in Spirit initiative*. Retrieved from https://nwac.ca/wp-content/uploads/2015/07/2010-What-Their-Stories-Tell-Us-Research-Findings-SIS-Initiative.pdf

Ormiston, N. T. (2010). Re-conceptualizing research: An Indigenous perspective. *First Peoples Child & Family Review, 5*(1), 50–56.

Purdy, C. (2003, November 26). Serial killer who roamed Saskatoon met with indifference by police, media: Journalist-author accepts award for book about slain Aboriginal women. *Edmonton Journal*. Retrieved from http://www.missingpeople.net/serial_killer_who_roamed_saskato.htm

Richardson, C., & A. Wade. (2009). Taking resistance seriously: A response-based approach to social work in cases of violence against Indigenous women. In J. Carriere & S. Strega (Eds.), *Walking this path together: Anti-racist and anti-oppressive child welfare practice* (pp. 204–220). Halifax, NS: Fernwood Publishing.

Sikka, A. (2009). *Trafficking of Aboriginal women and girls in Canada*. Ottawa, ON: Institute on Governance. Retrieved from https://iog.ca/docs/May-2009_trafficking_of_aboriginal_women-1.pdf

Sinclair, R. (2007). Identity lost and found: Lessons from the Sixties Scoop. *First Peoples Child & Family Review, 3*(1), 65–82.

Smith, A. (2005). *Conquest: Sexual violence and American Indian genocide*. Cambridge, MA: South End Press.

Thomas, D. R. (2006). A general inductive approach for analyzing qualitative evaluation data. *American Journal of Evaluation, 27*(2), 237–246.

TRC (Truth and Reconciliation Commission of Canada). (2015). *Final report of the Truth and Reconciliation Commission of Canada*. Vol. 1: *Summary: Honouring the truth, reconciling for the future*. Winnipeg, MB: Lorimer.

Walmsley, C. (2005). *Protecting Aboriginal children*. Vancouver, BC: UBC Press.

Wesley-Esquimaux, C., & Smolewski, M. (2004). *Historic trauma and Aboriginal healing*. Ottawa, ON: Aboriginal Healing Foundation. Retrieved from http://www.ahf.ca/downloads/historic-trauma.pdf

Wilson, S. (2008). *Research is ceremony: Indigenous research methods*. Winnipeg, MB: Fernwood Publishing.

CHAPTER 8

Factors Associated with the Child Welfare Placement Decision in Alberta

Bruce MacLaurin, Hee-Jeong Yoo, and Morgan DeMone

Introduction and Context of Child Welfare Placements

Placement of children in out-of-home care has been a primary form of intervention in Canadian child welfare systems since the first legislation in the 1880s (MacLaurin, 2002; MacLaurin & Bala, 2004). The changing rates of children who are seen to be in need of this expensive and intrusive form of intervention may reflect, in part, the provincial and territorial orientation regarding the role of the state in the lives of children and families (MacLaurin & Bala, 2004). Different value orientations are closely related to the social and political climate of the time and suggest alternative approaches to meet the best interests of the child. These shifting orientations have a critical impact on the decisions that are made, as well as on outcomes for children (Bala, 1999; Fernandez, 1999; Spratt, 2001). Shifts in child welfare legislation, policy, and practice have been described as the swing of a pendulum—the shift from a less interventionist to a more interventionist approach highlights the delicate balance between ensuring the safety of the child and supporting parental and family rights (Bala,

Suggested Citation: MacLaurin, B., Yoo, H.-J., & DeMone, M. (2018). Factors associated with the child welfare placement decision in Alberta. In D. Badry, H. Montgomery, D. Kikulwe, M. Bennett, & D. Fuchs, (Eds.), *Imagining child welfare in the spirit of reconciliation* (pp. 163–184). Regina, SK: University of Regina Press.

1999; Dumbrill, 2006; Trocmé, 1997). Historically, the momentum of the pendulum shifts has too frequently been driven by inquests or provincial/territorial fatality reviews rather than by foundations of evidence and knowledge (Gove, 1995a; Gove, 1995b; Hughes, 2006; Panel of Experts on Child Protection, 1998).

Historical Context of the Overrepresentation of Indigenous Children

There is a significant overrepresentation of Indigenous children reported, investigated, and placed in child welfare care in Canada (Blackstock, Trocmé, & Bennett, 2003; Sinha, Trocmé, Fallon, & MacLaurin, 2013; Sinha et al., 2011; Trocmé et al., 2010a). This current overrepresentation reflects a history of colonial policy designed to assimilate Indigenous peoples into mainstream Canadian society (Milloy, 1999). Policies that began with the residential schools have contributed to the systematic removal of Indigenous children from their homes over more than a century. The residential schools were followed by the Sixties Scoop, a period that witnessed high numbers of Indigenous children being placed in the care of the provincial and territorial child welfare systems (Blackstock, 2011; Milloy, 1999). These policies have had a severe and ongoing impact on the health of Indigenous peoples (LaBoucane-Benson, Sherren, & Yerichuk, 2017). The well-being of communities is further challenged by inequitable on-reserve funding for Indigenous children (Milloy, 1999; TRC, 2015).

Numbers of Children in Care

In 2013, an estimated 62,428 children were in out-of-home care on any one day across Canada—a rate of 8.5 children in care per 1,000 children (Jones, Sinha, & Trocmé, 2015; Mulcahy & Trocmé, 2009). The rate of children in out-of-home care in Canada increased between the mid-1990s and 2004, rising from 5.5 per 1,000 in the early 1990s to level off between 8.5 and 8.8 between 2004 and 2013. The marked increase in placements over the past twenty-five years may be attributed in part to the dramatic increase in the number of child welfare investigations that have occurred over this period (Trocmé et al., 2010b). For Indigenous children, there are higher rates of placement (Blackstock, 2009; Blackstock, Loxley, Prakash, & Wien, 2005; Sinha et al., 2013), changes in the types and severity of reported maltreatment (Fallon et al., 2013; MacLaurin et al., 2013; Sinha et al., 2013; Trocmé, Kyte, Sinha, & Fallon, 2014; Trocmé et al., 2013), and worker and organizational differences (Fallon & Trocmé, 2011; Fallon et al., 2015; Fluke, Chabot, Fallon, MacLaurin, & Blackstock, 2010), as well as increased duration of placements resulting in more children in care (MacLaurin & Bala, 2004). Out-of-home-placement trends in Canada reflect complex dynamics with respect to a changing response to professional knowledge, the development of a broader scope of service alternatives, shifts in the dominant values associated with child and family services, and changes in legislation and policy (MacLaurin & Bala, 2004). These changes have occurred in the midst of an ongoing debate about how well children in care are served with respect to their immediate safety, as well as their longer-term well-being and development.

Outcomes of Child Welfare Placements in Care

Outcome research on out-of-home care reflects different levels of success. The decision of out-of-home placement has a meaningful impact upon a child's development and well-being (Perlman & Fantuzzo, 2013). Children in care are reported to experience poorer short-term outcomes, including greater behavioural problems (Rubin, O'Reilly, Luan, & Localio, 2007), less engagement in relationships (Stott & Gustavsson, 2010), decreased cognitive functioning (Berger, Bruch, Johnson, James, & Rubin, 2009), and decreased educational performance and frequent school transfers (Pecora et al., 2006). As well, these children and youth experience disrupted or disjointed sibling and parental connections (Wilmshurst, 2002) and high turnover in professional relationships (Fanshel, Finch, & Grundy, 1990). Other research, however, suggests that important gains can be made among youth placed in care through out-of-home placements (Aldgate, Colton, Ghate, & Heath, 1992; Barber, 2005; Courtney and Dworsky, 2006; Hair, 2005; Noftle et al., 2011; Preyde, Cameron, Frensch, & Adams, 2011; Taussig, Clyman, & Landsverk, 2001; Timms & Thoburn, 2003) and that there is little evidence to indicate that maltreated children admitted to care experience more negative long-term outcomes than children who have experienced maltreatment but are not placed in care (Bullock, Courtney, Parker, Sinclair, & Thoburn, 2006). Over the past two decades, Canadian child welfare systems have adopted an outcome orientation designed to guide and improve decisions for children and families at risk. The question of which children and youth require placement in out-of-home care has been better refined to ask what form of service is best suited to which specific children, in terms of which aspects of development and under what conditions (Trocmé et al., 2009; Wald, 1988). Further work is needed to determine which children are referred to care in Canada and for what reasons.

Focus of This Analysis

This chapter reports on secondary data analyses of the most recent cycle of the Alberta Incidence Study of Reported Child Abuse and Neglect (AIS-2008) (MacLaurin et al., 2013). The AIS is a provincial study that was designed to determine the incidence and characteristics of child maltreatment in Alberta in 2008. This analysis will report on the incidence rates, placement decisions, primary categories of substantiated maltreatment, and Aboriginal heritage of children investigated for maltreatment, which are highlighted in Tables 1, 2, 3, and 4. Child, family, household, and case factors for children in a formal placement are then compared to those for children not in a formal placement. These bivariate analyses are highlighted in Tables 5, 6, 7, and 8, and Pearson's chi-square test of independence was calculated to determine significant interactions. The dichotomous placement variable included (1) formal child welfare placement (formal kinship care, family foster care, group home, and residential or secure treatment) and (2) no formal child welfare placement (informal kinship care, no placement, and placement considered but not acted on).

Methodology of the AIS-2008

The AIS-2008 is the second cycle of a provincial study that examines the incidence of reported child abuse and neglect in Alberta for children seventeen years and younger. Using a multi-stage sampling design, 2,239 child maltreatment investigations were collected from fourteen randomly selected child intervention offices over a three-month case selection period (October 1 to December 31, 2008). Offices were stratified by jurisdiction and size to ensure that all subpopulations were represented fairly in the study, with additional consideration for Delegated First Nations Agencies

(DFNA). Information on the characteristics of investigated children and families was collected directly from the investigating caseworker using a standardized Maltreatment Assessment Form. This analysis is based on annually and regionally weighted estimates of child investigations. A total of 27,147 child maltreatment investigations occurred in Alberta for 2008, and of this number 2,383 investigations resulted in a formal child welfare placement, while 24,764 investigations noted no child welfare placement during the initial investigation phase.

The AIS-2008 data set provides a unique opportunity to examine the child welfare response to reported maltreatment in Alberta; however, several factors should be considered when interpreting findings from this secondary analysis. The AIS-2008 (1) tracked reports investigated by child intervention services and did not include reports that were screened out, only investigated by police, or never reported; (2) examined the investigation phase only and cannot determine what happened following this initial six-to-eight-week period; (3) was based on the assessments provided by the investigating child intervention workers, which could not be independently verified; and (4) was weighted using regionalization and annualization weights.

Findings

Incidence of Child Welfare Investigations in Alberta

There were 27,147 child investigations conducted in Alberta in 2008—an incidence rate of 35.02 per 1,000 children in the province (see Table 1). This included 22,761 (39.36 per 1,000) investigations for maltreatment, as well as an additional 4,386 (5.66 per 1,000 children) risk-only investigations. Fifty-three per cent of all investigations—or an incidence rate of 18.58 per 1,000 children in Alberta in 2008—were substantiated by the investigation worker. Another 8 per cent of all investigations remained suspected at the end of the investigation phase. In these cases, the balance of evidence did not indicate that maltreatment had definitely occurred; however, the worker could not rule out this possibility and indicated that it was suspected. An additional 23 per cent of investigations were unfounded, where the balance of evidence indicated that maltreatment did not occur.

Table 1: Type of Investigation and Level of Substantiation in Child Maltreatment Investigations and Risk of Future Maltreatment Investigations in Alberta in 2008

Maltreatment and Risk-Only Investigations	Alberta 2008		
	#	**Rate per 1,000 Children**	**%**
Substantiated Maltreatment	14,403	18.58	53%
Suspected Maltreatment	2,160	2.79	8%
Unfounded Maltreatment	6,198	8.00	23%
Total Maltreatment Investigations	**22,761**	**29.36**	**84%**
Risk of Future Maltreatment	793	1.02	3%
No Risk of Future Maltreatment	2,501	3.23	9%
Unknown Risk of Future Maltreatment	1,092	1.41	4%
Total Risk Investigation Only*	**4,386**	**5.66**	**16%**
Total Investigations	**27,147**	**35.02**	**100%**

Alberta Incidence Study of Reported Child Abuse and Neglect 2008.
Percentages are column percentages.
**Risk investigations were not specified in the Alberta Incidence Study of 2003.*
Based on a sample of 2,239 child maltreatment and risk of future maltreatment related investigations in 2008, with information about the type and level of substantiation.

Placement Decisions

Workers indicated for the AIS-2008 if a placement occurred at any point during the maltreatment investigation. At the end of the investigation phase, a subtotal of 2,383 child investigations—or 3.07 per 1,000 children in Alberta in 2008—had resulted in a formal child welfare placement (see Table 2). A subtotal of 24,764 investigations—or 31.95 per 1,000 children—had no formal child welfare placement during the span of the investigation phase. Of these, however, there were 1,139 child investigations in which a child received an informal placement, meaning that an informal placement was arranged within the family support network, but the child welfare authority did not have formal custody of or legal responsibility for the child.

Table 2: Placement in Child Maltreatment Investigations and Risk of Future Maltreatment Investigations in Alberta in 2008

Placement Status	#	**Rate per 1,000 Children**	%
No Placement Required	23,025	29.70	85%
Placement Considered	600	0.77	2%
Informal Kinship Care	1,139	1.47	4%
Subtotal: No Child Welfare Placement	**24,764**	**31.95**	**91%**
Kinship Foster Care	398	0.51	2%
Foster Care	1,430	1.84	5%
Group Home	387	0.50	1%
Residential Secure Treatment	168	0.22	1%
Subtotal: Child Welfare Placement	**2,383**	**3.07**	**9%**
Total Investigations	**27,147**	**35.02**	**100%**

Alberta Incidence Study of Reported Child Abuse and Neglect 2008.
Percentages are column percentages.
Based on a sample of 2,239 child maltreatment related investigations in 2008, with information about child welfare placement.

Types of Substantiated Maltreatment

Table 3 presents the estimates and incidence rates for the primary categories of substantiated maltreatment in Alberta in 2008. The maltreatment typology in the AIS-2008 uses five major categories: physical abuse; sexual abuse; neglect; emotional maltreatment; and exposure to intimate partner violence. Specific definitions of each of the five categories and twenty-nine forms of maltreatment can be reviewed in the AIS-2008 Guidebook (MacLaurin et al., 2013).

An estimated 14,403 substantiated child maltreatment investigations took place in Alberta in 2008 (18.58 investigations per 1,000 children). Neglect comprises the largest proportion of substantiated maltreatment investigations (37 per cent), representing an estimated 5,328 cases (6.87 investigations per 1,000 children). In 34 per cent of substantiated investigations, exposure to intimate partner violence was identified as the primary concern (an estimated 4,883 investigations or 6.30 investigations per 1,000 children). Emotional maltreatment was identified as the primary category of maltreatment in 14 per cent of substantiated investigations (an estimated 1,974 investigations or 2.55 investigations per 1,000 children). In 13 per cent of substantiated investigations, the primary form of maltreatment identified was physical abuse (an estimated 1,933 cases or 2.49 investigations per 1,000 children). Sexual abuse was identified as the primary maltreatment form in 2 per cent of substantiated investigations (an estimated 285 investigations or 0.37 investigations per 1,000 children). Trends in reported and substantiated child maltreatment in Canada reflect increases in the categories of neglect, exposure to intimate partner violence, and emotional maltreatment, while physical abuse remains relatively stable and child sexual abuse has decreased over recent cycles (MacLaurin et al., 2013).

Table 3: Primary Category of Substantiated Maltreatment in Child Maltreatment Investigations and Risk of Future Maltreatment Investigations in Alberta in 2008

Primary Category of Maltreatment	#	Rate per 1,000 Children	%
Physical Abuse	1,933	2.49	13%
Sexual Abuse	285	0.37	2%
Neglect	5,328	6.87	37%
Emotional Maltreatment	1,974	2.55	14%
Exposure to Intimate Partner Violence	4,883	6.30	34%
Total Substantiated Investigations	**14,403**	**18.58**	**100%**

Alberta Incidence Study of Reported Child Abuse and Neglect 2008.
Percentages are column percentages.
Based on a sample of 1,133 substantiated child maltreatment related investigations in 2008, with information about the primary category of maltreatment.

Overrepresentation of Indigenous Children in Child Welfare Investigations

Children's Indigenous heritage was documented by the AIS-2008 in an effort to better understand some of the factors that bring children from these communities into contact with the child welfare system. Aboriginal children as a group are important to examine given the concerns about their overrepresentation in the foster and group care systems. Thirty-five per cent of substantiated maltreatment investigations involved children of Aboriginal heritage (see Table 4): 16 per cent of substantiated investigations involved children with First Nations status; 10 per cent involved First Nations non-status children; 8 per cent involved Métis children; and 1 per cent involved Inuit children. Estimates for children of other Aboriginal heritage were too low to reliably report. Table 4 shows that the incidence rate of substantiated child maltreatment investigations was more than five times higher in Aboriginal child investigations than in those involving non-Aboriginal children (72.57 per 1,000 Aboriginal children versus 13.21 per 1,000 non-Aboriginal children).

Table 4: Aboriginal Heritage of Children in Substantiated Child Maltreatment Investigations in Alberta in 2008

Aboriginal Heritage	#	**Rate per 1,000 Children**	%
First Nation, Status	2,336	NA	16%
First Nation, Non-Status	1,480	NA	10%
Métis	1,084	NA	8%
Inuit	110	NA	1%
Other Aboriginal	–	NA	0%
Subtotal: All Aboriginal	**5,109**	**72.57**	**35%**
Non-Aboriginal	**9,294**	**13.21**	**65%**
Total Substantiated Investigations*	**14,403**	**18.58**	**100%**

Alberta Incidence Study of Reported Child Abuse and Neglect 2008.
Percentages are column percentages.
**Based on a sample of 1,133 substantiated child maltreatment investigations with information about the child's Aboriginal heritage.*
Columns may not add up to a total because low-frequency estimates (fewer than 100 weighted investigations) are not reported but are included in the total.
Estimates of fewer than 100 weighted investigations are not shown.

Child Factors

Age of child as well as all child functioning concerns were found to be statistically significant factors in placement decisions, as tested by the chi-square test of independence ($p \leq .05$). Child functioning concerns include academic concerns (39 per cent), attachment issues (38 per cent), intellectual/developmental disability (34 per cent), depression (32 per cent), and aggression toward others (29 per cent). There was no significant interaction for placement and Aboriginal heritage. In investigations involving children younger than one year old, a higher percentage entailed

Table 5: Child Factors Associated with Formal Placement Cases and No Placement Cases in Alberta in 2008

	Formal Placement		**No Placement**	
Age of Child*	#	%	#	%
<1 Year	343	14%	1,981	8%
1-3 Years	420	18%	4,816	20%
4-7 Years	375	16%	5,445	22%
8-11 Years	333	14%	5,621	23%
12-15 Years	714	30%	5,312	21%
16-17 Years	198	8%	1,589	6%
Most Noted Child Functioning Concerns*				
Academic Difficulties	932	39%	5,573	23%
Attachment Issues	905	38%	2,566	10%
Intellectual/Developmental Disability	810	34%	3,542	14%
Depression	763	32%	3,798	15%
Aggression	693	29%	3,479	14%
At Least One Child Functioning Concern*	1,818	76%	10,430	42%
Aboriginal Heritage**	869	36%	7,392	30%
Alberta Incidence Study of Reported Child Abuse and Neglect 2008	2,383	100%	24,764	100%

Alberta Incidence Study of Reported Child Abuse and Neglect 2008.
**p less than or equal to .05.*
***p is not signficant.*

placement (14 per cent) than no placement (8 per cent). Similarly, in cases involving children between the ages of twelve and fifteen, the incidence of placement investigations (30 per cent) was higher than non-placement investigations (21 per cent). At least one child functioning concern was noted in 76 per cent of child investigations that noted a placement. In the AIS-2008, not all ethnoracial statuses are represented equally. A higher percentage of placement investigations (33 per cent) than non-placement investigations (30 per cent) involved children of Aboriginal heritage; however, this interaction was not significant.

Family Factors

A statistically significant interaction ($p \leq .05$) was found for the placement decision with noted caregiver risk factors and family structure with one caregiver. No significant interaction for placement was found with age of the primary caregiver or family structure with two caregivers (refer to Table 6). Caseworkers were asked to report on a total of nine risk factors for those caregivers living in the home. Rates of caregiver risk factors were consistently higher for the placement group than the non-placement group. In cases of placement, the children had previously lived with caregivers who experienced difficulty with few social supports (68 per cent of investigations), alcohol abuse (55 per cent), mental health issues (55 per cent), drug and solvent abuse (54 per cent), domestic violence (40 per cent), a history of parental foster or group care (25 per cent), physical health issues (25 per cent), and cognitive impairment (20 per cent). There was little difference in family structure between placement investigations and non-placement investigations.

Table 6: Family Factors Associated with Formal Placement Cases and No Placement Cases in Alberta in 2008

	Formal Placement		**No Placement**	
Age of Primary Caregiver**†	#	%	#	%
16-21 Years	112	5%	1,147	4%
22-30 Years	756	32%	7,245	29%
31-40 Years	1,104	46%	11,611	47%
41-50 Years	298	13%	4,100	17%
>50	99	4%	638	3%

Noted Household Caregiver Risk Factors*				
Few Social Supports	1,618	68%	9,011	36%
Alcohol Abuse	1,304	55%	7,995	32%
Mental Health Issues	1,300	55%	7,828	32%
Drug/Solvent Abuse	1,281	54%	5,304	21%
Victim of Domestic Violence	1,116	47%	9,828	40%
Perpetrator of Domestic Violence	951	40%	6,887	28%
History of Foster Care/Group Home	606	25%	2,904	12%
Physical Health Issues	602	25%	3,125	13%
Cognitive Impairment	478	20%	2,618	11%
At Least One Household Caregiver Risk Factors*	**2,207**	**93%**	**18,598**	**75%**
Family Structure with Two Caregivers[a]**	**1,548**	**65%**	**15,744**	**64%**
Biological Parents	822	34%	9,319	38%
Biological Grandparents	-	-	123	0%
Biological Parent with Partner	507	21%	4,967	20%
Other	100	4%	522	2%
Family Structure with One Caregiver*[a]	**819**	**34%**	**8,929**	**36%**
Biological Parent	756	32%	8,520	34%
Biological Grandparent	-	-	228	1%
Other	-	-	181	1%
Alberta Incidence Study of Reported Child Abuse and Neglect 2008	**2,383**	**100%**	**24,764**	**100%**

Percentages are column percentages, based on the total weighted number of investigations.

**p less than or equal to .05.*

***p is not significant.*

[†]*Column numbers may not add up due to rounding.*

[a]*Group subtotals will sometimes vary from the total due to unknown or missing data.*

Household Factors

A statistically significant interaction ($p \leq .05$) was found for the placement decision with all household risk factors (refer to Table 7). Caseworkers were asked to report on six key household safety concerns, including accessibility of drugs and drug production or trafficking. At least one household safety factor was noted in 31 per cent of placement investigations and in 12 per cent of non-placement investigations. The placement group demonstrated higher rates of the following key household risks: overcrowded

Table 7: Household Factors Associated with Formal Placement Cases and No Placement Cases in Alberta in 2008

	Formal Placement		No Placement	
	#	%	#	%
At Least One Household Safety Factors*	731	31%	2946	12%
Home Overcrowded*	477	20%	2893	12%
Runs Out of Money for Basic Necessities*	851	36%	5,621	23%
Source of Income*				
Full Time	494	21%	8,164	33%
Part Time/Multiple Jobs/ Seasonal	306	13%	3,326	13%
Employment Insurance/Social Assistance/Other Benefits/ Unknown	1,167	49%	9,289	38%
No Income	416	17%	3,985	16%
Type of Housing*				
Own Home	557	24%	7,906	32%
Private Rental	988	41%	11,223	45%
Other	838	35%	5,635	23%
Alberta Incidence Study of Reported Child Abuse and Neglect 2008	**2,383**	**100%**	**24,764**	**100%**

Percentages are column percentages, based on the total weighted number of investigations.

**p less than or equal to .05.*

housing (20 per cent); running out of money for basic necessities by the end of the month (36 per cent); reliance on less stable sources of income, including employment insurance, assistance, benefits, and "unknown" (41 per cent); and no income (17 per cent). A higher percentage of children who were placed in care had lived in homes that reflected housing risk factors: 35 per cent lived in public housing, band housing, unknown housing, and temporary hotel/shelter. A lower proportion of children who were placed had lived in a home that was owned by caregivers or was a private rental than had children who were not placed. Household risk factors are a consistent concern associated with placement in formal child welfare care.

Case Factors

A statistically significant interaction ($p \leq .05$) was found for the placement decision with all case factors: categories of maltreatment, risk investigations, substantiation, severity of harm, duration of maltreatment, previous opening, police involvement, and the decision for ongoing services. Placement investigations noted various categories of maltreatment investigations as the primary form of maltreatment (refer to Table 8). Neglect was the form of maltreatment noted most frequently in the group that was placed in child welfare care (54 per cent), followed by physical abuse (15 per cent), emotional maltreatment (14 per cent), exposure to intimate partner violence (7 per cent), and sexual abuse (3 per cent). Relatively few placements occurred for risk-only investigations (6 per cent). Forty per cent of placement investigations noted severe emotional harm requiring therapeutic treatment, and an additional 15 per cent noted moderate emotional harm that did not require intervention. A higher percentage of placement investigations (7 per cent) than non-placement investigations (1 per cent) noted serious physical harm requiring medical treatment. Seventy-four per cent of placement investigations noted chronic and ongoing forms of suspected or substantiated maltreatment occurring over extended periods of time, compared to 41 per cent of non-placement investigations. Seventy-seven per cent of placement investigations had been previously reported to child protection services, which is a reflection of repeated reports and investigations of maltreatment that build over time. Police involvement was noted when there was a police investigation and/or when charges were either laid or considered. Little difference was noted for police involvement related to intimate partner violence between

Table 8: Case Factors Associated with Formal Placement Cases and No Placement Cases in Alberta in 2008

Categories of Maltreatment Investigations*†	**Formal Placement**		**No Placement**	
	#	%	#	%
Neglect	1,294	54%	7,147	29%
Physical Abuse	363	15%	4,134	17%
Emotional Maltreatment	322	14%	2,584	10%
Exposure to Intimate Partner Violence	172	7%	5,891	24%
Sexual Abuse	78	3%	776	3%
Risk Investigations*	154	6%	4,233	17%
Substantiated Maltreatment Investigations*	2,093	88%	12,310	50%
Severity of Emotional Harm*†				
Harm, Treatment Required	956	40%	2,988	12%
Harm, No Treatment Required	346	15%	2,061	8%
No Harm	1,081	45%	19,716	80%
Severity of Physical Harm*				
Harm, Treatment Required	168	7%	281	1%
Harm, No Treatment Required	228	10%	759	3%
No Harm	1,987	83%	23,724	96%
Duration of Maltreatment*				
Single Incident	392	16%	4,133	17%
Multiple Incidents	1,760	74%	10,127	41%
Case Previously Opened*	1,824	77%	14,195	57%
Police Involvement*				
Police Involvement for Intimate Partner Violence	476	20%	5,099	21%
Police Involvement for Child Maltreatment	669	28%	1,873	8%
Ongoing Child Welfare Services*				
Case to Stay Open	2,178	91%	6,024	24%
Streamed to Differential Response	266	11%	2,692	11%
Alberta Incidence Study of Reported Child Abuse and Neglect 2008	**2,383**	**100%**	**24,764**	**100%**

Percentages are column percentages, based on the total weighted number of investigations.

**p less than or equal to .05.*

†Column numbers may not add up due to rounding.

children who were placed and children who were not placed; however, police involvement related to child maltreatment was significantly higher in placement investigations (28 per cent) than in non-placement investigations (8 per cent). Ninety-one per cent of placement investigations were referred for ongoing services upon completion of the investigation.

Discussion

This chapter reports on a secondary data analysis of 27,147 child maltreatment investigations from the AIS-2008, a provincial data set representative of child welfare in Alberta for 2008. Data includes a broad range of child, family, household, and case-level data associated with and predictive of the key forms of maltreatment. This analysis addressed the complexity of child welfare placement decision-making and the clinical risk factors to be considered when determining which children and youth require a temporary or longer-term out-of-home placement (Chabot et al., 2013; Fallon et al., 2015; Graham, Dettlaff, Baumann, & Fluke, 2015).

Findings from this study support previous research that the highest placement rates are associated with children under the age of one (Horwitz, Hurlburt, Cohen, Zhang, & Landsverk, 2011; Palusci, 2011), as well as with children between twelve and fifteen (Esposito et al., 2013; Fast, Trocmé, Fallon, & Ma, 2014). Cases in which children are placed in care demonstrate higher levels of risk to the child related to academic difficulties, attachment issues, intellectual and developmental disability, depression, and aggression to others. As well, these children and youth live in situations with heightened levels of caregiver risk as well as poorer household conditions related to poverty and well-being—a point that is well supported by the literature (Esposito et al., 2013; Fast et al., 2014; Fluke et al., 2010; Rivaux et al., 2008). A high proportion of investigations in which children were placed in out-of-home care identified neglect as the primary form of maltreatment (Drake, Jonson-Reid, Way, & Chung, 2003; Horwitz et al., 2011). Placement cases reflected significantly higher rates of physical and emotional harm—and specifically, severe emotional and physical harm requiring treatment—than did non-placement cases. This is supported by previous research that suggests evidence of mental or emotional harm is strongly associated with child placement (Black, Trocmé, Fallon, & MacLaurin, 2008; Tonmyr, Williams, Jack, & MacMillan,

2011). Finally, children of Indigenous heritage are investigated and placed at a higher rate than non-Indigenous children, which is a trend consistently noted in Canadian child welfare research findings (Chabot et al., 2013; Fallon et al., 2015; Fluke et al., 2010).

Conclusion

Historically, there has been little comprehensive provincial data that supports analysis of child placements for children investigated for alleged maltreatment in Alberta. The ongoing cycles of the AIS provide critical baseline information for future and ongoing research about children placed in the care of child welfare. This chapter has provided a descriptive summary of the child, caregiver, household, and case factors associated with a worker's decisions to place a child, based on the "best interests of the child" definitions in Alberta legislation. Building on ongoing work in this area, future analyses will examine the interactions among these risk factors using predictive models of placement.

Discussion Questions

1. What has contributed to the overrepresentation of Indigenous children in care?
2. Why is it important to regularly collect information on child welfare placement histories?
3. What are some of the challenges children in care face in relation to risks in academic achievement?
4. What is the most common form of child abuse documented in this research?
5. What are important factors to consider in relation to age and child placement?

References

Aldgate, J., Colton, M., Ghate, D., & Heath, A. (1992). Educational attainment and stability in long-term foster care. *Children & Society, 6*(2), 92–104.

Bala, N. (1999). Reforming Ontario's Child and Family Services Act: Is the pendulum swinging back too far? *Canadian Family Law Quarterly, 17*(2), 121–172.

Barber, J., & Delfabbro, P. (2005). Children's adjustment to long-term foster care. *Children and Youth Services Review, 27*(3), 329–340.

Berger, L. M., Bruch, S., Johnson, E., James, S., & Rubin, D. (2009). Estimating the "impact" of out-of-home placement on child well-being: Approaching the problem of selection bias. *Child Development, 80*(6), 1856–1876.

Black, T., Trocmé, N., Fallon, B., & MacLaurin, B. (2008). The Canadian child welfare system response to exposure to domestic violence investigations. *Child Abuse & Neglect, 32*(3), 393–404.

Blackstock, C. (2009). After the apology: Why are so many First Nations children still in foster care? *Children Australia, 34*(1), 22–29.

Blackstock, C. (2011). Wanted: Moral courage in Canadian child welfare. *First Peoples Child & Family Review, 6*(2), 35–46.

Blackstock, C., Loxley, J., Prakash, T., & Wien, E. (2005). *Wen:de: We are coming to the light of day*. Ottawa, ON: First Nations Child and Family Caring Society of Canada.

Blackstock, C., Trocmé, N., & Bennett, M. (2003). *Child welfare response to Aboriginal and non-Aboriginal children in Canada: A comparative analysis*. International Symposium on Family Violence, Montreal, QC.

Bullock, R., Courtney, M., Parker, R., Sinclair, I., & Thoburn, J. (2006). Can the corporate state parent? *Children and Youth Services Review, 28*(11), 1344–1358.

Chabot, M., Fallon, B., Tonmyr, L., MacLaurin, B., Fluke, J., & Blackstock, C. (2013). Exploring alternate specifications to explain agency-level effects in placement decisions regarding Aboriginal children: Further analysis of the Canadian Incidence Study of Reported Child Abuse and Neglect Part B. *Child Abuse & Neglect, 37*(1), 61–76.

Courtney, M., & Dworsky, A. (2006). Early outcomes for young adults transitioning from out-of-home care in the USA. *Child & Family Social Work, 11*(3), 209–219.

Drake, B., Jonson-Reid, M., Way, I., & Chung, S. (2003). Substantiation and recidivism. *Child Maltreatment, 8*(4), 248–260.

Dumbrill, G. (2006). Parental experience of child protective intervention: A qualitative study. *Child Abuse & Neglect, 30*(1), 27–37.

Esposito, T., Trocmé, N., Chabot, M., Shlonsky, A., Collin-Vézina, D., & Sinha, V. (2013). Placement of children in out-of-home care in Québec, Canada: When and for whom initial out-of-home placement is most likely to occur. *Children and Youth Services Review, 35*(12), 2031–2039.

Fallon, B., Chabot, M., Fluke, J., Blackstock, C., Sinha, V., Allan, K., & MacLaurin, B. (2015). Exploring alternative specifications to explain agency-level effects in placement decisions regarding Aboriginal children: Further analysis of the Canadian Incidence Study of Reported Child Abuse and Neglect Part C. *Child Abuse & Neglect, 49*(November), 97–106.

Fallon, B., & Trocmé, N. (2011). Factors associated with the decision to provide ongoing services: Are worker characteristics and organization location important? In K. Kufeldt & B. McKenzie (Eds.), *Child welfare: Connecting research, policy, and practice* (pp. 57–73). Waterloo, ON: Wilfrid Laurier University Press.

Fallon, B., Van Wert, M., Trocmé, N., MacLaurin, B., Sinha, V., Lefebvre, R.,...& Goel, S. (2015). *Ontario Incidence Study of Reported Child Abuse and Neglect – 2013: Major findings* (OIS-2013). Toronto, ON: Child Welfare Research Portal.

Fanshel, D., Finch, S. J., & Grundy, J. F. (1990). *Foster children in a life course perspective.* New York, NY: Columbia University Press.

Fast, E., Trocmé, N., Fallon, B., & Ma, J. (2014). A troubled group? Adolescents in a Canadian child welfare sample. *Children and Youth Services Review, 46*(November), 47–54.

Fernandez, E. (1999). Pathways in substitute care: Representation of placement careers of children using event history analysis. *Children and Youth Services Review, 21*(3), 177–216.

Fluke, J., Chabot, M., Fallon, B., MacLaurin, B., & Blackstock, C. (2010). Placement decisions and disparities among Aboriginal groups: An application of the decision-making ecology through multi-level analysis. *Child Abuse & Neglect, 34*(1), 57–69.

Gove, T. J. (1995a). *Report of the Gove inquiry into child protection in British Columbia.* Vol. 1: *Matthew's story.* Victoria, BC: British Columbia Ministry of Services to Children and Families.

Gove, T. J. (1995b). *Report of the Gove inquiry into child protection in British Columbia.* Vol. 2: *Matthew's legacy.* Victoria, BC: British Columbia Ministry of Services to Children and Families.

Graham, J., Dettlaff, A., Baumann, D., & Fluke, J. (2015). The decision making ecology of placing a child into foster care: A structural equation model. *Child Abuse & Neglect, 49*(November), 12–23.

Hair, H. (2005). Outcomes for children and adolescents after residential treatment: A review of research from 1993 to 2003. *Journal of Child & Family Studies, 14*(4), 551–575.

Horwitz, S., Hurlburt, M., Cohen, S., Zhang, J., & Landsverk, J. (2011). Predictors of placement for children who initially remained in their homes after an investigation for abuse or neglect. *Child Abuse & Neglect, 25*(3), 188–198.

Hughes, E. N. (2006). *BC children and youth review: An independent review of BC's child protection system.* Victoria, BC: British Columbia Ministry of Children and Family Development.

Jones, A., Sinha, V., & Trocmé, N. (2015). *Children and youth in out-of-home care in the Canadian provinces* (CWRP Information Sheet #167E). Montreal, QC: Centre for Research on Children and Families, McGill University.

LaBoucane-Benson, P., Sherren, N., & Yerichuk, D. (2017). *Trauma, child development, healing and resilience: A review of literature with focus on Aboriginal peoples and communities.* Edmonton, AB: PolicyWise for Children & Families.

MacLaurin, B. J. (2002). Historical and contextual factors associated with child welfare decisions in Canada (Unpublished paper). Calgary, AB, University of Calgary.

MacLaurin, B., & Bala, N. (2004). Children in care. In N. Bala, M. K. Zapf, R. J. Williams, R. Vogl, & J. P. Hornick (Eds.), *Canadian child welfare law* (pp. 111–138). Toronto, ON: Thompson Educational Publishing.

MacLaurin, B., Trocmé, N., Fallon, B., Sinha, V., Feehan, R., Enns, R.,...& Budgell, D. (2013). *Alberta Incidence Study of Reported Child Abuse and Neglect – 2008 (AIS-2008): Major findings*. Calgary, AB: University of Calgary.

Milloy, J. S. (1999). *A national crime: The Canadian government and the residential school system, 1879 to 1986*. Winnipeg, MB: University of Manitoba Press.

Mulcahy, M., & Trocmé, N. (2009). *Children and youth in out-of-home care in Canada* (CECW Information Sheet #76). Toronto, ON: Centre of Excellence for Child Welfare.

Noftle, J., Cook, S., Leschied, A. W., St. Pierre, J., Stewart, S. L., & Johnson, A. (2011). The trajectory of change for children and youth in residential treatment: Implications for policy and program. *Journal of Child Psychiatry & Human Development, 42*(1), 65–77.

Palusci, V. (2011). Risk factors and services for child maltreatment among infants and young children. *Children and Youth Services Review, 33*(8), 1374–1382.

Panel of Experts on Child Protection. (1998). *Protecting vulnerable children*. Toronto, ON: Ontario Ministry of Community and Social Services.

Pecora, P., Williams, J., Kessler, R., Hiripi, E., O'Brien, K., Emerson, J.,...& Torres, D. (2006). Assessing the educational achievements of adults who were formerly placed in family foster care. *Child & Family Social Work, 11*(3), 220–231.

Perlman, S., & Fantuzzo, J. (2013). Predicting risk of placement: A population-based study of out-of-home placement, child maltreatment, and emergency housing. *Journal of the Society for Social Work & Research, 4*(2), 99–113.

Preyde, M., Cameron, G., Frensch, K., & Adams, G. (2011). Parent-child relationships and family functioning of children and youth discharged from residential mental health treatment or a home-based alternative. *Residential Treatment for Children & Youth, 28*(1), 55–74.

Rivaux, S., James, J., Wittenstrom, K., Baumann, D., Sheets, J., & Henry, J. (2008). The intersection of race, poverty and risk: Understanding the decision to provide services to clients and to remove children. *Child Welfare, 82*(2), 151–168.

Rubin, D., O'Reilly, A., Luan, X., & Localio, A. (2007). The impact of placement stability on behavioral well-being for children in foster care. *Pediatrics, 119*(2), 336–344.

Sinha, V., Trocmé, N., Fallon, B., & MacLaurin, B. (2013). Understanding the investigation-stage overrepresentation of First Nations children in the child welfare system: An analysis of the First Nations component of the Canadian Incidence Study of Reported Child Abuse and Neglect 2008. *Child Abuse & Neglect, 37*(10), 821–831.

Sinha, V., Trocmé, N., Fallon, B., MacLaurin, B., Fast, E., Thomas Prokop, S.,...& Richard, K. (2011). *Kiskisik Awasisak: Remember the children. Understanding the overrepresentation of First Nations children in the child welfare system*. Ottawa, ON: Assembly of First Nations.

Spratt, T. (2001). The influence of child protection orientation on child welfare practice. *British Journal of Social Work, 31*(6), 933–954.

Stott, T., & Gustavsson, N. (2010). Balancing permanency and stability for youth in foster care. *Children and Youth Services Review, 32*(4), 619–625.

Taussig, H., Clyman, R., & Landsverk, J. (2001). Children who return home from foster care: A 6-year prospective study of behavioural health outcomes in adolescence. *Pediatrics, 108*(1), E10–E17.

Timms, J., & Thoburn, J. (2003). *Your shout! A survey of the views of 706 children and young people in public care.* London, United Kingdom: National Society for the Prevention of Cruelty to Children.

Tonmyr, L., Williams, G., Jack, S., & MacMillan, H. (2011). Infant placement in Canadian child maltreatment-related investigations: Family profiles and service provisions. *International Journal of Mental Health & Addiction, 9*(October), 441–459.

TRC (Truth and Reconciliation Commission of Canada). (2015). *Honouring the truth, reconciling for the future: Summary of the final report of the Truth and Reconciliation Commission.* Winnipeg, MB: TRC.

Trocmé, N. (1997). Staying on track while the pendulum swings: Commentary on Canadian child welfare policy trends. *OACAS Newsmagazine, 3*(2), 13–14.

Trocmé, N., Fallon, B., MacLaurin, B., Sinha, V., Black, T., Fast, E.,...& Holroyd, J. (2010a). Characteristics of children and families. In *Canadian Incidence Study of Reported Child Abuse and Neglect – 2008: Major findings* (pp. 36–43). Ottawa, ON: Public Health Agency of Canada.

Trocmé, N., Fallon, B., MacLaurin, B., Sinha, V., Black, T., Fast, E.,...& Holroyd, J. (2010b). Characteristics of substantiated maltreatment. In *Canadian Incidence Study of Reported Child Abuse and Neglect – 2008: Major findings* (pp. 30–35). Ottawa, ON: Public Health Agency of Canada.

Trocmé, N., Fallon, B., Sinha, V., Van Wert, M., Kozlowski, A., & MacLaurin, B. (2013). Differentiating between child protection and family support in the Canadian child welfare system's response to intimate partner violence, corporal punishment, and child neglect. *International Journal of Psychology, 48*(2), 128–140.

Trocmé, N., Kyte, A., Sinha, V., & Fallon, B. (2014). Urgent protection versus chronic need: Clarifying the dual mandate of child welfare services across Canada. *Social Sciences, 3*(3), 483–498.

Trocmé, N., MacLaurin, B., Fallon, B., Shlonsky, A., Mulcahy, M., & Esposito, T. (2009). *National child welfare outcomes indicator matrix (NOM).* Montreal, QC: Centre for Research on Children and Families, McGill University.

Wald, M. S. (1988). Family preservation: Are we moving too fast? *Public Welfare, 46*(3), 33–38.

Wilmshurst, L. A. (2002). Treatment programs for youth with emotional and behavioural disorders: An outcome study of two alternative approaches. *Mental Health Services Research, 4*(2), 85–96.

CHAPTER 9

A Strained Relationship: Southern Sudanese Communities and Child Welfare Systems in Two Urban Centres in Western Canada

David Este and Christa Sato

Introduction

As a result of immigration, Canadian society has become increasingly diverse on several dimensions, including race, language, and religious faith. In 2016, the country admitted 296,346 new permanent residents. The "economic class" emerged as the top category of immigrants to the country, with 155,994 (52.6 per cent). Individuals admitted under the "family class" accounted for 78,004 (26.3 per cent) of newcomers. Finally, refugee claimants—government- and privately sponsored refugees admitted under the humanitarian category—comprised 21.0 per cent of newcomers (IRCC, 2017). The three top countries of origin—Philippines, India, and Syria—accounted for 39.3 per cent of permanent residents admitted in 2016 (IRCC, 2017). The projected figure for 2018 regarding the number of individuals who will be admitted into Canada ranges between 290,000 and 330,000 (IRCC, 2017).

Suggested Citation: Este, D., & Sato, C. (2018). A strained relationship: Southern Sudanese communities and child welfare systems in two urban centres in Western Canada. In D. Badry, H. Montgomery, D. Kikulwe, M. Bennett, & D. Fuchs, (Eds.), *Imagining child welfare in the spirit of reconciliation* (pp. 185–204). Regina, SK: University of Regina Press.

With the diversity that exists in Canada, child welfare agencies are challenged to ensure that the programs and services provided are responsive to the needs of individuals and families from ethnocultural communities involved with child protection systems. It is noted within the literature that racialized and ethnic-minority children are overrepresented in child welfare systems (Chaze, 2009; Clarke, 2011; Maiter & Stalker, 2011), especially in the large Canadian cities of Toronto, Montreal, and Vancouver. Moreover, Clarke (2011) stressed that the increasing involvement of Black children in the child welfare system suggests that closer attention must be paid to this overrepresentation. Hence, the purpose of this chapter is to explore Southern Sudanese community members' perceptions of and experiences with the child welfare systems in Calgary and Brooks, Alberta.

This chapter is organized in the following manner: the next two sections focus on Southern Sudanese migration to Canada and descriptions of the two sites in Alberta where the study was conducted: Brooks and Calgary. A review of the existing literature on the relationship between child welfare systems in Canada and immigrant/refugee communities is then provided. Next an overview of the methods used to conduct the study is given. The final two sections of the chapter include the presentation of the study's major results followed by a discussion in which recommendations are put forward to improve the relationship between child welfare authorities and the Sudanese communities in Brooks and Calgary.

Background/Context

Southern Sudanese communities began to emerge in Canada in the early 1990s. The major impetus for migration to Canada was the ongoing brutal civil war in the republic of Sudan. Conditions of severe drought, mass killings, and acts of environmental destruction perpetuated by forces loyal to the national government located in Khartoum forced over half a million Sudanese (the majority from the southern region) to escape to neighbouring countries such as Chad, Uganda, Ethiopia, and Kenya (Este & Tachble, 2009). Children were separated from their families and eventually became known as the "lost boys and girls of Sudan" (Luster, Qin, Bates, Johnson, & Rana, 2008; Luster, Qin, Bates, Rana, & Lee, 2010). The civil war ended in 2005 when a comprehensive peace accord was signed between the government of Sudan and the Sudan People's Liberation

Movement (Ensor, 2014). On July 9, 2011, the Republic of South Sudan became an independent country. However, there has been ongoing war and clashes between rival ethnic groups, as well as famine, which the United Nations has described as a catastrophe caused by civil war and economic collapse, resulting in the displacement of South Sudan citizens (South Sudan Profile, 2018).

The provinces of Ontario and Alberta are homes to the largest Southern Sudanese communities in Canada. Cities with the largest communities are Toronto, Calgary, and Edmonton. For the purposes of our study, semi-structured interviews were conducted with respondents residing in Calgary and Brooks, Alberta. In the next section, we provide National Household Survey (NHS) population data for Brooks and Calgary; however, it is important to note that Southern Sudanese and other African diasporas in Alberta are underestimated and that the actual sizes of these communities are much larger than reported (M. Embaie, personal communication, September 2017).

Southern Sudanese in Alberta

Brooks is a small, unique city in Alberta, as it has a sizable immigrant and refugee community. According to the 2011 NHS, roughly 3,420 newcomers resided in the city, representing 15 per cent of the total population (Statistics Canada, 2013). The presence of the Lakeside Meat Packing plant served as a major attractor for immigrants/refugees to settle in Brooks in that it offered opportunities for employment. As of 2011, approximately 270 Sudanese resided in Brooks, with the majority employed at Lakeside.

In Brooks, a key organization for Sudanese community members is the Brooks Sudanese Christian Church. The church assists Sudanese newcomers as they adapt to their new home. Sudanese also access services from the Language Centre for Newcomers, which was founded by a member of the community. Brooks and County Immigrant Services is the primary immigrant-serving agency utilized by immigrants and refugees who venture to the city.

According to the 2011 ethnic origins data (provided by the NHS), 3,245 Sudanese resided in Calgary. Prior to 2000, the Sudanese community in the city was relatively small. In the early part of the century, the size of the community increased as a result of two waves of migration, in 2000 and

2002 (Simich, Este, & Hamilton, 2010). During this period, Calgary experienced a surge in economic growth, and this served as an attractor for Southern Sudanese newcomers.

There are at least three non-profit organizations formed by members of the community that assist with the settlement and adaptation process in Calgary. The Sudanese Social Club provides assistance, guidance, and support to these individuals and families as needed. The club also organizes events for the community. The second organization in the city is the African Sudanese Association of Calgary, which provides an array of settlement and interpretation services for Sudanese community members. The final organization is the Calgary South Sudanese Community Association. One of the primary aims of this group is to serve vulnerable Sudanese populations in Calgary and the surrounding area. Services offered include adult education, literacy programs, parental education, and community engagement programs designed to help Sudanese become more acquainted with Canadian society.

The next section provides a brief overview of the Canadian literature on child welfare and immigrant, refugee, and racialized families.

Literature Review

In Canada, child welfare organizations are being challenged to ensure that the services they provide are responsive to the changing racial, ethnic, religious, and cultural composition of the nation's population. Canadian research exploring immigrant, refugee, and racialized families and child welfare systems is limited; however, some notable exceptions have attempted to fill this paucity of literature (Chaze, 2009; Clarke, 2011; Dumbrill, 2008; Maiter, 2004; Maiter & Stalker, 2011; Maiter, Stalker, & Alaggia, 2009). More specifically, literature that explores the perceptions and experiences of Sudanese community members in relation to child welfare systems is virtually non-existent. In an article by Este and Tachble (2009) that examined Sudanese perceptions of fathering, the contentious issue of child welfare was noted by participants, but it was not a major topic explored in their study. Nevertheless, valuable insights can be gleaned from the existing bodies of literature; thus, we present a brief overview of Canadian scholarship focused on immigrant, refugee, and racialized families' relationships with child welfare.

In reviewing the literature, Chaze (2009) explored the relationship among barriers to employment for visible minority immigrants, poverty, mothering discourse, and child welfare intervention. The author attributed child welfare intervention among visible minority immigrant mothers to their inability to find suitable employment, leading to the increased likelihood of the family living in poverty, subsequent interventions by child welfare services, and North American mothering discourses that contribute to misperceptions that immigrant mothers are "bad mothers."

Maiter and colleagues have published a series of articles on their qualitative study that examined the experiences of minority immigrant families receiving child welfare services (Maiter, 2004; Maiter & Stalker 2011; Maiter, Stalker, & Alaggia, 2009). The sample consisted of twenty South Asian immigrants (twelve women, eight men) in Canada who had child welfare involvement. The first article (Maiter, 2004) focuses on the concepts of cultural sensitivity and competence in child protection and their relevance for South Asian parents. The following paragraph captures the essence of the study:

> *Since South Asian participants in the study do not identify child protective services as a source of help, they may be unlikely to report situations of maltreatment. Child protective services are viewed as creating greater problems for families rather than as being helpful to families. This review can result in underreporting of maltreatment by community members and a reluctance to help child protective services.* (Maiter, 2004, p. 77)

In a later article, Maiter et al. (2009) specifically examine the stressors perceived by participants as contributing to child welfare interventions among twenty South Asian immigrants to Canada who had child welfare involvement. Findings from this study highlight the loneliness, betrayal, hopelessness, and financial struggles that precipitated local child welfare intervention in the lives of newcomer families in Toronto. Further, the authors contextualize these perceived stressors within a framework of conservation of resource (COR), arguing that the erosion of resources increases newcomer minority families' vulnerability and may result in child welfare intervention. They conclude that "child maltreatment in minority immigrant families can be reduced by efforts focused in a wide variety of ways to prevent the spiral of resource loss, and to increase opportunities for resource gain" (Maiter et al., 2009, p. 35). In their 2011 article, Maiter and Stalker contend that child welfare systems have struggled historically in providing appropriate services for immigrant and racialized families. Major themes presented in this article include participants' experiences of child protection intervention, worker-client relationships, perceptions of cultural responsiveness, access to supports, and ways to improve service (Maiter & Stalker, 2011).

In addressing the relationship between refugee parents and child welfare, Dumbrill (2008) conducted a participatory action photovoice study with eleven refugee parents (nine women, two men) in Ontario who had had direct and indirect experience with child protection services. The sample consisted of refugee parents who had migrated from West Africa and from southwest and central Asia. Based on participants' views of parenting and their experiences of child welfare services, Dumbrill identified three major themes: understanding the hopes and fears participants had for their children, understanding their settlement challenges, and working with refugee parents in the development of child welfare policies and services.

Research that examines child welfare involvement with different Black communities in Canada is limited. However, in her study with nine participants of Afro-Caribbean descent (three mothers, three youth, three child welfare workers), Clarke (2011) noted five themes: perceived differential treatment, criminalization, surveillance, control, and poverty. While the mothers raised the lack of awareness and understanding of the role of professionals, and the need for more training of young workers, the youth discussed issues of separation and anger, as well as the perceived loss of culture as a result of being removed from their family homes. The child welfare workers highlighted a lack of structural analysis, misunderstanding of Afro-Caribbean culture, and the lack of understanding of the impact of immigration patterns (Clarke, 2011).

Finally, Este and Tachble (2009) examined the experiences of twenty Sudanese refugee men as fathers in Calgary. Through interviews, individuals shared insights on the meaning of fatherhood, values that guide their behaviours as fathers, interactions with and aspirations for their children, and challenges encountered as fathers in Canadian society. Of the challenges reported, discipline of their children is directly related to the focus of the article. Respondents in this study maintained children have more rights in Canada, making it difficult to discipline them. The fathers stressed that parents, family members, and neighbours should have the right to discipline children without any constraints placed upon them. They believed that this issue has resulted in considerable tension between the Sudanese community in Calgary and the local child welfare system (Este & Tachble, 2009).

However, none of these studies specifically addresses the nature of child welfare relationships with the Sudanese community. This chapter aims to contribute to the literature by focusing on the perceptions and experiences of Southern Sudanese community members' relationships with child welfare systems in the province of Alberta. This chapter is drawn from a study that explored the settlement and adaptation experiences of Southern Sudanese, elaborated in the following section.

Methods

The study followed a pragmatic qualitative research design, as prescribed by Patton (2002) and Creswell (2007), which allows flexibility in determining research strategies provided they are used ethically. A criterion sampling strategy was used to identify and recruit members of the community to participate in this study. Eligible participants had to be eighteen years of age or older; to have resided in Canada at least six months and up to a maximum of ten years; and to have a primary residency in Calgary or Brooks. Recruitment was facilitated through the help of staff at two non-profit organizations in Calgary and one in Brooks that were extensively engaged with the Sudanese community. Second, information about the study was shared with key agency staff in meetings with the research team and distributed through posters and presentations at local community events. A third recruitment strategy was employed using personal connections of the lead author and the interviewer for the project (a leader in Calgary's Sudanese community).

A total of twenty-two (twelve in Calgary and ten in Brooks) in-depth, semi-structured interviews with Southern Sudanese adults were conducted for this study. The interviews lasted sixty to ninety minutes and were audio-recorded, translated as needed, and transcribed. An inductive approach was used for the data analysis (Lincoln & Guba, 1985). In describing this process, Thomas (2006) remarked that "inductive analysis refers to approaches that primarily use detailed readings of raw data to derive concepts, themes, or a model through interpretation made from the raw data by an evaluator or researcher" (p. 238). A directed a priori coding framework for organizing interview data was first conducted on thirty-one categories based on five interview topics: (1) migration and settlement (arrival, feelings about Canada, challenges, opportunities); (2) concepts of family (definitions, roles and decision-making, impact of changes); (3) concept of health (community health, healthy families, illness causes and response, changes in health); (4) social support interventions (barriers, impacts, supports needed); and (5) perceptions of the roles of community and government. Responses were coded and thematically analyzed; we used the computer software Atlas.ti to help us manage and analyze the data.

Major Findings

Three major themes emerged from questions exploring the relationship between communities in Calgary and Brooks and the respective local child welfare systems: (1) core Sudanese family values, (2) issues between the Sudanese community and local child welfare authorities, and (3) strategies and recommended solutions. Each theme is discussed in further detail below; however, a profile of the study participants is provided first.

Table 1: Profile of Study Participants (N=22)

	Calgary	Brooks
Gender	9 males 3 females	8 males 2 females
Age Range	19–41 years (males) 23–34 years (females)	

As illustrated in Table 1, a total of seventeen men and five women, ranging from nineteen to forty-one years of age, participated in the study. The interviewees' time in Canada ranged from ten months to six years. The majority of respondents had completed at least secondary school and claimed their English proficiency was good. Additionally, most individuals from Brooks were employed at Lakeside Meat Packing Plant.

Core Sudanese Family Values

One of the salient themes that emerged from the data was core values that were intrinsic to Sudanese families, including the importance of education and respect.

Importance of Education

A consistent message imparted by participants was the value of education as paramount within Southern Sudanese families. Essentially, coming to Canada represented an opportunity for the children in their families to obtain education leading to a better life. This was elicited in the following comment by a female participant in Calgary: "You want them to be successful children, wish them a good education and a better life." In a similar vein, a Sudanese father from Brooks stressed the role he intended to play in supporting his children with their schooling. He remarked, "I will try my best to support them so that they can get a better education and get a good job when they finish their studies, not to work a physical job like what I am doing." Clearly, interviewees expressed the desire to provide a better life for their children, where education was perceived to be an avenue for improving the social and economic well-being of the family, especially for the children.

Importance of Respect

Respect was also a value that was strongly enforced by Sudanese families, which manifested in the interview responses. For example, one individual demarcated the ways he instilled cultural tenets about respect from his home country in his children, who were now growing up in Canada. The male respondent vocalized:

> *From the place I am and the way I was brought up, I have to teach my children how to respect other people. I have to teach the children how to act with me and their mother. They should have to respect us, and if they give us respect, they will give respect to other people.* (Male participant, Calgary)

A concrete illustration shared by another Sudanese father of his expectations for how his children should treat elders was described as follows:

"they [children] should show respect to elders. For instance, in our Dinka culture, when a child is talking to elders, he or she should not look up to the face of elders." The two quotes highlight interviewees' perceptions of how the younger generation should treat their elders with respect, which was based on participants' experiences growing up in Sudan.

In brief, the importance of understanding core Sudanese family values shared through the lens of the participants provides a cultural context that precipitates issues between members of the Sudanese community and local child welfare authorities, as discussed in the next section of the chapter.

Issues between the Sudanese Community and Local Child Welfare Authorities

Not surprisingly, different cultural approaches toward raising children within Sudanese families as compared to the Canadian mainstream led to tensions between the Sudanese community and local child welfare authorities, which represent the second theme from our findings. More specifically, linked to the theme of the tensions between child welfare and the Sudanese community are subthemes of the changing nature of parent-child relationships; styles of disciplining; apprehension of children; and the breakdown of Sudanese families.

Changing Nature of Parent-Child Relationships

A major value that guides the parenting practices in Sudanese families is the importance that is placed on ensuring children are respectful. Despite the importance of respect within Sudanese families, the majority of respondents maintained that the practice of being respectful was being eroded in their children as a result of living in Canadian society. One Sudanese respondent remarked, "You talk to your kids, they talk back to you. They talk to you, they look at your face. And to the elders, it is a bad thing that the kids are no longer respecting them" (male participant, Brooks). This quote stresses the shifting nature of parent-child relationships among Sudanese families in Canada, particularly in the ways that cultural values like respect were perceived by adults to be dissipating among their children's generation. Further, the notion of respect was tied to their cultural values; therefore, the lack of respect shown by Sudanese children toward elders in their community contributed to feelings of losing their cultural values. This was exemplified in the following quote: "We are losing the respect that our elders are supposed to be accorded....[W]e need to re-educate ourselves to be able to get the good values from our culture" (male participant, Calgary). This subtheme underscores some of the challenges associated with reinforcing Sudanese family values (the importance of education and respect) in a different cultural context, focusing particularly on the changing nature of parent-child relationships. Consequently, these shifting family dynamics were often a precursor to child welfare intervention, as many Southern Sudanese parents turned to corporal punishment as a form of disciplining their children.

Style of Disciplining

The lack of respect displayed by Sudanese children contributed to family discord, which in some instances resulted in the involvement of child welfare authorities. Undoubtedly, one of the most contentious issues that emerged with respect to child welfare involvement in Sudanese communities pertained to the study participants' methods of disciplining their children. In particular, Sudanese parents felt that their rights to discipline their children in the manner to which they were accustomed were limited or completely removed. A mother from Brooks noted, "Here you cannot beat your child. The child will say 'no' and 'you cannot do that [beat me].' The government will come in." Another participant commented on discipline styles in Southern Sudan as compared to Canada: "And my father [in Sudan] can beat me, nobody can complain about that. Here [in Canada], now it is not like you can beat your child" (male participant, Brooks). Additionally, participants maintained that in Canada their children possessed rights they did not have while living in Sudan. This was expressed by a female participant in Calgary, who observed, "In terms of disciplining in Canadian culture, our way is seen as abusing.... [T]he Canadian system is difficult for us. Children decide what they want to do. We do not do that back in Sudan." As elicited in these quotes, parents voiced their strong displeasure regarding the criticism they received from child welfare representatives on how they disciplined their children. The ongoing tensions were further exacerbated when local authorities apprehended their children as a result of Sudanese parents' physical style of discipline.

Apprehension of Children

Overwhelmingly, study respondents asserted that a major issue facing the community was the poor relationships with local child welfare authorities stemming from the interference of child welfare in family life and the apprehension of Sudanese children. In describing the interactions with child protection services, a male participant from Calgary stated, "Our community has so many difficulties especially dealing with child welfare. Kids are being taken away from families." Sudanese community members believed there was no need for child welfare personnel to interfere in matters perceived to be family affairs. Sudanese respondents felt that elders in the community were better positioned than child welfare authorities to deal with these issues, as captured in the following comment: "Instead of coming into our houses and interfering,...they should ask the elders of the community to deal with the problems in the community" (male participant, Brooks). Thus, interviewees viewed intervention by child welfare through the apprehension of Sudanese children as an issue that was conducive to the breakdown of families within their community.

Breakdown of Families

Regardless of the mandate of child welfare to protect the well-being of children in the province of Alberta, Sudanese study participants strongly contended that the involvement of child welfare intensified family discord, leading to breakdown within Sudanese families. In describing the nature of family breakdown, one male participant from Calgary said, "The biggest problem that I as a person have noted is the breakdown of families....[M]ost Sudanese children have been taken away from their parents, and it is a big concern to me." Another respondent highlighted these problematic encounters with child welfare authorities, who were viewed as playing a major role in the disintegration of Sudanese families living in Canadian society:

> *We Sudanese come here [to Canada], and we got a lot of problems with child welfare because whatever happens in families child welfare came in and took the children and separated people, separated families, which we do not have in our culture.* (female participant, Calgary)

In brief, this section highlighted the issues identified by participants related to the child welfare system and Sudanese communities at the two sites where the study was conducted. However, the respondents also discussed a series of steps they believed would improve these relationships, which is the focus of our final theme presented in the major findings.

Strategies and Recommended Solutions

During the interviews, participants shared various strategies and recommended solutions for improving the strained relationships between Sudanese communities and local child welfare authorities. Importantly, strategies proposed to address the strained relationships from the perspectives of Sudanese community members offer valuable insights that could help reconcile some of the competing tensions inherent in those relationships. Participants identified five key strategies: (1) Sudanese families working collaboratively with the child welfare system; (2) child welfare employing Sudanese staff; (3) child welfare using translators and providing services in the families' first language; (4) child welfare acquiring knowledge of Sudanese culture; and (5) community/family problem solving.

Collaboration with the Child Welfare System

In recognizing the ongoing tensions between members of the Southern Sudanese community and local child welfare systems in Alberta, participants surmised that an effective strategy to improve these relationships was working together, collaboratively. For instance, as a Sudanese male from Calgary suggested,

> *Well, the only way we can do it is if we can work hand-in-hand with child welfare. If child welfare can provide educational workshops for the Sudanese families, then our people can work in preventing child welfare from coming to take kids away from their parents. So we need at least some educational workshops from places like child welfare, family law, or even from the police.*

As illustrated, some participants recognized the importance of working in collaboration with child welfare officials as a way to develop meaningful resolutions between the two parties.

Employment of Sudanese Staff by Child Welfare

A consistent message imparted by the respondents was the need for the child welfare system to hire more members from the community:

> *Sudanese social workers [could work] with the social services, including child welfare. This may make it easier for the system [child welfare] to understand us. This huge apprehension would not happen again because there would be understanding and dialogue and bringing information forward....[T]he system would be aware and create a program that responds to their needs.* (Male participant, Calgary)

Importantly, study respondents stressed the urgency of mainstream systems such as child welfare having an enhanced understanding of the ways in which apprehension affects the community and creating services that are culturally responsive to the Sudanese communities they encounter. A recommendation put forth by a Sudanese woman participant from Brooks was as follows: "Outreach workers are needed. They should go to the homes and see how people are living. How the children are being treated." The inclusion of outreach workers collaborating with child protection workers could potentially contribute to improved relationships with Sudanese community members.

Use of Sudanese Translators and First-Language Services

The use of translators was viewed as a way of improving communication between Sudanese families and child welfare employees, as expressed in this comment: "They should have some translators for child welfare, people who can translate the language—ethnic language" (male participant, Brooks). Additionally, interviewees acknowledged the challenges that English-language services posed, as barriers to the community's communication with local child welfare authorities; therefore, an individual advanced the need for "Sudanese translators who can translate English to their language to the people who do not wish to know English" (male participant, Calgary).

The responses captured in interviews with Sudanese community members highlighted the limited services available in first languages. Thus, a proposed strategy to effectively deal with this issue was to provide services in a family's first language: "We have many languages in Sudan.... [S]ervices can be provided for the majority, for example, [in] the Dinka, the Nuer, and Arabic [languages]" (female participant, Calgary). Moreover, the use of translators who can understand and contextualize the issues that surface between Sudanese families and child protection staff may be a valuable resource in mitigating miscommunication that may arise due to language barriers.

Acquisition of Knowledge of Sudanese Culture by Child Welfare Staff

Several interviewees stressed the need for child welfare staff to be more knowledgeable about Sudanese culture. For example, one participant stated,

> *Child welfare workers have to understand our culture and the importance of respect...and that's a very important issue parents are facing here as our younger kids are starting to behave more Canadian. They do not have respect towards the elderly people.* (Male participant, Brooks)

Indicated in this excerpt is the belief that solutions for resolving these strained relationships involve a two-way process of enhanced knowledge and understanding of the different cultural expectations when it comes to raising children. In other words, the onus should not be placed solely on Sudanese families to learn and adapt to Canadian ways of raising and disciplining children. In building mutual understanding and bridging relationships between the two entities, participants felt strongly that there must be a willingness on the part of child welfare authorities to acquire knowledge of Sudanese culture as an avenue toward improving mutual relationships.

Community/Family Problem Solving

Virtually all respondents claimed that the most effective strategy in dealing with the adverse relationship between the Sudanese community and child welfare authorities was the community problem-solving process, which is used in Southern Sudan. This was reflected in the words of a Sudanese female participant: "The only solution for us to deal with the problems with child welfare is for the problems to be solved through the community—that is the only solution that the Sudanese can feel happy [and] healthy [about]" (female participant, Calgary). Clearly, participants felt that Sudanese community members were better positioned than Canadian mainstream institutions and systems to solve family issues that emerged within their communities: "Family problems—we try to solve them by our community, not going to the government and making them more difficult" (male participant, Brooks). Instead, intervention by government in the affairs of family was perceived by interviewees as making the situation worse, rather than solving the problems. They held a firm belief that the community as a collective possessed the authority and ability to deal with family issues.

Discussion and Conclusion

As Alberta's population continues to become more diverse racially, culturally, linguistically, and spiritually, human service organizations will continue to be challenged to ensure that the services they provide address the unique needs of the diverse communities who use their services. This chapter contributes to the existing literature by examining the adaptation of Sudanese community members to Canada. More specifically, this work fills a void by focusing explicitly on the relationships between local child welfare authorities and the Sudanese community in Calgary and Brooks, Alberta. Findings from the study presented in this chapter emphasize the contexts that precipitate child welfare involvement in Sudanese communities, highlight the issues that arise between the two parties, and finally propose strategies and recommendations from the perspectives of Sudanese community members for how to improve their problematic relationships with local child welfare authorities.

All of the participants from the two study sites, in Calgary and Brooks, were refugees from Southern Sudan (now the Republic of Sudan) who chose to settle in Canada. The majority of participants had spent time in refugee camps, and these participants encountered a number of challenges in adapting to Canadian society. Some of the obstacles they experienced were, for example, the existence of language barriers, the search for meaningful and well-paid employment that matched their education credentials and prior work experience, the loss of a family support system, and various cultural differences (Este & Tachble, 2009). The involvement of child welfare services in affairs that are typically considered to be dealt with appropriately within the family was also a major adjustment for Sudanese refugees.

As this chapter clearly demonstrates, dealing with the child welfare system appeared to be quite problematic for the Sudanese in Calgary and Brooks. A similar view is seen in other Canadian research on the relationships between child welfare and immigrant/racialized communities (Chaze, 2009; Clarke, 2011; Maiter et al., 2009). This study's participants possessed virtually no knowledge about the mandate and responsibilities of child protection services in Canada, where the state (provincial governments) plays an active role in the welfare and protection of children and youth.

For some of the respondents in this study, child welfare was perceived to be part of the government apparatus and very intrusive in the affairs of the family. Based on their experience with the government of Sudan (prior to the granting of independence of the Republic of South Sudan), the participants were quite suspicious of the child protection workers. The involvement of child welfare services in affairs typically dealt with in the family was also a major adjustment for Sudanese refugees. The Sudanese parents we spoke with strongly maintained that only they as parents or members of their extended family possessed the inherent right to raise their children. Just as strong was the belief that, if families encountered difficulties in raising their children, the Sudanese community as a collective entity possessed the knowledge and skills required to resolve those types of issues. This intervention was identified by virtually all of the study's participants.

Additionally, child welfare's interactions with the Sudanese community were perceived as being punitive, especially when a family's failure to adhere or adapt resulted in the apprehension of their children. A lack of understanding of different parenting practices within Sudanese culture often led to the families' miscommunication with child welfare authorities and the authorities' failure to recognize the assets that contribute to strong family bonds and cohesion within Sudanese families. Unfamiliarity with child and family services and a lack of knowledge about the role, responsibilities, and rights of parents on the part of Sudanese communities in Canada coupled with a lack of cultural knowledge of Sudanese on the part of child welfare exacerbated the already strained relationships.

Given the mandate of child welfare systems, it is imperative that representatives from this system and Sudanese community members engage in ongoing dialogue as a critical step in improving the tensions that currently prevail between the two parties. There is a need for Sudanese communities and child welfare authorities to work together to reduce the tension that exists between them. We contend that the formation of a working group consisting of Sudanese parents and child welfare personnel (including frontline and management) may be an effective intervention. The primary purpose of the group would be to engage in dialogue whereby the Sudanese would share with child welfare specific information about parenting practices that prevail in the Republic of South Sudan; family structure, roles, and processes associated with Southern Sudanese families; and the challenges the Sudanese encounter in adjusting to life in their new environment. However, this proposed working group would be effective only if the members continue to engage in meaningful, ongoing dialogue that takes concrete steps toward the incorporation of the strategies put forward by Sudanese study participants. Without these actions, it is highly likely that the strained relationship will continue to persist.

From a policy perspective, prior to coming to Canada, refugees need to be informed about not only the child welfare system but also acceptable parenting approaches and behaviours in Canadian society. This type of information needs to be reinforced as part of any orientation that refugees receive once they arrive at their designated destinations in Canada. Collectively, these strategies will help refugee communities and child welfare develop meaningful and positive relationships.

Discussion Questions

1. What are the major issues that need to be addressed to improve the relationship between the child welfare system and Southern Sudanese communities in Alberta?
2. In what ways can enhanced knowledge about Southern Sudanese family values facilitate stronger relationships with local child welfare institutions?
3. How can barriers limiting Sudanese integration into Canadian society be effectively addressed in a culturally responsive manner by local child welfare systems?
4. What steps should be taken to improve the relationships of Southern Sudanese communities and local child welfare systems?

Acknowledgement

The authors of this chapter acknowledge the contributions of Dr. Laura Simich and Dr. Hayley Hamilton for their involvement in the original research for this project.

References

Chaze, F. (2009). Child welfare intervention in visible minority immigrant families: The role of poverty and the mothering discourse. *Journal of the Association for Research on Mothering, 11*(2), 56–65.

Clarke, J. (2011). The challenge of child welfare involvement for Afro-Caribbean families in Toronto. *Children and Youth Services Review, 33*(2), 274–283.

Creswell, J. (2007). *Qualitative inquiry and research design: Choosing among five approaches* (2nd ed.). Thousand Oaks, CA: Sage.

Dumbrill, G. (2008). Your policies, our children: Messages from refugee parents to child welfare workers and policymakers. *Child Welfare, 88*(3), 145–168.

Ensor, M. (2014). Displaced girlhood: Gendered dimensions of coping and social change among conflict-affected South Sudanese youth. *Refuge, 1*(1), 15–24.

Este, D., & Tachble, A. (2009). Fatherhood in the Canadian context: Perceptions and experiences of Sudanese refugee men. *Sex Roles, 60*(7–8), 456–466.

IRCC (Immigration, Refugees and Citizenship Canada). (2017). *2017 annual report to Parliament on immigration.* Ottawa, ON: IRCC. Retrieved from http://www.cic.gc.ca/english/resources/publications/annual-report-2017/index.asp

Lincoln, Y., & Guba, E. (1985). *Naturalistic inquiry*. Thousand Oaks, CA: Sage.

Luster, T., Qin, D., Bates, L., Johnson, D., & Rana, M. (2008). The lost boys of Sudan: Ambiguous loss, search for family, and reestablishing relationships with family members. *Family Relations, 57*(4), 444–456.

Luster, T., Qin, D., Bates, L., Rana, M., & Lee, J. (2010). Successful adaptation among Sudanese unaccompanied minors: Perspectives of youth and foster parents. *Childhood, 12*(2), 197–211.

Maiter, S. (2004). Considering context and culture in child protection services to ethnically diverse families: An example from research with parents from the Indian subcontinent (South Asians). *Social Work Research and Evaluation, 5*(1), 63–80.

Maiter, S., & Stalker, C. (2011). South Asian immigrants' experience of child protection services: Are we recognizing strengths and resilience? *Child & Family Social Work, 16*(2), 138–148.

Maiter, S., Stalker, C., & Alaggia, R. (2009). The experiences of minority immigrant families receiving child welfare services: Seeking to understand how to reduce risk and increase protective factors. *Families in Society: The Journal of Contemporary Social Services, 90*(1), 28–36.

Patton, M. Q. (2002). *Qualitative research and evaluation methods* (3rd ed.). Thousand Oaks, CA: Sage.

Simich, L., Este, D., & Hamilton, H. (2010). Meanings of home and mental well-being among Sudanese refugees in Canada. *Ethnicity & Health, 15*(2), 199–212.

South Sudan profile – Timeline. (2018, January 17). *BBC News*. Retrieved from http://www.bbc.com/news/world-africa-14019202

Statistics Canada. (2013). *Immigration and ethnocultural diversity in Canada: National household survey 2011*. Catalogue no. 99-010-X2011001. Ottawa, ON: Minister of Industry.

Thomas, D. (2006). A general inductive approach for analyzing qualitative evaluation data. *American Journal of Evaluation, 27*(2), 237–246.

CHAPTER 10

The Linkage between FASD and Homelessness for Individuals with a History of Child Welfare Care

Dorothy Badry, Christine A. Walsh, Meaghan Bell, and Kaylee Ramage

Introduction

The number of children and youth in care in Alberta is substantial. As of June 2017, 7,245 children and youth were in care in the province of Alberta, the majority of whom were in foster care (3,504) and kinship care (2,198), with almost 2,000 Support and Financial Assistance Agreements (SFAAS) (Alberta, 2017). When young people are aging out of the child welfare system, there is some hope that adulthood may be an easier journey than the one that led to them being raised in care, mostly apart from their family of origin. Children with fetal alcohol spectrum disorder (FASD), a disability resulting from prenatal alcohol exposure, are a particularly vulnerable group and often face considerable adversities in adulthood. Although exact estimates are unknown, a significant population of the children and youth in care have suspected or diagnosed FASD (Popova, Lange, Burd, &

Suggested Citation: Badry, D., Walsh, C., Bell, M., & Ramage, K. (2018). The linkage between FASD and homelessness for individuals with a history of child welfare care. In D. Badry, H. Montgomery, D. Kikulwe, M. Bennett, & D. Fuchs, (Eds.), *Imagining child welfare in the spirit of reconciliation* (pp. 205–227). Regina, SK: University of Regina Press.

Rehm, 2014). However, the needs of youth with FASD who are leaving the child welfare system are not well understood. The knowledge base is insufficient to inform programming and policy development. This gap contributes to their vulnerability and increases their risk for further exploitation.

While a perception exists that many adults with FASD who experience homelessness have histories of child welfare involvement, the trajectories to housing insecurity for this population are neither well understood nor clearly established in the literature. Often the support services that children and youth with FASD receive are terminated in adulthood (Burns, 2009). Adults with FASD are at increased risk of experiencing conflict with the law, are often homeless, and frequently live on the margins of society, with limited social and economic supports (IHE, 2013; Popova, Lange, Bekmuradov, Mihic, & Rehm, 2011). Adults with FASD have difficulty finding housing and, once housed, typically live in unstable and unsustainable housing arrangements and continue to be vulnerable to homelessness (Burns, 2009). As Burns (2009) explicates,

> *When youth [with FASD] reach the age of majority, the notion of being able to access suitable housing and eventually become independent and function day to day with no supports is unrealistic for many. This expectation can also set them up for lifelong disappointments of facing revolving doors of temporary housing, homelessness, or placing the responsibility on other adult caregivers.* (p. 24)

There is a need for research that examines the linkage between FASD and youth leaving the child welfare system who move into unstable, tenuous housing with an outcome of homelessness in adulthood. To address this knowledge gap, we conducted a mixed-methods exploratory study to examine the support needs of adults with FASD within the episodically and chronically homeless population. The study also examined the impact of FASD on service utilization, program compliance, and housing outcomes within the Calgary Homeless-Serving System of Care. Findings from this research can also be used to guide policies and programming targeted at youth with FASD leaving the child welfare system.

This chapter shares findings of a mixed-methods study conducted in partnership with the Calgary Homeless Foundation (CHF) and the Faculty of Social Work, University of Calgary. This study included a quantitative analysis of the demographic profile of clients with FASD in the Homeless Management Information System (HMIS) and qualitative interviews both with adults with FASD experiencing homelessness and with service providers in the housing and FASD sectors. The aim of this research is to contribute to the development of an FASD-informed model of care, which includes promoting appropriate and sustainable housing that recognizes and supports individuals' needs and disabilities. This chapter can offer insight into the many challenges young people with FASD may face in leaving care and becoming appropriately housed.

Literature Review

Canada has been progressive in responding to the needs of individuals with FASD in terms of a public health priority. However, persons with FASD are extremely challenged in functioning independently due to the neurological consequences of alcohol exposure, including problems with memory, planning, and understanding cause and effect (Kodituwakku, 2009).

Many individuals with FASD often do not have visible signs of a disability and are thus characterized as "non-compliant" and "hard to serve" rather than as someone with a disability. Specifically, the needs of individuals with FASD who experience homelessness are not well understood within the homeless-serving sector, and many challenges exist in providing effective supports. FASD is often unrecognized within the sector, and frontline workers typically receive limited or no training on FASD as a disabling condition. This lack of awareness of FASD and client needs for care can play a role in housing instability. Developing an FASD-informed continuum of care is critical in our efforts to effectively serve individuals who are in need of socially supportive housing.

The 2008 Government of Alberta FASD 10-Year Strategic Plan (2007–17) focuses on intervention, prevention, and care for individuals, children, and families, in recognition that FASD is a lifelong condition (Alberta, 2008). In Alberta, the FASD Cross-Ministry Committee has been progressive and very active in promoting awareness, training, knowledge development, exchange, and mobilization through the FASD Learning Series and annual conferences. Additionally, FASD Service Networks exist across Alberta and support FASD prevention, with a goal of reducing incidence and providing support to caregivers and families (fasd.alberta.ca). Individuals with FASD have particular vulnerabilities associated with the disability, including mental health conditions, substance-use disorders, and behavioural challenges that may contribute to social isolation, and this population often lives in poverty on the margins of society (Grant et al., 2013).

An underlying concern driving this research was the belief that many individuals with FASD also have chronic problems related to homelessness, while their needs may not be recognized or attributed to a disability. The other concern in raising the topic of FASD and homelessness relates to the human toll of this disability for adults who may not be diagnosed or even know that a disability factors into their social/emotional functioning and daily life challenges.

Homelessness is a major issue in Canada and has prompted municipal and provincial action plans to end homelessness (Gaetz, 2010). Calgary established a ten-year plan to end homelessness (2008–18) (CHF, 2008), in response to the 800 per cent increase in homelessness in the city between 1992 and 2008. A recent point-in-time count estimated that more than 3,200 people are homeless in Calgary on any given night (CHF, 2016). Although precise estimates of the number of homeless individuals with FASD in Calgary are not available, the need to identify clients with FASD at intake into the Calgary System of Care has been identified. As a first step, the CHF, with input and support from Alberta Human Services, added an item to the HMIS to identify this population at intake. Educational materials to explain this change and information regarding FASD as well as some of the challenges concerning assessment and diagnosis were provided to all agencies in the Calgary System of Care.

FASD and the Child Welfare System

The child welfare system plays a crucial role in responding to FASD, as this system often becomes involved with children and families where active substance abuse is a serious problem. Goodman et al. (2013) identified that children with FASD are far more likely to require out-of-home placement (70 per cent) than when FASD is not a concern (27 per cent). In the Alberta child intervention system, the identification of FASD as a disabling condition is broadly recognized as an indicator that children and families require support (Badry, 2009). Fuchs, Burnside, Reinink, and Marchenski (2010) found that youth with FASD leaving care continued to have difficulties such as engaging in risky behaviours (e.g., inappropriate sexual behaviours, early pregnancy, criminal activities, and not attending/finishing school). Further, Fuchs et al. found that, in Manitoba's provincial child welfare system, children with an FASD diagnosis who were in permanent care (89 per cent) came into care younger (2.5 years) than children with no disability (3.6 years) or other disabilities (4.3 years) and become permanent wards at approximately four years of age.

FASD and Mental Health

Individuals with FASD have a higher risk of developing mental health issues; some research suggests that as many as 94 per cent of affected individuals with an FASD diagnosis had at least one mental health diagnosis in adulthood (Jonsson, Dennett, & Littlejohn, 2009). As such, individuals with FASD need mental health support that is responsive to their diagnoses and adapts supports and intervention to individual needs, with efforts to provide integrated care when possible. Due to the neuropsychological problems associated with FASD, there are genuine concerns about suicide among this population (Huggins, Grant, O'Malley, & Streissguth, 2008). Huggins et al.'s (2008) study of eleven young adults with FASD aged eighteen to thirty found that general risk factors for suicide align closely with many of the challenges for individuals with FASD, including mental health problems, impulsivity, historical trauma, abuse, and environmental factors such as loss of social relationships and social isolation. The researchers indicate that service providers who are trained in FASD and understand the disability recognize the need for consistent, structured support in creating and maintaining stability.

Gelb and Rutman (2011) noted the "interplay between the effects of FASD and other risk factors that leads to high risk behaviors or situations" (p. 18), suggesting that the primary effects of FASD contribute to high-risk behaviours. This relationship, for many, is coupled with the psychosocial impacts of limited social contacts and poor role models, often leading to a sense of hopelessness and low self-esteem and a normalization of abuse and violence (Gelb & Rutman, 2011). In addition, individuals with FASD face multiple challenges, and their vulnerabilities are linked to life experience that includes poor parental role modelling, disturbed development of trust and identity, avoidant coping behaviour, and dysfunctional relationships in adolescence and adulthood (Sullivan, 2007). The primary neurocognitive challenges of FASD—such as poor impulse control, poor judgment, poor receptive language, and poor understanding of cause and effect—can lead to risk factors that contribute to experiences of poverty and homelessness that in turn increase risk of abuse and exploitation. Recognizing that many of these issues are a concern for individuals with child welfare involvement offers some insight into the reasons why individuals with FASD have vulnerabilities to homelessness as adults.

Further, individuals with mental health disorders and cognitive disabilities tend to be overrepresented in the criminal justice system as both offenders and victims (Hayes, Shackell, Mottram, & Lancaster, 2007; Herrington, 2009). Due to their disability, adults with FASD often have a diminished capacity to foresee consequences, make informed choices, and learn from their mistakes (IHE, 2013), all of which contributes to their involvement with the justice system. Rudin's (2012) study of 253 individuals with FASD found that 60 per cent reported a history of being charged, convicted, or in conflict with the law.

Risk factors for homelessness identified by the CHF (2008) include "poverty, physical disability or mental illness or addiction, difficult childhood history like fetal alcohol syndrome [FASD] and abuse, time in foster care, family conflict, lack of supportive relationships, [and] lack of education" (p. 5). Also, triggers for homelessness among this population include "financial crisis, moving for economic or social opportunity, health crisis, family conflict, landlord/roommate conflict, unchecked addiction and mental illness, [and] crime (either as victim or perpetrator)" (CHF, 2008, p. 5). These risk factors and triggers for homelessness are deeply intertwined with those experienced by individuals with FASD.

Methods

This mixed-methods study involved three stages. First, a comprehensive narrative literature review was conducted of FASD and promising practices for delivering FASD-informed care to people experiencing homelessness, the results of which were presented in the literature review section.

Second, an analysis of the HMIS data for the Calgary Homeless-Serving System of Care was completed. The HMIS, created by the CHF (2017a), collects information from clients accessing programs or services. This data collection is mandatory for all programs operating under the umbrella of the CHF. Third, in-depth qualitative, exploratory interviews (Patton, 2002) were conducted with sixteen individuals who had either suspected or diagnosed FASD and who self-identified as having experienced homelessness. Participants were recruited through several agencies engaged with service provision in the homeless-serving sector and were provided with a twenty-dollar gift card at the conclusion of the interview. In addition to providing basic demographic information, the Life History Screen (LHS)—a structured screening instrument consisting of twenty-seven items that "describe life history outcomes observed in individuals who suffer from an FASD" (Grant et al., 2013, p. 44)—was administered. The LHS includes items related to "childhood history, maternal drinking, education, substance use, employment and psychiatric symptomatology" (Grant et al., 2013, p. 37). In the present study, the LHS was used after consultation with and approval from the lead developer, to elicit each individual's history in relation to known indicators of FASD diagnosis. Finally, in-depth, qualitative exploratory interviews were conducted with key informants (*N*=19), including frontline staff, policy-makers, and subject experts within the housing and FASD sectors. Qualitative interviews were audio-recorded and transcribed verbatim.

The study received approval from the institutional research ethics board at the University of Calgary, and all participants provided written informed consent.

Findings

The findings report on two distinct activities related to the research. We discuss, first, the quantitative analysis of data related to the HMIS through the Calgary Homeless Foundation and, second, the qualitative interviews with sixteen individuals who self-selected into the study through our recruitment of participants. A third activity undertaken was qualitative interviews with key informants, both frontline staff and policy-makers working within the housing and FASD sectors, whose observations are also integrated into our findings.

Homeless Management Information System

We retrieved intake data from the HMIS database for forty-six supportive housing programs funded through the CHF from April 1, 2012, to March 31, 2015. Most information in the HMIS is self-reported by clients accessing supportive housing programs in Calgary: one item was used to identify the number of individuals with suspected or diagnosed FASD. The item to assess FASD ("Do you have FASD?") had five response categories: yes, diagnosed; yes, suspected/undiagnosed; no; don't know; or declined to answer. Of the 2,437 records at initial intake, 3 per cent indicated suspected FASD, and 1 per cent indicated diagnosed FASD; 9 per cent did not know their FASD status, and 87 per cent responded negatively. More males reported suspected (3.4 per cent) (*n*=46) or diagnosed (1.7 per cent) (*n*=23) FASD than females, whose rates were 2.65 per cent (*n*=28) and 1.5 per cent (*n*=16) for suspected or diagnosed FASD, respectively. Females had higher rates of unknown FASD status (10.2 per cent) (*n*=109) than males (7.5 per cent) (*n*=103). Of the 113 individuals with diagnosed or suspected FASD, 33 per cent were Caucasian and 59 per cent Indigenous. Table 1 offers the age distribution of individuals in the HMIS database; it is clear that the majority of individuals fall in the age range of thirty-six to fifty. In Table 2, it is clear that individuals with an FASD diagnosis leave supportive housing approximately three months sooner than individuals without an FASD diagnosis.

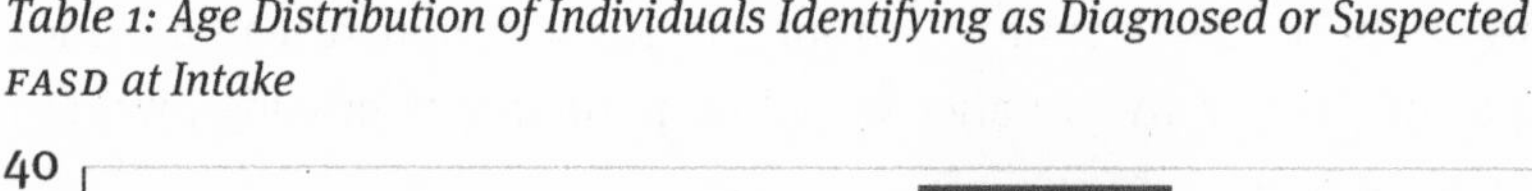

Table 1: Age Distribution of Individuals Identifying as Diagnosed or Suspected FASD at Intake

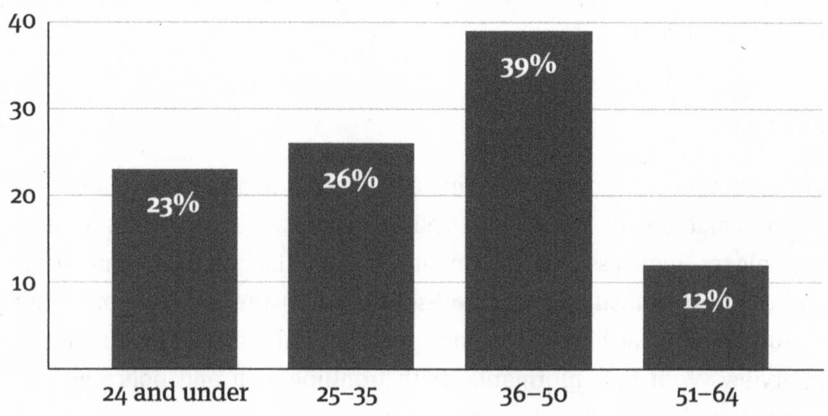

Source: HMIS database

Table 2: Length of Stay in Supportive Housing Program

	Diagnosed FASD	Suspected FASD	No FASD diagnosis
Number of days (intake to exit)	205	295	292

Source: HMIS database

Qualitative Interviews: Participants and Key Informants

Sixteen individuals who self-reported as diagnosed (*n*=12) or suspected (*n*=4) FASD completed the qualitative interviews. The sample consisted of nine men and seven women, and the average age was forty years. In terms of education, two individuals had completed only junior high education, four had reached high school but did not complete it, five had grade 12 or a General Equivalency Diploma (GED), and five indicated having some post-secondary education. Almost all of the participants reported addiction issues (94 per cent); 63 per cent reported mental health issues, and 50 per cent indicated having a physical disability. Approximately 68 per cent reported previous involvement in the criminal justice system, and half of the participants reported past child welfare involvement. The length of homelessness among participants ranged from one to twenty-four years, with a median of thirteen years. Thirteen of the participants were housed at the time of the interviews; this was most often through housing supports provided to those with previous involvements in the justice system. Eleven individuals in the study were parents, three of whom were accessing various parenting supports. The service providers involved in the study came from a variety of agencies engaged in adult justice, women's health, and community-based agencies in the homeless-serving sector.

The thematic analysis produced the following themes: challenges of understanding FASD as a disability (by service providers); housing system challenges faced by adults with FASD; impact of FASD diagnosis; systems involvement of homeless individuals with FASD; addictions and mental health; vulnerability of homeless women with FASD; supports for homeless adults with FASD; and hope, resilience, and success. Each of the themes is described more fully in the following section with illustrative quotes from the transcripts of service providers and participants.

Challenges of Understanding FASD as a Disability

Individuals with FASD face many challenges due to their disability. FASD is often viewed as an "invisible disability," and, as such, service providers and other natural supports may not understand that a person has neurological impairment. This impacts the service providers' ability to provide effective services for the individual and could lead to frustration and apathy, as one service provider explains:

> *If you are working with a client who has FASD and you don't understand where the trouble is coming from, what possibly could be happening here, then your work will be for naught almost for sure. It just doesn't make sense for us to keep providing a service that doesn't meet their needs.*

Service providers and other helping professionals may not realize the extent to which an individual with FASD has a disability because the individual appears and often claims to understand the information provided. In addition, individuals with FASD may not think to tell service providers about their diagnosis or needs, which may further complicate providing or even being offered support, as one service provider illustrates:

> *When she's seeing a doctor she's never seen before, she doesn't think to tell them about her FASD. So they give her instructions. You would never know when you're talking to her that she does not comprehend you. But they think that she's getting their instructions, but she doesn't come back.*

One service provider notes that behaviour is often misinterpreted by other service providers:

> *Really often the consequences of having an FASD and the kind of behaviour that it creates [are] misunderstood. It's seen as a lack of motivation—that people are lazy or bad.*

Ultimately, the failure by service providers to understand and recognize that the negative behaviours are a result of a disability can lead to an individual with FASD losing services or housing. The consequences are even direr for some individuals, as one service provider indicated:

> *[Parole] conditions don't really matter in the moment. It is frustrating because they're kind of being punished for something they can't control.*

Key informants also identified a lack of recognition of the complexity of FASD within the criminal justice system, within the healthcare system, within shelters and housing programs, and within natural supports. Service providers indicated that it was difficult to recognize FASD, especially if there were limited interactions with the individual (e.g., interactions with lawyers). Some service providers were unsure of how to recognize individuals with FASD if they did not have a diagnosis, and others did not recognize the impact of the disability on the individual's behaviour or circumstances. One service provider suggested that FASD-informed practice "means we have to believe that there is a disability. We're finding that a lot of people don't [believe the person has a disability]."

Housing System Challenges Faced by Adults with FASD

Participants identified several systems-level barriers to becoming housed, including access to housing, limited resources, long waiting times, and a lack of informed practice and knowledge of FASD among housing providers. Individuals with FASD found the process to acquire supportive housing very strenuous and complicated. They reported having to access multiple housing sources before they could be housed. In addition, participants noted that they were often not recognized as needing additional support in obtaining and maintaining housing.

The Service Prioritization Decision Assessment Tool (SPDAT), a tool used in Calgary to prioritize and triage clients into supportive housing programs, "helps determine the level of service a client requires and type of program needed to end their homelessness" (CHF, 2017b, para. 5). Completing the SPDAT was noted as problematic by service providers and clients, and service providers noted that individuals did not always know about their diagnosis and thus scored lower on the SPDAT and were then not prioritized for housing programs offered through the homeless-serving sector. Or, conversely, the individual was placed into a supportive housing program that did not match the intensity of supports required.

Service providers and adults living with FASD identified a lack of informed practice within systems. Participants indicated that they were often not well understood by the professionals that they had to work with, and their needs were not always met. As one participant explained,

> *[The worker] just says, "Go get a job."...I said, "Look lady, it's the first time in years I've had a home. I just got out of jail, I don't really have any resume that's relevant and recent, and I'm facing some health issues, and I'm in recovery right now from my drug addictions."...She said, "Well, you had a job last year." I said, "Yeah, I did. I was doing really well last year, but I still didn't have a home, and I wasn't making enough to get a home. It killed me, and I ended up using again."*

In particular, gaps exist in service provision to support young people with FASD transitioning to adulthood. In recognition of the importance of this stage for preparing the individual for more independence, one service provider commented,

> *There is a gap between the ages of fourteen and nineteen, where services are starting to dwindle for these individuals. Families are starting to get exhausted. There's often breakdown....[T]hey want to be adults, but their mind just doesn't allow for that, so there's a real dichotomy with making decisions and problem solving, and all kinds of issues flare up.*

Service providers noted the links between client behaviours and housing, recounting examples of their clients being blamed for crimes for which they were not responsible. The consequences for maintaining housing were noted by service providers:

> *[Letting others stay in their housing] resulted in losing their [financial support] money to "friends" and [in] losing their places because they let others stay there that caused noise or damages.*

When other family members or friends come into their place and create trouble, it is that person's responsibility to deal with that, and they can't. So they are always losing their place.

Systems Involvement of Homeless Individuals with FASD

The majority of participants in this study had experienced substantial involvement with the criminal justice system, the health system, and/or the child welfare system. Involvement with the criminal justice system, in particular, was seen as a barrier to sustainable housing. Unknown release dates, incarceration, and lack of supports in the criminal justice system, as service providers described, can lead the individuals back into homelessness and can separate them from supports.

Many of the study participants had childhood histories of involvement with the child welfare system. For one participant, his involvement in foster care and frequent placements as a child led to feelings of rejection:

Having gone from home to home and for some reason never really belonging anywhere...[y]ou end up asking a question within your soul, "Why are they not keeping me, why am I not staying here, why am I not welcome here anymore?"

Indigenous participants also shared how being removed from their biological families and being placed in the foster care system resulted in a loss of culture and identity. As one participant expressed, "It creates a whole identity crisis, with no roots or family or people to identify with culturally." Experiencing multiple placements and trauma in the child welfare system directly impacted participants' housing stability. One participant described "running away and living on the streets. I guess it was my choice, but it wasn't my choice. Because I didn't know where else to go."

The way in which individuals with FASD interacted with the healthcare system, although associated with their disability, resulted in a significant cost to the healthcare system. Service providers highlighted this link:

It makes sense—she's immediate. "This is what I feel right now, so I'm going to go to the hospital and ask for that help." So just in being able to understand this [immediate need] and make a different plan. The levels of resources we spend are [high], especially for

FASD. Our highest system users, we just figured out that they may have FASD and have other cognitive issues.

Experiences with Addictions and Mental Health

The majority of adult participants with FASD indicated that they had previous or current issues with substance use. A key informant with diagnosed FASD described his experience with alcohol addiction from an early age:

> *My brother got me drunk when I was eight years old, and I drank eight beers. That was the significance of the whole thing. I was eight years old and drank eight beers, [and then] when I was twelve years old I drank twelve beers.*

Addictions were described by both participants and service providers as very difficult to overcome. One service provider indicated that, to be successful in housing, individuals with FASD had to have dealt with their addictions. In the intersection between addictions treatment and housing, it was seen as beneficial for the clients to have their space in the housing program held for them during the residential treatment program. In this way, even if they were not successful in completing the addictions treatment program, they still had a place to live and did not need to start over and risk returning to homelessness. One service provider noted the dire implications of losing housing as a consequence of the cycle of addiction:

> *[Some] agencies...they'll hold their place while they're in the addiction [treatment program], and then they come back to their place, their clothing. If they slip and use, they're right back into addiction, but their place is held for them. Other places will just say "You're out of here," and all of their belongings get thrown out. It's like you have no value. You start all over again.*

Service providers noted that traditional models for addictions treatment were not FASD-informed, and therefore "individuals with FASD do not thrive" in these programs. There were, however, limited alternative options for support. Service providers noted that barriers included the auditory nature of many programs (i.e., no workbook that can be used for reminders or refreshers), the autonomy needed to continue in the program, strict rules about appointments, and the group work.

Vulnerability for Homeless Women with FASD

The issue of gender and the vulnerabilities of women who are homeless and living with FASD were highlighted by study participants. A number of women in the study shared experiences of various forms of victimization.

> *[Men] sexually abused me....I'm lucky I just made it through everything. I wish things would have been different.*

> *Then I ended up in prostitution...made money to survive basically.*

> *I was in a super abusive relationship...and I got away, and I drank.*

Women in the study were also impacted by cross-generational FASD, where their own children or grandchildren were affected by FASD. They expressed concern about the risk of victimization for their own children, as one woman elaborated:

> *[I want to live] somewhere constant, not [moving around all the time] and stressing [my son] out. That's the thing I'm most worried about now, because of his diagnosis. That he can fall into the same traps that I did....I don't want that to happen.*

Recommended Housing Supports for Adults with FASD

Service providers identified a number of housing supports for adults with FASD.

Flexibility in rules

> *They were taking him from a housing program he had been at for two years, and the maximum you could stay at that place is two years, so...he needs to go to independent housing now. But nobody knew that he had an FASD assessment....You're setting him up [for failure]...so let's put the [assessment recommendations] in place and transition him in a way that's going to be helpful.* (Service provider)

Financial management (trusteeship)

> *They get them on [income supports], and we just create $1,600 a month of vulnerability, not service....If you manage their money, you take away half of their problems because you remove that vulnerability.* (Service provider)

Harm reduction

> *We're going to have to get used to a harm reduction conversation.... If we can help agencies have conversations with the FASD population based upon what's doable, I'm...probably going to also have an opportunity to have conversations with you about [other positive changes].* (Service provider)

Guest management

> *A lot of folks [with FASD] have trouble saying no to anybody...so they let anybody in....The biggest thing that works is [at the front] they can say "No, that person is not allowed in this building, so if you want to be with them you have to go out of the building." So...it keeps their housing a safe place to be.* (Service provider)

Life skills intervention

> *There's always [the need] to assess the person's ability to live independently and then putting different interventions in place.* (Service provider)

Social networks (community and natural supports)

> *We can't be the only person in the circle and the support system. Even if it's just somebody taking them for coffee who is a family member or friend, [it] will give them something to do in that time when they have nothing to do.* (Service provider)

Built-in supports

> *People are very different, and some folks maybe need day-to-day support in every area.* (Service provider)

Cultural and spiritual supports

> *I had these struggles going on, and I was also discovering my culture. I had something bigger than me....I didn't care where it was—I could pray anywhere. Whereas before I could do drugs or drink anywhere, now I can pray anywhere.*
>
> *I started going to these sweats, and I started feeling better and better about being in there....I just found the ability to take stuff and process it in the way that works for me.* (Participant)

Hope, Resilience, and Success

Despite the significant traumas and chaos that many of the adult informants with FASD had experienced, they expressed that they remained hopeful for their future and sought stability in their lives, for their families, and in their housing. As one participant elucidated,

> *Today I'm happy. I can say, "I have a good life. I've been through this, and I've also helped other people."*

Another participant who was homeless at the time of the interview indicated that he was "just focused on surviving." He explained that he had faced several setbacks to getting his own place and found the process frustrating and difficult, but he was still working toward this goal:

> *I'm just happy. I'm content just to do what I gotta do to survive each day right now....I got my ladder, I'm climbing up, and the rung breaks, and I fall back to the bottom. I get another ladder, I start climbing up again, again it breaks, and I fall back to the bottom again. So I'm trying to find a nice sturdy ladder I can climb out of right now.*

The voices and viewpoints of participants and service providers offer rich insight into the lived experiences of individuals with FASD in the homeless-serving sector. In summary, the needs of individuals with FASD are often served within the child welfare system, but supports either drop off or end in young adulthood, and housing becomes a concern. Given the assertion by Fuchs et al. (2010) that children with FASD become permanent wards at about four years of age, and the need for lifelong care being established early in the child's life, it is necessary to consider the implications over the lifespan. Based on our research, it is clear that FASD is not well understood as a disability and that workers in the homeless-serving sector do not know what types of supports are required to assist the individual to navigate the housing system and all its requirements. We know individuals with FASD have challenges with addictions and mental health, and gender-based violence is a deep concern for women. In our interviews with service providers, we identified the following housing supports: flexibility in rules, financial management, harm reduction approaches, support with relationships to reduce vulnerabilities, and life skills interventions. Cultural and spiritual supports were strongly identified by service providers for Indigenous clients, and daily support is required on an ongoing basis for individuals with FASD in the homeless-serving sector.

Discussion

Individuals who live with FASD have often spent much of their lives disenfranchised from family, and this continues into adulthood through their experiences with homelessness. While many children raised in foster care have benefited from supportive interventions in child welfare care, the reality is that these supports are less available in adulthood (Fuchs et al., 2010). The need to address FASD effectively means that, when FASD is identified in childhood, planning and interventions must take into account a lifespan perspective. The question to consider is how to prepare youth with FASD for adulthood in light of the high level of support and supervision required while they were in care. Systems that serve children, youth, and adults need to tackle this question to support persons with FASD in transitioning to adulthood. The hope is that this transition will include safe, stable, supportive, and secure housing.

Findings of this study support the critical role that knowledge about FASD plays when assessing individuals on various intake forms, including the SPDAT, as earlier noted. Because FASD can affect language comprehension and cause verbalization difficulties, it is also possible that individuals do not understand all of the questions being asked, and thus the assessment does not always reflect the level of vulnerability.

Study findings reinforce concerns in the literature that individuals with an unrecognized diagnosis of FASD are often perceived and judged as non-compliant when accessing supportive services, which jeopardize the limited supports they receive.

As demonstrated in this study, adults with FASD have a number of serious, complex, and overlapping issues, and there is a strong connection between (a) substance use, (b) exposure to violence, and (c) gender. For example, in a study by Brownstone (2005) of fourteen women with FASD in Saskatchewan, all had histories of physical abuse and substance abuse. Gelb and Rutman (2011) highlight the concern that women with FASD often have a history of multiple traumas, frequent experiences of domestic violence, and high rates of depression and stress, coupled with limited resources and challenges in linking behaviour with risk; these factors influence the trajectory of substance-use problems. This multiplicity of risk creates a highly vulnerable population.

Key recommendations identified in this research focus on increased awareness of FASD in relation to housing insecurity, specifically among those tasked with serving this population. This requires specific training and education on FASD among the sector. Further, FASD-specific housing supports, as well as a complex case management approach including assertive outreach strategies, are needed to promote housing access and stability. It is important to understand the linkage between a childhood history of child welfare involvement and homelessness in adulthood (Fuchs et al., 2010; Popova et al., 2011). The inclusion of the Life History Screen in this research has been valuable, and as such it may be an important tool for FASD screening in the homeless-serving sector.

Also, the literature is clear that early screening for FASD is effective in providing timely and effective supports to interrupt the documented trajectories for youth in care with undiagnosed FASD as they negotiate the transition to adulthood. Thus, addressing FASD among youth in care is critical. Further, the limited understanding of FASD as a disability within adult service systems needs to be addressed using a lifespan approach. In addition to the specific needs for awareness and training noted previously, social action and advocacy approaches are needed to challenge systems to respond to the unique and complex needs of adults with FASD. In moving forward, a recalibration and repositioning of services should foreground FASD as a significant public health problem founded on the notion that supporting individuals with this disability is also a fundamental aspect of prevention.

Hope Terrace opened in Edmonton in 2016 and is owned and operated by Homeward Trust, and the Bissell Centre provides supported housing services and supervision to individuals with FASD in a single complex of apartments (Baxter & Badry, 2017). The program, the first of its kind in Canada, offers a place and space for individuals with FASD who require 24/7 support. Although many challenges have been documented, this program has increased housing stability and community building for individuals who are otherwise vulnerable and isolated. Hope Terrace can inspire the development of other housing projects for adults with FASD who require housing support.

This exploratory research highlighted the voices of participants and service providers. While they offer some hope in terms of moving forward to provide the necessary supports and services for this vulnerable population, they also remind us we have a long way to go. An approach grounded in the lived experience of individuals with FASD must adopt a lifespan approach to ensure that evidence-informed, gender-based, and culturally sensitive services are provided across a continuum from childhood to adulthood. It is our hope that these supports will alleviate some of the challenges that individuals with FASD face. The ultimate goal is for individuals with FASD, as for all Canadians, to find themselves with a place to call home.

Discussion Questions

1. Why is it important to assess individuals for FASD in the child welfare and homeless-serving sector?
2. What are some of the practices you can employ as a social worker or human service professional to best understand individuals with FASD who experience homelessness?
3. What factors contribute to individuals with FASD leaving housing sooner than those without FASD?
4. What can you do to prevent homelessness for individuals with FASD?
5. Why is qualitative research important with vulnerable populations?

References

Alberta. (2008). *FASD 10-year strategic plan*. Retrieved from http://fasd.alberta.ca/documents/FASD-10-year-plan.pdf

Alberta. (2017). *Child intervention information and statistics summary: 2017/18 first quarter (June) update*. Retrieved from http://www.humanservices.alberta.ca/documents/child-intervention-info-stats-summary-2017-18-q1.pdf

Badry, D. (2009) Fetal alcohol spectrum disorder standards: Supporting children in the care of Children's Services. *First Peoples Child & Family Review, 4*(1), 47–56.

Badry, D. (2013). *The FASD (fetal alcohol spectrum disorder) Community of Practice (CoP) in Alberta Human Services: Leading from Within initiative*. Edmonton, AB: Alberta Centre for Child, Family & Community Research. Retrieved from http://fasd.alberta.ca/documents/FinalReportFASDCoPLFW 2012-2013.pdf

Badry, D., & Bradshaw, C. (2011). *Inventory of literature on the assessment and diagnosis of FASD among adults: A national and international systematic review*. Ottawa, ON: Public Health Agency of Canada. Retrieved from http://www.phac-aspc.gc.ca/hp-ps/dca-dea/prog-ini/fasd-etcaf/publications/ad-ed/pdf/fasd-etcaf-eng.pdf

Badry, D., Walsh, C., Bell, M., & Ramage, K. (2015). *Promising practices in delivering housing and support interventions to chronically and episodically homeless with FASD* (Research report). Edmonton, AB: Alberta Centre for Child, Family & Community Research.

Baxter, A., & Badry, D. (2017, October 26). Housing initiatives for individuals with FASD. Paper presented at the National Conference on FASD: Climbing with Courage and Exploring with Hope, Calgary, AB.

Brownstone, L. (2005). *Feasibility study into housing for people with FASD*. Regina, SK: Brownstone Consulting.

Burns, C. (2009). *Report on supportive housing opportunities for adults with FASD*. Cold Lake, AB: Lakeland Centre for FASD. Retrieved from https://lcfasd.com/wp-content/uploads/2017/07/Report-on-Supportive-Housing-Opportunities-for-adults-with-FASD.pdf

CHF (Calgary Homeless Foundation). (2008). *Calgary's 10 year plan to end homelessness 2008–2018*. Retrieved from http://homelesshub.ca/resource/calgary%E2%80%99s-10-year-plan-end-homelessness-2008-2018

CHF (Calgary Homeless Foundation). (2016, November 29). Homelessness count drops. Calgary still epicentre in province (Blog post). Retrieved from http://calgaryhomeless.com/blog/homelessness-count-drops-calgary-still-epicentre-province/

CHF (Calgary Homeless Foundation). (2017a). *Calgary Homeless Management Information System: Data collection policy, version 2.0*. Retrieved from http://calgaryhomeless.com/content/uploads/HMIS-Data-Collection-Policy-April-1-2017.pdf

CHF (Calgary Homeless Foundation). (2017b). *Coordinated access and assessment*. Retrieved from http://calgaryhomeless.com/ending-homelessness/our-role/coordinated-access-assessment/

Fuchs, D., Burnside, L., Reinink, A., & Marchenski, S. (2010, November). *Bound by the clock: The voices of Manitoba youth with FASD leaving care*. Report prepared for the Public Health Agency of Canada. Retrieved from http://cwrp.ca/sites/default/files/publications/en/MB-Youth_with_FASD_Leaving_Care.pdf

Gaetz, S. (2010). The struggle to end homelessness in Canada: How we created it and how we can stop it. *Open Health Services and Policy Journal, 3*, 21–26.

Gelb, K., & Rutman, D. (2011). *Substance using women with FASD and FASD prevention: A literature review on promising approaches in substance use treatment and care for women with FASD*. Victoria, BC: Research Initiatives for Social Change Unit, University of Victoria. Retrieved from http://www.uvic.ca/hsd/socialwork/assets/docs/research/Substance%20Using%20Women%20with%20FASD-LitReview-web.pdf

Goodman, D., MacLaurin, B., Trocmé, N., Fallon, B., Sinha, V., Enns, R., et al. (2013). Characteristics of investigations with noted child functioning concern of FAS/FAE in Alberta in 2008. Calgary: University of Calgary.

Grant, T. M., Novick Brown, N., Graham, J. C., Whitney, N., Dubovsky, D., & Nelson, L. A. (2013). Screening in treatment programs for fetal alcohol spectrum disorders that could affect therapeutic progress. *International Journal of Alcohol and Drug Research, 2*(3), 37–49. doi:10.7895/ijadr.v2i3.116

Hayes, S., Shackell, P., Mottram, P., & Lancaster, R. (2007). The prevalence of intellectual disability in a major UK prison. *British Journal of Learning Disabilities, 35*(3), 162–167.

Herrington, V. (2009). Assessing the prevalence of intellectual disability among young male prisoners. *Journal of Intellectual Disability Research, 53*(5), 397–410.

Huggins, J. E., Grant, T., O'Malley, K., & Streissguth, A. (2008). Suicide attempts among adults with fetal alcohol spectrum disorders: Clinical considerations. *Mental Health Aspects of Developmental Disabilities, 11*(2), 33–42.

IHE (Institute of Health Economics). (2013). *Consensus statement on legal issues of fetal alcohol spectrum disorder (FASD)*. Retrieved from https://www.ihe.ca/advanced-search/consensus-statement-on-legal-issues-of-fetal-alcohol-spectrum-disorder-fasd

Jonsson, E., Dennett, L., & Littlejohn, G. (Eds.). (2009). *Fetal alcohol spectrum disorder (FASD): Across the lifespan: Proceedings from an IHE Consensus Development Conference 2009*. Edmonton, AB: Institute of Health Economics.

Kodituwakku, P. W. (2009). Neurocognitive profile in children with fetal alcohol spectrum disorders. *Developmental Disabilities Research Reviews, 15*(3), 218–224. doi:10.1002/ddrr.73

Patton, M. Q. (2002). *Qualitative evaluation and research methods*. Thousand Oaks, CA: Sage.

Popova, S., Lange, S., Bekmuradov, D., Mihic, A., & Rehm, J. (2011). Fetal alcohol spectrum disorder prevalence estimates in correctional systems: A systematic literature review. *Canadian Journal of Public Health, 102*(5), 336–340.

Popova, S., Lange, S., Burd, L., & Rehm, J. (2014). Canadian children and youth in care: The cost of fetal alcohol spectrum disorder. *Child Youth Care Forum, 43*(1), 83–96. doi:10.1007/s10566-013-9226-x

Public Health Agency of Canada. (n.d.). Fetal alcohol spectrum disorder in Canada–New project funding: Backgrounder. Retrieved from https://www.canada.ca/en/public-health/news/2017/05/fetal_alcohol_spectrumdisorderincanadanewprojectfunding1.html

Rudin, J. (2012). Looking backward, looking forward: The Supreme Court of Canada's decision in R. v. Ipeelee. *Supreme Court Law Review, 57*. Retrieved from http://digitalcommons.osgoode.yorku.ca/sclr/vol57/iss1/17/

Streissguth, A. P., Barr, H. M., Kogan, J., & Bookstein, F. L. (1996). *Understanding the occurrence of secondary disabilities in clients with fetal alcohol syndrome (FAS) and fetal alcohol effects (FAE): Final report*. Seattle, WA: University of Washington School of Medicine.

Sullivan, A. K. (2007). Fetal alcohol spectrum disorders (FASD) in the adult: Vulnerability, disability, or diagnosis–a psychodynamic perspective. In K. D. O'Malley (Ed.), *ADHD and Fetal alcohol spectrum disorders (FASD)* (pp. 237–268). New York, NY: Nova Science.

PART IV

Education

CHAPTER 11

The Development of a Training Video: Demonstrating Essential Skills for Child Welfare Practice

Cathy Rocke and Judy Hughes

Reconciliation in Child Welfare: Essential Skills for Developing Relationships with Parents

The Canadian child welfare system serves an essential function: to ensure that children are safe in their homes. This system is also highly controversial for its historical and continued role in the removal of Indigenous children from their families and communities (Blackstock, 2009; Blackstock, Brown, & Bennett, 2007; Kline, 1992). Because of the current disproportionately high numbers of Indigenous families involved with the Canadian child welfare system and Indigenous children placed into foster care (Sinha, Trocmé, Fallon, & MacLaurin, 2013; Trocmé, Knoke, & Blackstock, 2004), the system is an important site at which to begin to address reconciliation. The first five recommendations in the Truth and Reconciliation Commission's report focus on child welfare and are designed to reduce the number of Indigenous children in care (TRC, 2015). Models of reconciliation

Suggested Citation: Rocke, C., & Hughes, J. (2018). The development of a training video: Demonstrating essential skills for child welfare practice. In D. Badry, H. Montgomery, D. Kikulwe, M. Bennett, & D. Fuchs, (Eds.), *Imagining child welfare in the spirit of reconciliation* (pp. 231–248). Regina, SK: University of Regina Press.

of the system often focus on broader-level reforms, including self-determination for Indigenous nations, the restoration of language and culture, and structural interventions to improve living conditions for Indigenous families (Blackstock, Brown, & Bennett, 2007). Although it is necessary for individual social workers, agencies, and professional organizations to support and advocate for efforts aimed at reconciliation, less guidance is provided to social workers when intervening directly with Indigenous families and communities at the individual level. Particularly difficult for child welfare workers is dealing with the resistance that many parents exhibit when challenged about their parenting and the subsequent conflict that can ensue between the worker and parent(s). For Indigenous parents, the resistance and conflict are often rooted in historical trauma (Evans-Campbell, 2008) that arises from the impact of the residential school system, the Sixties Scoop, and generational involvement with the child welfare system (TRC, 2015).

In this chapter, we describe the development of a set of teaching resources—three demonstration videos and an accompanying student workbook and instructor handbook—that was designed specifically to help social work students build effective relationships with parents and to better understand and respond to the power and conflict that are inherent in relationships between parents and child welfare workers. The video and education resources were developed as a joint project between Indigenous and non-Indigenous practitioners and academics. The teaching resource has been designed so that instructors can use the videos in their entirety to explore the practices demonstrated by the child welfare workers in each section. We have also isolated separate sections of the videos that could be used to focus classroom discussion on important issues in child welfare practice, in five special topic areas: confidentiality and case documentation, development of trust within a mandated setting, domestic violence in child welfare settings, fathers' and mothers' rights, and best interests of the child. The student workbook contains discussions of the theoretical and research literature that forms the background material for each of the sections in the videos along with discussion questions for students to use both before and after viewing each video. In the instructor manual, we have included many of the insights and explanations that were provided by the experienced child welfare workers about their use of the skills and practices demonstrated in the video and suggested classroom exercises that can be used to stimulate discussion with students. Preliminary research on the efficacy of the teaching research is currently being completed with upper-level undergraduate students and workers within an Indigenous child welfare agency.

Disproportionate Representation of Indigenous Children in Canadian Child Welfare Systems

In what would become known as the Sixties Scoop, high numbers of Indigenous children were removed from their families and communities by provincial child welfare systems, leading to losses in identity, language, cultural traditions, and intergenerational family and community relationships (Blackstock, 2009; Blackstock et al., 2007; Kline, 1992). Because of this history, Indigenous children are disproportionally overrepresented in the care of Canadian child welfare systems. In 2003, Indigenous children represented 5 per cent of the child population but 18 per cent of maltreatment investigations and 17 per cent of substantiated investigations (Sinha et al., 2013). Indigenous children are also more likely than non-Indigenous children to be placed into out-of-home care (Trocmé et al., 2004). These rates are highest in the Prairie provinces: for example, in Alberta, 9 per cent of the child population is Indigenous, compared to 69 per cent of children in care; in Saskatchewan, 25 per cent of the child population is Indigenous, compared to 65 per cent in care; and in Manitoba, 23 per cent of the child population is Indigenous, compared to 87 per cent in care (ACCWG, 2015).

Reforming the child welfare system and, in particular, reducing the numbers of Indigenous children are crucial. Research conducted in Manitoba reveals that children and youth placed in foster care—many of whom are Indigenous—do not have long-term positive outcomes; these youths are less likely to finish high school, resulting in a greater likelihood of teen birth and a greater likelihood of being in receipt of income assistance as adults (Brownell et al., 2010). Such outcomes suggest that without address the cycle of continued risk and disadvantage will continue into the next generation. The difficulty for intervention at the individual level is that many of the issues impacting parents' ability to adequately care for their children are rooted in structural or historical issues. For example, most parents who come to the attention of child welfare authorities are living in poverty (Fallon et al., 2013; Holland, 2011), and in Canada most Indigenous families are referred to child welfare due to neglect (Blackstock, Trocmé, & Bennett, 2004; Trocmé et al., 2004). Both factors—poverty and neglect—are also strongly linked to inadequate and unsafe housing, greater dependence on social assistance, higher numbers of younger parents, more parents who were maltreated as children, and higher rates of alcohol and drug use, as well as the lack of prevention services in the remote and reserve communities where many Indigenous peoples are living (Lavergne, Dufour, Trocmé, & Larrivée, 2008; Sinha et al., 2013; Stokes & Schmidt, 2011; Trocmé et al., 2004). Such structural issues suggest that changes are beyond the efforts of individual child welfare workers (Sinha et al., 2013; Stokes & Schmidt, 2011).

We believe, however, that change in the child welfare system is possible at the individual level, beginning in the relationships between child welfare workers and parents. The teaching resource we developed was designed specifically to address difficulties in parent-worker relationships and the power of child welfare workers when intervening with parents. A central dilemma of the child welfare system is the mandate provided to child welfare workers to ensure children's best interests, which requires workers to investigate parents' home environments and their parenting abilities (Maiter, Palmer, & Manji, 2006; Mullins, 2011; Spratt & Callan, 2004) while also developing a working relationship where interventions to reduce the child protection risk can be negotiated. The child welfare mandate also includes the power to remove children from their parents' care—a power that is considered one of the most coercive of state powers (Bala, 2004; Dumbrill, 2006). Parents may react with anger or distress when provided with information that they have harmed or placed their children at risk (Dumbrill, 2006; Karp, 1984; Mirick, 2014). In this chapter, we describe the development of the video, student handbook, and instructor manual as well as highlight three critical skills in child welfare practice: relationship building, confrontation, and dealing with conflict.

Development of the Demonstration Best Practice Video for Child Welfare

In university classrooms, students are often provided with academic readings in the form of journal articles and book chapters. The difficulty is that these descriptions of best practices in academic papers are not easily translatable into practice (Brownson & Jones, 2009; Buckley, Tonmyr, Lewig, & Jack, 2014; Cooper, Gordon, & Rixon, 2015). To help students integrate theory into practice (Kinney & Aspinwall-Roberts, 2010; Petracchi & Collins, 2006), role-play activities are used in which students take turns "performing" the roles of clients and professional social workers (Eun-Kyoung, Blythe, & Goforth, 2009; Kinney & Aspinwall-Roberts, 2010; Vapalahti, Marttunen, & Laurinen, 2013). In some approaches, professional actors or course instructors assumed roles as clients (Kinney & Aspinwall-Roberts, 2010; Petracchi & Collins, 2006; Todd, 2012; Villadsen, Allain, Bell, & Hingley-Jones, 2012). These simulation activities are a means to place students in situations that simulate contact with "real" clients yet provide a safe environment in which to practise skills and obtain timely feedback (Todd, 2012). When evaluated, students describe these simulated activities as useful for their professional development (Kinney & Aspinwall-Roberts, 2010; Petracchi & Collins, 2006; Vapalahti et al., 2013). However, these exercises can fall short of simulating the complexity of human need and the emotion that is characteristic of interactions between social workers and their clients.

Because of the static nature of these traditional role-play approaches, we wanted to develop a teaching resource that addressed this gap. The idea for the development of the practice demonstration video came directly from a research project that included qualitative interviews with eighty-four mothers who were clients in the child welfare system and thirty-seven child welfare workers in Manitoba and British Columbia (Hughes & Chau, 2012; Hughes & Chau, 2013; Hughes, Chau, & Poff, 2011). In the analysis of this data, a gap was recognized between the child welfare workers' described practices and the accounts provided by the women—60 per cent of whom were Indigenous women—about their experiences as mothers.

To create the demonstration video, we brought together a theatre student, who was hired to portray two different mothers involved with the child welfare system (based on anonymized copies of the mothers' research interview transcripts) and two experienced child welfare workers. Katherine Hallick has over thirty years of social work experience, from frontline practice to supervisory positions. She has also provided competency-based training for child welfare workers. Marlene Moore has fifteen years of experience working in frontline practice directly with high-risk families and youth and currently works as a child welfare worker. Our initial intent was to develop a scripted video where trained actors would portray the roles of both workers and clients. Our concern with this approach was that highly scripted videos can make the performance portrayed unattainable to students (Badger & MacNeil, 2002; Gelman & Tosone, 2006). Instead, we decided to video-record the interactions as they occurred between the workers and the actor hired to portray the mothers. We wanted a portrayal that preserved the authenticity of practice situations. The workers were provided with only a short summary/intake sheet with information similar to that provided to workers in agencies in Manitoba. Recording of the video was completed in an apartment to further provide authenticity. After each of the recorded interviews was completed, a meeting was held with the workers to review and discuss the recordings, providing the workers with an opportunity to explain the reasoning behind the practices they demonstrated in the video recording. We also obtained feedback from the actor who portrayed the mothers about the impact of these practices on her.

At the end of filming, we had three digitally recorded segments. The first segment demonstrates how a child welfare worker engages and builds a relationship with a mother and then further attempts to develop a common understanding between herself and the mother about the reasons for the child welfare referral and how best to address the identified risks. The second segment also shows an initial meeting in which the worker concentrates on engaging the mother, but here the focus is on providing services and supports as the worker engages in safety planning to reunify a child and her mother. The final video segment demonstrates how a child welfare worker can inappropriately escalate an interaction with a parent and then the skills that can be used to de-escalate and diffuse emotional situations. In developing the video demonstrations, we focused on parent-worker engagement and parental resistance as important aspects of child welfare practice.

Relationship Building between Child Welfare Workers and Parents

Relationships between parents and child welfare workers are crucial. The quality of the relationship between the worker and the parents has been linked to positive outcomes in child welfare practice (Howe, 2010; Platt,

2012; Tuck, 2013; Turney, 2012). Information about children's welfare is best obtained directly from parents, and without trust in and willingness to engage with the worker, parents may withhold or hide information (Forrester, Kershaw, Moss, & Hughes, 2008; Turney, 2012). As well, engagement is vital to ensure that parents accept referrals and attend services and programs that can support them to reduce risks to their children (Buckley, Carr, & Whelan, 2011; de Boer & Coady, 2007; Howe, 2010; Platt, 2012).

Although necessary, developing trust between parents and child welfare within a mandated setting is difficult and requires that social workers develop specific engagement skills. In the first video scenario, the child welfare worker is meeting the mother for the first time after receiving a referral about the physical abuse of her daughter. The worker uses herself—her personality—to engage the mother from the moment of first meeting her. She initially uses small talk and humour to try to put the mother at ease. The worker stated afterward that the first part of the interaction was totally scripted by her because she wanted (1) the mother to have time to relax and (2) the focus to be on her as the worker and not on the mother. Her intention was to be silly and deliberate in asking for help from the mother (e.g., asking about her own earring that felt like it had come loose). The worker also said that she began the interview by asking easy questions, such as names and ages, to get the mother to relax and to begin to engage her before shifting to more difficult questions about harm. The actor role-playing the mother acknowledged that this had helped her relax and that she had thought, "Okay, this is going to be a while; I do not have to say anything." Overall, the purpose was to engage and disarm the mother, because the worker thought she was not ready for the more difficult discussion about the welfare of her daughter, and so the worker wanted this first part to be less formal.

In the first video demonstration, the worker needed to create a relationship to obtain information about the safety of the daughter. In the second video, the worker similarly began her interview by attempting to engage the mother and establish the mother's co-operation in working with her, so that the mother and daughter could be reunited. To begin, as the worker stated later, she introduced herself by explaining who she was (providing her business card) and verifying some basic information about the mother. The worker stated that she always begins interviews by asking parents how they became involved with the agency, because in her experience the parents' stories are always different from what is written in the family's file. A suggested statement to begin this process was provided by the worker: "Let's share our perspectives. I have information from the workers who were here previously that I need to talk to you about, but I really want to hear your perspective first."

Trotter (2004) identified three specific skills that workers can use in order to continue to engage parents in difficult discussions about harm or risk of continued harm to their children. First, social workers need to be honest with parents during their initial meeting regarding the purpose of the contact, the expectations placed on them as clients, the limits of confidentiality, and the issues that are negotiable and non-negotiable. Second, social workers should engage in collaborative problem solving, beginning with the client's definition of the problem, which often entails the worker listening to a range of issues that is important to the client and/or the family. Using a collaborative problem-solving approach, workers then focus on the issues that led up to the abuse or neglect, rather than just the incident(s) of abuse or neglect. Third, the worker must balance the use of confrontation with encouragement to encourage prosocial behaviour. Together, these three skills include the worker highlighting and encouraging positive client behaviour when addressing the issues without minimizing the abuse and/or neglect that has occurred.

Early in the questioning of the mother in the first video demonstration, the worker stated that she was trying to be transparent with the mother by letting her know what she has read in the file, but she also let the mother know that she would listen to her to ensure that the information is accurate. When the worker shifted to asking the mother difficult questions about bruises on her daughter, she continued to engage her. Throughout this section of the recorded interaction, the worker asked the mother to join her in understanding what happened to her daughter, rather than accusing the mother of harming the child. The worker also stated that she provided the mother with positive messages throughout the interview. Many times, throughout the interaction, the worker reassured the mother: "My plan is to return your daughter home."

Balancing relationships with parents and investigating harm to children are difficult, particularly because child welfare workers are charged with the responsibility of ensuring children's safety. Across Western countries, the "best interests of the child" notion is a central organizing principle for social policies and practices that specify that children's welfare and safety are the primary considerations in decision-making about child custody. This child-centred concept is often the touchstone of child protection policy and legislation and of frontline child welfare workers' practices (Alaggia, Jenney, Mazzuca, & Redmond, 2007). Indigenous groups have long argued that the concept has reflected the values of those from mainstream European backgrounds. As a result, decisions based on this particular cultural notion of children's best interests have had detrimental effects on Indigenous children and their families and have contributed to the historical and continued presence of the large number of First Nations, Métis, and Inuit children in agency care (Kline, 1992; Sinclair, Bala, Lilles, & Blackstock, 2004).

Both of the workers participating in our video demonstrations acknowledged that a "best interests of the child" mandate could present a challenge to child welfare workers in terms of knowing who the client is and when children's rights are more important than parents' rights. As she interviewed the mother, the worker in the first video demonstration not only confronted the mother about risks to her daughter but also continually used language that attempted to draw the mother into working with her to keep her daughter safe. At various moments during the interaction, the worker stated to the mother, "We're going to figure [out] how to keep your kids safe" and "You cannot drink around your child, but we're going to figure out what's going on about the drinking and get that under control." The worker also stopped at various points in this confrontation to check in with the mother and offer empathy: "This is making you uncomfortable, right?" "Why would I be asking you this, right? You said you look fine, but [I know] you're not."

Other basic communication skills that a worker must demonstrate include empathy, appropriate self-disclosure, humour, and optimism (Trotter, 2004). Through using these skills, workers can demonstrate not only that they are listening but also that they understand the difficulties experienced by parents (Levitt, 2001; Weger, Castle, & Emmett, 2010). Empathy is not just a practice skill but an approach to practice that begins with having a compassionate attitude and a genuine willingness to understand the life experiences and circumstances of another (Shebib, 2013). For Indigenous parents and families, this requires that the social worker have an understanding of their historical trauma and the ability to recognize that risks to children are the result not of individual failure or inadequate parenting but of intergenerational trauma that many have faced through the residential school system and the Sixties Scoop (Evans-Campbell, 2008). Humour can be used effectively to diffuse tension in an interview or to help clients take a less serious view of their situation, but its use must be carefully considered because the use of humour can be inappropriately timed and seem insensitive (Rocke, 2015; Shebib, 2013). Research on the use of these skills in interactions between child welfare workers and parents demonstrates their effectiveness in reducing client resistance (Forrester et al., 2008), creating positive experiences for parents (Studsrød, Willumsen, & Ellingsen, 2014), and supporting higher engagement between child welfare workers and parents (Gladstone et al., 2012).

Confrontation

The term "confrontation" implies conflict and negative impact. However, the need to confront parents is a necessary skill for child welfare workers to develop. Parents tend to get distressed or angry when confronted with the information that child welfare believes they have harmed or placed their children at risk (Dumbrill, 2006; Karp, 1984; Mirick, 2014). When workers are uncomfortable with confrontation, they might also react with anger and hostility, or they might engage in a number of evasive behaviours in order to avoid negative reactions from parents. Some of these behaviours can include refraining from asking parents difficult questions or from challenging inconsistencies in parental behaviours, giving parents unrealistic assurances about future interventions (e.g., "your children will not be removed"), crossing professional boundaries, or not engaging with hostile family members. As a result, workers run the risk of missing potentially important information, excluding or denying important information about the family when consulting with superiors, and not engaging with the child of interest by forming an alliance with the parent (Beckett, 2007).

In the second video demonstration, the mother actively resisted the efforts of the worker. Instead of responding with anger and using her power as a child welfare worker, the worker listened carefully to each of the concerns stated by the mother. Afterward, the worker stated that she had been deliberate in not responding. In turn, she acknowledged the mother's concerns and validated that it is difficult to be involved with the child welfare system. This worker continually conveyed to the mother that she wished to be a support to her: "We're going to work together to get Tina back into your care, and we're going to do that together. I'm going to help you." The worker stated later that she had been deliberate in validating the mother when the mother said she had been to the hospital to seek help for depression. Many times during the interview, she also took the opportunity to engage the mother: "It seems you have a great relationship, I want to support you." "It seems like a strong relationship, we can make it stronger." This then allowed her to ask questions that are more difficult—"There is a little thing under here, this depression, can we talk about that?"—and to offer support: "What do you think about doing this?" There is a point in the interview where the mother asked to be updated about her daughter's schoolwork and asked for a picture of her. The second worker explained to us that mothers ask for these updates and pictures because they want their child welfare workers to acknowledge their roles as mothers. The worker stated that she offers to do this for parents and has provided parents with copies of report cards, pictures of the children, and opportunities to sign permission slips.

Karp (1984) suggests that, instead of reacting with equal anger or using power coercively, child welfare workers invite parents to discuss their fears and concerns as a way of exploring what the parent is feeling. When confrontation is done in an effective and constructive rather than accusatory fashion, the likelihood of a parent being defensive is reduced. Presenting parents with specific examples of their behaviours that have placed their children at risk is helpful. Timing is also important; confrontation should only be used after some time has been spent developing a relationship with the client. Social workers also need to examine their motives for using confrontation, which will increase the likelihood that confrontation is used for the benefit of clients rather than for the benefit of workers (e.g., to defend oneself).

Conflict

Knowing how to deal effectively with conflict begins with understanding our own personal conflict styles. Conflict styles are defined as "patterned responses, or clusters of behaviour, that people use in conflict" (Wilmot & Hocker, 2011, p. 144). They develop over our lifetime and are impacted by a number of factors, including our life experiences, family background, and personal philosophy. By the time we are adults, our personal preference for either avoiding or engaging in conflict has been set. Research has identified five different conflict styles, along with tactics used within these styles. Tactics are described as the "individual moves people make to carry out their general approach" (Wilmot & Hocker, 2011, p. 144).

The five styles of conflict response are avoidance, competition, compromise, accommodation, and collaboration (Kilmann & Thomas, 1975). Avoidance is the most common conflict style. Child welfare workers often engage in avoidance-type strategies when they lack the skills necessary to deal with conflict and confrontation effectively. Common tactics used within an avoidance style include denial of the conflict, changing and avoiding contentious topics, being non-committal, and making jokes to ease the tension (Wilmot & Hocker, 2011). It is important to understand that there is a difference between avoidance and postponement of conflict; sometimes when emotions are running high and there is time, postponement can be a good strategy. In contrast, the competitive conflict style is characterized by aggressive behaviour. Common tactics used in this style are threats. People often use threats because they believe they will be effective in getting the results that they want. The use of threats in child welfare practice is both inappropriate and unethical. The power to intervene in families has been deemed as the most intrusive state power that currently exists in Canadian society (Bala, Zapf, Williams, Vogl, & Hornick, 2004). It is therefore important that child and family services workers exercise great caution in the exercise of this power.

In the final video segment, the worker was asked to deliberately escalate conflict and anger between herself and the mother. The video was then briefly stopped, and the worker was asked to de-escalate the situation. To de-escalate the conflict, the worker knew that she needed to first apologize and then take responsibility (as the worker) for the conflict. Child welfare workers often hear from parents that the "previous worker was an idiot" or "my last worker did not give me visits or any help." Both workers suggested it is okay for workers to acknowledge that the system and prior workers may have made mistakes and then to say to a parent, "I am open to exploring this together if you want, I am more than willing to do that, but I would like to move forward—you and I—in a different way. And I know that that probably does not seem fair to you, and there might be some recourse that you have if the agency violated your rights, then you do have legal recourse to challenge us on that, and I will certainly help you to do that piece, but right now I would like us to work together on keeping your children safe."

The collaborative conflict style has been determined to be the most constructive conflict-engagement style. This style requires the most highly developed communication skills. The goal of collaboration in child welfare practice is to honour parents by seeking to understand their perception of the situation and utilizing a strengths-based and problem-solving approach to seek solutions to the issues that have brought the family to the attention of child welfare authorities (Wilmot & Hocker, 2011).

Conclusion

Blackstock, Cross, George, Brown, & Formsma (2006) identified four aspects of reconciliation that are needed in child welfare: truth telling, acknowledging, restoring, and relating. The goals of the educational resources described in this chapter build on the restoring and relating aspects, respectively, "to design and implement earnest steps to redress past harms and set frameworks in place to prevent their recurrence," as well as the requirement for "Indigenous and non-Indigenous people to work jointly to implement a set of core values, a vision, and a structure for best practice" (Blackstock et al., 2006, pp. 9, 10). As mentioned earlier, the teaching resources described in this chapter were developed as a joint project between Indigenous and non-Indigenous practitioners and academics with the goal of identifying child welfare practices that can be used to teach social work skills rooted in critical best practices and Indigenous ways of knowing. The skills identified in this chapter can be used with all families involved in the child welfare system; however, child welfare workers working with Indigenous families need to frame their interactions within an understanding of how the colonial history of Canada affects Indigenous peoples today.

Reconciliation in the child welfare system requires more than structural change. Reconciliation also requires that frontline child welfare workers have the skills to develop trust and working relationships with the parents with whom they work. A working relationship also includes being able to deal with conflict, acknowledging, and mitigating the power inherent in child welfare work.

Discussion Questions

1. What are some of the most essential basic skills social workers need when engaging parents in difficult discussions about harm or risk of continued harm to their children?
2. What are some of the key skills social workers need in working with Indigenous families in child welfare practice?
3. What is the collaborative conflict style, and why is it important in engagement with families?
4. What tools can you use as a social worker in supporting a family's strengths and abilities?

References

ACCWG (Aboriginal Children in Care Working Group). (2015, July). *Aboriginal children in care: Report to Canada's premiers. Aboriginal Children in Care Working Group.*

Alaggia, R., Jenney, A., Mazzuca, J., & Redmond, M. (2007). In whose best interest? A Canadian case study of the impact of child welfare policies in cases of domestic violence. *Brief Treatment & Crisis Intervention, 7*(4), 275–290.

Badger, L. W., & MacNeil, G. (2002). Standardized clients in the classroom: A novel instructional technique for social worker educators. *Research on Social Work Practice, 12*(3), 364–374.

Bala, N. (2004). Child welfare law in Canada: An introduction. In N. Bala, M. K. Zapf, R. J. Williams, R. Vogl, & J. P. Hornick (Eds.), *Canadian child welfare law: Children, families, and the state* (2nd ed.) (pp. 1–25). Toronto, ON: Thompson Educational Publishing.

Bala, N. (2011). Setting the context: Child welfare law in Canada. In K. Kufeldt & B. McKenzie (Eds.), *Child welfare: Connecting research, policy, and practice* (2nd. ed.) (pp. 1–18). Waterloo, ON: Wilfrid Laurier University Press.

Bala, N., Zapf, M. K., Williams, R. J., Vogl, R., & Hornick, J. P. (Eds.). *Canadian child welfare law: Children, families, and the state* (2nd ed.). Toronto, ON: Thompson Educational Publishing.

Beckett, C. (2007). *Child protection: An introduction* (2nd ed.). London, United Kingdom: Sage.

Blackstock, C. (2009). The occasional evil of angels: Learning from the experiences of Aboriginal peoples and social work. *First Peoples Child & Family Review, 4*(1), 28–37.

Blackstock, C., Brown, I., & Bennett, M. (2007). Reconciliation: Rebuilding the Canadian child welfare system to better serve Aboriginal children and youth. In I. Brown, F. Chaze, D. Fuchs, J. Lafrance, S. McKay, & S. Thomas Prokop (Eds.), *Putting a human face on child welfare: Voices from the Prairies* (pp. 59–87). Regina, SK: University of Regina Press.

Blackstock, C., Cross, T., George, J., Brown, I., & Formsma, J. (2006). *Reconciliation in child welfare: Touchstones of hope for Indigenous children, youth, and families.* Ottawa, ON: First Nations Child & Family Caring Society.

Blackstock, C., Trocmé, N., & Bennett, M. (2004). Child maltreatment investigations among Aboriginal and non-Aboriginal families in Canada. *Violence against Women, 10*(8), 901–916.

Brownell, M. D., Roos, N. P., MacWilliam, L., Leclair, L., Ekuma, O., & Fransoo, R. (2010). Academic and social outcomes for high-risk youths in Manitoba. *Canadian Journal of Education/Revue canadienne de l'éducation, 33*(4), 804–836.

Brownson, R. C., & Jones, E. (2009). Bridging the gap: Translating research into policy and practice. *Preventive Medicine, 49*(4), 313–315.

Buckley, H., Carr, N., & Whelan, S. (2011). "Like walking on eggshells": Service user views and expectations of the child protection system. *Child & Family Social Work, 16*(1), 101–110.

Buckley, H., Tonmyr, L., Lewig, K., & Jack, S. (2014). Factors influencing the uptake of research evidence in child welfare: A synthesis of findings from Australia, Canada, and Ireland. *Child Abuse Review, 23*(1), 5–16.

Cooper, B., Gordon, J., & Rixon, A. (2015). *Best practice with children and families: Critical social work stories.* New York, NY: Palgrave.

de Boer, C., & Coady, N. (2007). Good helping relationships in child welfare: Learning from stories of success. *Child & Family Social Work, 12*(1), 32–42.

Dumbrill, G. C. (2006). Parental experience of child protection intervention: A qualitative study. *Child Abuse & Neglect, 30*(1), 27–37.

Eun-Kyoung, O. L., Blythe, B., & Goforth, K. (2009). Can you call it racism? An educational case study and role-play approach. *Journal of Social Work Education, 45*(1), 123–130.

Evans-Campbell, T. (2008). Historical trauma in American Indian/Native Alaska communities: A multilevel framework for exploring impacts of individuals, families, and communities. *Journal of Interpersonal Violence, 23*(3), 316–338.

Fallon, B., Ma, J., Allan, K., Pillhofer, M., Trocmé, N., & Jud, A. (2013). Opportunities for prevention and intervention with young children: Lessons from the Canadian Incidence Study of Reported Child Abuse and Neglect. *Child and Adolescent Psychiatry and Mental Health, 7*(4), 1–13.

Forrester, D., Kershaw, S., Moss, H., & Hughes, L. (2008). Communication skills in child protection: How do social workers talk to parents? *Child & Family Social Work, 13*(1), 41–51.

Gelman, C. R., & Tosone, C. (2006). Making it real: Enhancing curriculum delivery through the use of student-generated training videos. *Journal of Technology in Human Services, 24*(1), 37–52.

Gladstone, J., Dumbrill, G., Leslie, B., Koster, A., Young, M., & Ismaila, A. (2012). Looking at engagement and outcome from the perspectives of child protection workers and parents. *Children & Youth Service Review, 34*(1), 112–118.

Holland, S. (2011). *Child and family assessment in social work practice* (2nd ed.). Thousand Oaks, CA: Sage.

Howe, D. (2010). The safety of children and the parent-worker relationship in cases of child abuse and neglect. *Child Abuse Review, 19*(5), 330–341.

Hughes, J., & Chau, S. (2012). Children's best interests and intimate partner violence in the Canadian family law and child protection systems. *Critical Social Policy, 32*(4), 677–695.

Hughes, J., & Chau, S. (2013). Making complex decisions: Child protection workers' practices and interventions with families experiencing intimate partner violence. *Children and Youth Services Review, 35*(4), 611–617.

Hughes, J., Chau, S., & Poff, D. C. (2011). "They're not my favourite people": What mothers who have experienced intimate partner violence say about involvement in the child protection system. *Children and Youth Services Review, 33*(7), 1084–1089.

Karp. H. B. (1984). Working with resistance. *Training and Development Journal, 38*(3), 69–73.

Kilmann, R., & Thomas, K. W. (1975). Interpersonal conflict-handling behavior as reflections of Jungian personality dimensions. *Psychological Reports, 37*(3), 971–980.

Kinney, M., & Aspinwall-Roberts, E. (2010). The use of self and role play in social work education. *Journal of Mental Health Training, Education, and Practice, 5*(4), 27–33.

Kline, M. (1992). Child welfare law, "best interests of the child" ideology, and First Nations. *Osgoode Hall Law Journal, 30*(2), 375–425.

Lavergne, C., Dufour, S., Trocmé, N., & Larrivée, M.-C. (2008). Visible minority, Aboriginal, and Caucasian children investigated by Canadian protective services. *Child Welfare, 87*(2), 59–76.

Levitt, H. M. (2001). Sounds of silence in psychotherapy: The categorization of clients' pauses. *Psychotherapy Research, 11*(3), 295–309.

Maiter, S., Palmer, S., & Manji, S. (2006). Strengthening social worker-client relationships in child protective services: Addressing power imbalances and "ruptured" relationships. *Qualitative Social Work, 5*(2), 167–186.

Mirick, R. G. (2014). The relationship between reactance and engagement in a child welfare sample. *Child & Family Social Work, 19*(3), 333–342.

Mullins, J. L. (2011). A framework for cultivating and increasing child welfare workers' empathy towards parents. *Journal of Social Service Research, 37*(3), 242–253.

Petracchi, H. E., & Collins, K. S. (2006). Utilizing actors to simulate clients in social work student role plays: Does this approach have a place in social work education? *Journal of Teaching in Social Work, 26*(1–2), 223–233.

Platt, D. (2012). Understanding parental engagement in child welfare services: An integrated model. *Child & Family Social Work, 17*(2), 138–148.

Rocke, C. (2015). The use of humor to help bridge cultural divides: An exploration of a workplace cultural awareness workshop. *Social Work with Groups, 38*(2), 152–169.

Shebib, B. (2013). *Choices: Interviewing and counselling skills for Canadians.* Don Mills, ON: Pearson Education Canada.

Sinclair, M., Bala, N., Lilles, H., & Blackstock, C. (2004). Aboriginal child welfare. In N. Bala, M. K. Zapf, R. J. Williams, R. Vogl, & J. P. Hornick (Eds.), *Canadian child welfare law: Children, families, and the state* (2nd ed.) (pp. 199–244). Toronto, ON: Thompson Educational Publishing.

Sinha, V., Trocmé, N., Fallon, B., & MacLaurin, B. (2013). Understanding the investigation-stage overrepresentation of First Nations children in the child welfare system: An analysis of the First Nations component of the Canadian Incidence Study of Reported Child Abuse and Neglect 2008. *Child Abuse & Neglect, 37*(10), 821–831.

Spratt, T., & Callan, J. (2004). Parents' views on social work interventions in child welfare cases. *British Journal of Social Work, 34*(2), 199–224.

Stokes, J., & Schmidt, G. (2011). Race, poverty, and child protection decision-making. *British Journal of Social Work, 41*(6), 1105–1121.

Studsrød, I., Willumsen, E., & Ellingsen, I. T. (2014). Parents' perceptions of contact with the Norwegian child welfare services. *Child & Family Social Work, 19*(3), 312–320.

Todd, S. (2012). Practicing in the uncertain: Reworking standardized clients as improv theatre. *Social Work Education, 31*(3), 302–315.

TRC (Truth and Reconciliation Commission of Canada) (2015). *Truth and Reconciliation Commission of Canada: Calls to Action.* Retrieved from http://www.trc.ca/websites/trcinstitution/File/2015/Findings/Calls_to_Action_English2.pdf

Trocmé, N., Fallon, B., MacLaurin, B., Sinha, V., Black, T., Fast, E.,...& Holroyd, J. (2010). Characteristics of substantiated maltreatment. In *Canadian Incidence Study of Reported Child Abuse and Neglect – 2008: Major findings* (pp. 30–35). Ottawa, ON: Public Health Agency of Canada.

Trocmé, N., Knoke, D., & Blackstock, C. (2004). Pathways to the overrepresentation of Aboriginal children in Canada's child welfare system. *Social Service Review, 78*(4), 577–600.

Trotter, C. (2004). *Helping abused children and their families: Towards an evidence-based practice model.* Thousand Oaks, CA: Sage.

Tuck, V. (2013). Resistant parents and child protection: Knowledge base, pointers for practice, and implications for policy. *Child Abuse Review, 22*(1), 5–19.

Turney, D. (2012). A relationship-based approach to engaging involuntary clients: The contribution of recognition theory. *Child & Family Social Work, 17*(2), 149–159.

Vapalahti, K., Marttunen, M., & Laurinen, L. (2013). Online and face-to-face role-play simulations in promoting social work students' argumentative problem solving. *Journal of Comparative Social Work, 8*(1), 2–35.

Villadsen, A., Allain, L., Bell, L., & Hingley-Jones, H. (2012). The use of role-play and drama in interprofessional education: An evaluation of a workshop with students of social work, midwifery, early years, and medicine. *Social Work Education: The International Journal, 31*(1), 75–89.

Weger, H., Jr., Castle, G. R., & Emmett, M. C. (2010). Active listening in peer interviews: The influence of message paraphrasing on perceptions of listening skill. *International Journal of Listening, 24*(1), 34–49.

Wilmot, W., & Hocker, J. (2011). *Interpersonal conflict* (9th ed.). New York, NY: McGraw Hill.

CHAPTER 12

Transforming the Classroom: Supporting Critical Change in Social Work Education in the Spirit of Reconciliation for Child Welfare

Jennifer Hedges

Reconciliation is essentially about love.

—Dr. Chief Robert Joseph

Introduction

As a social work educator and doctoral student, I have profound learning experiences at every turn, which is both exciting and arduous. I read material every day that explains why social problems and inequities exist, yet they still do. In moments of reflection when I try to make sense of it all, I find myself asking, "What now?" The theme of the eighth biennial Prairie Child Welfare Consortium (PCWC) symposium, Imagining Child Welfare in the Spirit of Reconciliation, captured this struggle for me because *imagining* child welfare in the spirit of reconciliation represents a call to action, a real response to what is known about colonization, and a commitment to moving forward in a better way. The 2016 PCWC symposium

Suggested Citation: Hedges, J. (2018). Transforming the classroom: Supporting critical change in social work education in the spirit of reconciliation for child welfare. In D. Badry, H. Montgomery, D. Kikulwe, M. Bennett, & D. Fuchs, (Eds.), *Imagining child welfare in the spirit of reconciliation* (pp. 249–267). Regina, SK: University of Regina Press.

was a collaborative effort by Indigenous and non-Indigenous peoples to continue answering the "what now?" question.[1] In reflecting on the symposium itself, I saw its presentations, discussions, and relationships as an act of reconciliation that offered hope and inspiration. In this chapter, I will share part of my journey as a student exploring the relationship between social work education and the preparation of social workers for work in child welfare. I am challenged to consider my role as a non-Indigenous educator and researcher in how social work education can be a platform for transformative learning for students toward reconciliation. To illustrate this, I will present relevant literature and reflections on the themes that emerged throughout the symposium that have informed my learning about social work education. A critical theory lens is used to examine the historical and current landscape of social work education and child welfare as I consider future possibilities. As a non-Indigenous person, I acknowledge that I approach this topic from a place of privilege, and I am committed to learning from Indigenous peoples about how I can contribute to reconciliation.

Dr. Cindy Blackstock (2016), renowned advocate for Indigenous children, presented evidence that the Canadian government and the Canadian people—including the profession of social work, social work education, and the child welfare system—have known better yet have continued to repeat the same mistakes. She challenged social workers and researchers to confront this reality, to examine what blocks our moral courage, and to commit to doing things differently moving forward. During the opening plenary, Dr. Chief Robert Joseph (2016), ambassador for Reconciliation Canada, stated that "reconciliation starts with you, right here in this room, where you sit." He spoke about love and the promise he saw in the audience, calling us "to our highest consciousness to have open and deep discussion about the issue at hand...so that we can truly discover new ways

1 The terms "Indigenous" and "Aboriginal" are used throughout this chapter to refer to First Nations, Métis, and Inuit peoples in Canada (INAC, n.d.). These groups represent a wide variety of unique and diverse cultures, traditions, and languages. There is no one Indigenous worldview; however, Indigenous scholars acknowledge that Indigenous peoples share common challenges, and it is possible to consider some common ground (Hart, 2002). I use the terms "Indigenous" and "Aboriginal" with respect for this diversity and to reflect the language used in the sources cited.

forward collectively." With my background working as a child protection worker and now as an educator, I am tasked with the responsibility of examining my own roles and imagining alternative ways of teaching and practising in the spirit of reconciliation. Joseph stated, "We are reconciliation." As an educator, I can help create an environment that encourages students to value different ways of knowing, engage in meaningful reflection, and imagine alternatives to practice, specifically in child welfare. Education and child welfare have been significant tools used for harming Indigenous peoples; therefore, reconciliation should be at the centre of social work education.

Social Work Education as Reconciliation

> *How can you become what you cannot imagine?*
>
> —bell hooks

Senator Murray Sinclair, chief commissioner of the Truth and Reconciliation Commission of Canada (TRC), stated that education is the key to reconciliation (Macdonald, 2016). Social workers, however well intentioned, have contributed to the oppression of Indigenous peoples through the residential school system and the Sixties Scoop (Sinclair, 2004; Jennissen & Lundy, 2011). Education followed the same assimilation principles: "[W]estern theoretical hegemony manifests primarily in educational institutions....[T]he paradigm from which 'social work' has been taught and practiced is western in theory, pedagogy and practice" (Sinclair, 2004, p. 51). These important realities challenge social worker educators. Throughout history, social workers have been involved in oppressive practices despite holding core values oriented toward social justice. Without ongoing reflection and dialogue, social workers can be doing harm under the guise of social work:

> *Social workers fall into the trap of believing that just because they are social workers they are, therefore, non-racist and non-oppressive because the profession has a code of ethics to guide practice and because social work institutions proclaim they are committed to this ideology.* (Sinclair, 2004, p. 52)

The truth is that social work is rooted in both oppressive and anti-oppressive ideologies. A beginning place for acknowledging this truth is in social work education. During the PCWC symposium, Manitoba's deputy children's advocate Corey La Berge (2016) stated, "The passage of time does not absolve responsibility," and he charged participants to think about what story we are writing. This notion of responsibility is significant and holds social work educators accountable. What story is social work education writing? According to Blackstock (2016), reconciliation is about how people in a society, at a given time, react to injustice. She challenged social workers to consider our continued role in discriminating against Indigenous peoples: "Social work also needs to own its soul as well because we are more likely to be part of it than to fight against it....[W]e need to look in the mirror to see what is it about us that allowed us to carry on so long." Just as Chief Joseph called us to our highest consciousness, Sinclair (2004) referred to Freire's "development of critical consciousness through conscientization,"

> *a critical approach to liberatory education that incorporates helping the learner to move towards a new awareness of relations of power, myths, and oppression. By developing critical consciousness this way, learners work toward changing the world.* (p. 53)

Social work education should be more than learning specific knowledge, values, and skills. It is about experiences that transform the self into a way of being that lives and breathes justice in relations and service. Chief Joseph (2016) stated that social workers must "adopt reconciliation as a core value in [their] heart, [their] mind, and in [their] soul."

Kovach, Carriere, Montgomery, Barrett, and Gilles (2015) explain, "The attitude, effort and capacity of the postsecondary professor cannot be understated, for the professor becomes the initial exemplar for the new practitioner" (p. 7). The social work educator is on a journey of reconciliation as well and has a responsibility to teach and model critical reflection and reflexivity. Ives and Thaweiakenrat Loft (2013) state,

> *The task of social work educators is to challenge social work—and other—students to reconceptualize how they perceive their disciplines—past, present, and future....[T]his kind of reimagining of*

> *one's personal and professional self and practice approach is a small step in re(shaping) the reconciliation that must take place in order to heal relationships between Indigenous and non-Indigenous Peoples.* (pp. 250–251)

Pelech, Enns, and Fuchs (2014) argue that "social work education should be shaped by the times and the critical issues faced within modern society" (p. 249). One critical issue facing the current child welfare system is the overrepresentation of Indigenous and other minority children in care (Sinha, Trocmé, Fallon, & MacLaurin, 2013). Other concerns include the high turnover rates of frontline workers, limited acceptance of non-Western cultural practices, and continued lack of resources, all of which contribute to structural injustices such as sexism, racism, and poverty that further create barriers for service users (Bennett, Sadrehashemi, & Smith, 2009; Carriere & Strega, 2015; Lavergne, Dufour, Trocmé, & Larrivée, 2008). A question for social work education is how to prepare social workers for working successfully in this field to deliver services as well as reform. In an opinion piece in the *Toronto Star* titled "Reforming child welfare first step toward reconciliation," Blackstock and Grammond (2016) point out that, despite the human rights tribunal finding the federal government guilty in 2016 of discriminating against Indigenous children, child welfare policies continue to ignore "Indigenous jurisdiction regarding child welfare" (para. 10). The authors draw attention to positive and culturally relevant initiatives by Indigenous communities and caution against repeating the same colonial mistakes by reforming child welfare from the top down instead of collaborating with Indigenous peoples and communities. This is a significant point in time for social workers to imagine a different future through reconciliation.

Child welfare is a main area of practice in social work; therefore, social workers have the opportunity and responsibility to guide policy and practice. Social work education struggles to deliver a curriculum that not only balances the needs of social workers working within current systems but also develops critical thinkers who can deconstruct dominant oppressive discourses and imagine alternatives that uphold social work's values related to social justice. Social work education has been criticized for reinforcing a colonial and residual approach to social welfare that focuses on professionalization and competency-based child welfare work

(Sinclair, 2004). In the spirit of reconciliation, social work education has to support students in deconstructing these contested discourses. As hooks (2000) states, we need to work together to think of alternative ways of thinking and being; specifically, she asks, "How can you become what you cannot imagine?" (p. 70). This kind of imagining can begin in the social work classroom.

In 2017, the Canadian Association for Social Work Education (CASWE) released online a "Statement of Complicity and Commitment to Change" as a step toward engaging social work education in the reconciliation process. This statement acknowledges that "social work education, research and practice have been, and continue to be, complicit in our colonial reality. Such complicity contradicts the espoused values and ethics of social work, potentially negates the positive impact of social work interventions, and results in harmful policies and practices" (CASWE, 2017). The statement lists twelve commitments by the CASWE board toward reconciliation, including a commitment to "encourage and support Canadian schools of social work in revising mission statements, governance processes, curriculum, and pedagogy in ways that both advance the TRC recommendations and the overall indigenization of social work education" (CASWE, 2017). This is an important step toward social work education being accountable and moving awareness into action.

Coggins (2016) states that diversity must become central to social work education in order to reflect Canada's growing cultural diversity. Reconciliation requires that social work education move beyond cultural competence to develop in each student a sense of cultural humility and cultural safety (Este, 2007; Milliken, 2012). Milliken (2012) explains that cultural safety entails moving beyond oneself to listen to another with a deeper level of understanding; it forces you to examine yourself and the ways that you can emphasize and equalize power. This way of being would undoubtedly transform approaches to engagement in child protection practice. During a previous symposium, Indigenous scholars and practitioners joined for discussions about Indigenous child welfare (Gosek & Bennett, 2012). They explained that, in order to move forward, child welfare systems need to value Indigenous knowledges. It is not enough to just acknowledge diversity or roll it into the mainstream orientations; this has proven to be insufficient and, at worst, harmful. It was notable in these joint discussions that cultural competence models can limit the building of more meaningful relationships that are foundational for understanding and providing culturally appropriate responses. Indigenous worldviews, traditions, and Elders need to speak to how services can reflect community needs (Gosek & Bennett, 2012).

Critical Social Work Education

Reconciliation may begin with listening and learning history, but it can only be realized through action. During the 2016 PCWC symposium, Karen Joseph (2016), chief executive officer of Reconciliation Canada, cautioned, "You may have heard but not really understand." Knowledge Keeper Sherry Copenace (2016) explained that to understand you have to "listen with your heart." A critical approach to social work education can help transform the classroom so that educators and students are learning and experiencing reconciliation together. The early theoretical foundations of social work were based on general systems theory and an ecological framework (Leslie & Cassano, 2003). Critical social work, which has become more prominent since the 1970s, "takes a mainly social change view of social work" (Payne, 2014, p. 327). "Critical social work" can be used as an umbrella term to describe "approaches to social work practice that are informed by an eclectic range of critical social theories" (Pease & Nipperess, 2016, p. 5) influenced by radical, anti-oppressive, anti-racist, and feminist perspectives (Healy, 2014). Adams (2009) explains the importance of social work students developing a critical approach, in that it

> *enables the person "to recognise multiple perspectives, as part of the ability to work with multi facets of the whole context" (Fook et al., 2000; 213)....[T]his enables the practitioner-to-be to appreciate multiple perspectives on a given practice situation and the reality that they may be not only diverse but contradictory and ever-changing.* (p. 239)

One of the main theories expressed in social work education currently is anti-oppressive practice (de Montigny, 2011; Healy, 2014). Child protection, similar to education, is rooted in "paradigms of patriarchy, whiteness, privilege, positivism and ethnocentrism" (Barter, 2001, p. 264). Dumbrill (2003) identified child welfare as a "nemesis" of anti-oppressive practices.

He explained the dilemma facing social workers in practising from an anti-oppressive approach, which "attempts to dismantle systemic inequalities," in a system that privileges social control. For a course project during my doctoral studies, I interviewed three child protection workers about how their social work education had prepared them for child welfare practice. I found it interesting how each person talked about child protection work and the dual nature of the tension between helping and protecting. The child protection workers described this tension in their own way: "the head and the heart are always at war"; "it's like a double-edged sword"; and "it's like wearing two hats." Child welfare workers can share a kind of powerlessness with the children and families they serve (Bundy-Fazioli, Briar-Lawson, & Hardiman, 2009). McLaughlin, Gray, and Wilson (2015) found that a dual concept of social justice is held by child welfare workers as both a goal and a process, and workers expressed disconnect between social justice and everyday practice, which led to discouragement regarding their ability to engage in social change. This could be a reason why some workers do not stay in child welfare and an area where social work education could better prepare students to cope in this context.

Sinclair (2004) cautions that "anti-oppressive practice has an inherent danger. The danger lies in proclaiming an anti-oppressive stance, while doing nothing or little to address it" (p. 52). Yee and Wagner (2013) raise the question of anti-oppression teaching as a form of neoliberalism practised unconsciously. Although an anti-oppressive framework provides a way to examine oppression of different groups, it stems from Western ideology, and thus "the status quo remains entrenched...as it may inadvertently support neo-liberal and post-colonial structures in the wider society" (Yee & Wagner, 2013, p. 334). Dominelli (2002) argues that social workers have a responsibility to eliminate oppression in their practice and in society because, "if their impact on either clients or co-workers is oppressive, intentionality is immaterial" (Dominelli, 2002, p. 60). A choice has to be made between liberation and status quo (Dominelli, 1996). Social work educators have this same responsibility; therefore, it is necessary to turn a critical lens on their practice and the authenticity of the anti-oppressive frameworks they teach and model. Jennissen and Lundy (2011) state,

> *A social justice framework has become "mainstream" in Canadian social work to the extent that its meaning is often not clearly*

> *explicated, but taken for granted. The consequences [sic] of this has been that many social workers espouse practising from a social and economic justice framework, but this framework is not reflected in either their ideological positions or their practices. The term "social justice," in many respects, has become so all-embracing and without a strong theoretical base as to be almost meaningless.* (pp. 301–302)

This is concerning and requires a response by social work educators, because "we cannot separate knowledge from action, research from practice, or theory from wisdom" (Earls Larrison & Korr, 2013, p. 205). It is important to facilitate opportunities for students to integrate their learning and practise critical reflection. Social work is in a position to push forward culturally anchored approaches to child welfare, and social work education is a platform where these values and skills can be instilled. Social work education can help students deconstruct their perspectives and then reconstruct them through an anti-oppressive lens (Clarke et al., 2012). Contemplative, activist, and Indigenous pedagogies offer ways to ground social work education in social justice.

Contemplative Pedagogy

Contemplative pedagogy is a holistic experience that helps students realize their interconnectedness to self and others, leading to the embodiment of critical social work (Wong, 2013). Wong (2013) compares this approach of connecting the mind, body, heart, and spirit within and outside oneself to more traditional teaching that is limited to the mind. She argues for the need to seek spirituality and wholeness in the current neoliberal environment that dominates university education and social work. Wong notes being surprised to learn how significant this approach was for her students, who had already had extensive learning on critical social work theories in their previous academic setting. She indicates that the students in the study explained that the difference was not only the focus on wholeness and inter-being with others but also the way it moved learning from an intellectual idea to an active way of being. One student reflected on the way she does child welfare work and recognized how contemplative learning exercises changed her practice: she began to put service users first and paperwork second; while still valuing paperwork, she understood human engagement as her priority for practice. This illustrates a direct link between social work education and impact on practice (Wong, 2013). Gockel and Deng (2016) found that integrating mindfulness training in social work courses supported student well-being and self-care by helping students develop skills for managing anxiety and stress. These are important skills for social workers entering complex fields such as child welfare.

Activist Pedagogy

Activist pedagogy moves beyond "social critique" and "urges both students and faculty to think of the classroom as a site for 'doing' as well as 'thinking about doing'....[A]ctivist pedagogy sees action and applied knowledge as socially transformative" (Preston & Aslett, 2014, p. 515). Swift, Good Gingrich, and Brown (2015) describe activist pedagogy as reclaiming the social, engaging in history, and building alliances for resistance. They assert, "reflexivity is key to unveiling the falseness of the neoliberal autonomous individual. It is to know ourselves as social, which is to know our humanity" (p. 387). They advise educators to "learn, teach and emphasize language, values, attitudes and skills that equip us for challenge and knowledge about how the world actually works. We can think socially, resist collectively and work actively to create a collective soul" (p. 391). Educators are finding ways to resist neoliberal influences inside and outside the classroom. Sharing these creative responses is a way for social work to build a stronger knowledge base as to ways that social work education can respond and prepare students to continue thinking critically in the field. While social work theory may be embracing a more postmodern and collectivist approach to practice and decision-making, political and economic sources that govern and fund social services continue to demonstrate a modernist understanding of need. A process of deconstructing knowledges that justify oppressive paradigms is necessary to avoid "replacing one authoritarian with another, albeit in the name of new ideology" (Agger, 2013, p. 31). There has to be an imagining of an alternative approach that values diversity and a collectivist way of being.

Indigenous Pedagogy

Faith (2008) explains that, "as a product of its time and place, social work's theory base was mostly derived from the thought of one race, class and gender" (p. 247). Moving forward in social work education, "disruption" is necessary (Dumbrill & Green, 2008, p. 489). Sinclair (2004) states, "Aboriginal social work education is an emerging pedagogy framed within colonial history and Indigenous worldview" (p. 49). It uses a variety of approaches, "including the traditional ways of learning and knowing, involves guidance and teaching from community Elders, and is delivered in a community setting; such a curriculum will contribute to the decolonizing project of combating the structural oppression of Indigenous people" (Ives and Thaweiakenrat Loft, 2013, p. 241). Ives and Thaweiakenrat Loft (2013) explore ways in which social work education could build bridges between social work and Indigenous communities. They explain that context and history are essential to understanding Indigenous "cultural and social realities" (p. 240). Helping and healing "Indigenous methods of care" existed before social work (Faith, 2008, p. 247). It is important that, when multiple knowledges are presented in teaching, they should be valued in their own right and not as "secondary information to Western knowledges" (Baskin, 2016, p. 304). Indigenous ways of helping shape "new ways of thinking....[C]ross-cultural dialogue and exchange is moulding and shaping new forms of social work—localized and culturally relevant" (Baskin, 2016, pp. 18–19). Gray and Coates (2008) caution against intervention models designed to illuminate differences: "To teach something, we have to know or establish what it is....[C]ulturally appropriate social work can be seen as a form of resistance and a medium for transformation from externally imposed to locally developed models of practice and solutions" (pp. 21–22).

Clarke et al. (2012) use the metaphor "uprooting social work education" (p. 81) to explore ways that social work education could bridge the gap between mainstream and Indigenous social work. They use the image of a tree to examine social work's past, present, and future. The roots of the tree represent social work's colonizing roots as well as its efforts to reduce the negative effects of poverty. The roots represent "the historical legacy" that continues (p. 86). Aboriginal concepts of respect, reciprocity, reflexivity, and resistance frame the trunk of the tree. The leaves on the tree represent "current approaches to social work education and our vision for the future..., the diverse elements of both mainstream and Indigenous social work" (pp. 92–93). Some of these approaches include anti-oppressive practice, poststructuralism, postmodernism, strengths theory, constructivism, social justice, self-reflection, reflexivity, and Aboriginal values such as "storytelling, sharing circles, wholism, and holistic methods of healing" (p. 95). Clarke et al.'s collaborative art-based project "suggests ways of moving forward with an allied approach that bridges the gap between mainstream and Indigenous social work education....[T]his allowed us to engage creatively and critically with the tensions, contradictions and complexities of social work history" (pp. 96–97). Aims of the project were to reveal hidden Eurocentric dominant ways of knowing in education and to reveal the possibilities of integrating multiple ways of knowing for the benefit of everyone as a vision and hope for the future of social work education. In my Introduction to Social Work class, I share this article with students to read, and then we make our own tree. I draw the trunk and roots, as described in the article, on the board and give students as many cut-out leaves as they want, on which to write words representing their thoughts and actions toward the process of decolonization. Students take turns placing their leaves on the board, and we create a visual together as a class for discussion. This activity brings to life the learning from the article, and everyone in the class participates in uprooting social work education. Sinclair (2004) states that "a decolonizing pedagogy is a contemporary cultural imperative; that culturally appropriate and sociologically relevant teaching and healing models must evolve and translate into practice and service delivery that will meet the needs of future generations" (p. 49).

Alternative ways of teaching child welfare have been evolving. For example, schools of social work in British Columbia have developed BSW programs and post–bachelor degree certificates with a specialization in child welfare. These programs collaborate with child welfare agencies to break away from a Eurocentric social work education and challenge students to become reflexive workers who have cultural intelligence (Dumbrill & Green, 2008). These programs work toward building trusting relationships with Aboriginal citizens and increasing the number of Aboriginal child welfare social workers. The child welfare certificate contributes to increased self-confidence and abilities in practice, which supports higher retention rates for Aboriginal social workers (Pierce, Hemingway, & Schmidt, 2014). Further research is required to explore generalist and specialized paradigms of social work education for child welfare.

Stronger partnerships between social work education and child welfare agencies are necessary to advocate for and conduct research that supports legislation and policy changes that are culturally relevant for child welfare (SFNSCI, 2017). Academics may have access to resources that can help bring recommendations forward. These partnerships can also create a shared responsibility for providing education and training before and after students graduate that are specific to the local culture and needs of an agency (SFNSCI, 2017). Throughout the PCWC symposium, deliberate opportunities were created for participants to meet and discuss action steps for moving forward in reconciliation. Social work education programs can create these spaces as well and encourage such dialogue among students. Reconciliation should be an institutional priority that promotes opportunities, like the PCWC conference, to participate in acts of reconciliation.

Conclusion

Bellefeuille and Schmidt (2006) use the metaphor "between a rock and a hard place" to describe social work education and child welfare; they note that "the residual and at times adversarial nature of the child welfare system seems contrary to the ideals of the social work profession that strives to act as an advocate for the poor" (p. 3). There is a need in social work education for "cultivating humanity" in child welfare work that helps instill resilience as well as hope (Higgins, 2016). Lonne, Harries, Featherstone, and Gray (2016) describe ethical child welfare as seeing service users "as part of a 'web of care'" (p. xv). They question how prepared workers are for this "complex, rational, emotional and relational process" (p. 36). This way of thinking relationally is an important social work value and skill that can be developed in social work education. Indigenous ways of living relationally have much to offer in this endeavour.

Chief Joseph's (2016) assertion that "reconciliation is essentially about love" resonated with me. It is easy to take for granted that love is part of social work, but just as we teach students how to listen we also, and perhaps more importantly, have a responsibility to teach and be taught how to love. A better question for my research might be how can we prepare students to love in child welfare? Chief Joseph stated that reconciliation requires love with "courage and daring." Also speaking at the PCWC symposium, Karen Joseph (2016) explained we need to "provide those transformative experiences that link knowing better and create an emotional connection to it that allows us to do better, and that's how we go about creating change." Social work educators have both the privilege and the power to influence students.

> *Love, or a "love of humanity," has the same intent as formulations of social work grounded in postmodern critical theory, but it uses a different language. It uses a language of lived experience and personal commitment—a language that appeals to our hearts—a language passionate about, and incorporating, human rights and social justice.* (Morley & Ife, 2002, p. 69)

Morley and Ife (2002) describe "love of humanity" as a way of being conscious in the world—one that affirms human value and "is also about action. To love is not only to feel, but also to do, and it is only in the living out of one's essential humanity that love can be realised" (p. 71). Karen Joseph (2016) cautions, "Reconciliation is not for wimps, it takes courage....[I]f you are not uncomfortable in this process, chances are you are not doing it right." Admittedly, I took comfort in this because I often do make mistakes as I navigate becoming a stronger ally and advocate. I believe it is important that I share these experiences openly and honestly with my students so they realize that love for humanity is a journey, and achieving reconciliation is not possible unless everyone participates. A spirit of reconciliation has to be at the centre of social work education, so that it becomes a part of who social workers are in their lives, in everything they think, feel, and do. Although reconciliation can mean different things, the 2016 PCWC symposium highlighted, for me, that reconciliation has to be experienced in relation to child welfare practice in future directions, and this needs to be a priority. Reconciliation is about love: truth, trust, humility, respect, relationships, and hope. It is also about responsibility. Social work education has the opportunity and responsibility to write reconciliation into the story.

Discussion Questions

1. How can you incorporate critical pedagogies into your teaching or learning?
2. What "actions" are you taking to uproot social work education?

3. What does "reconciliation is love" mean to you?
4. How do you imagine reconciliation in social work education? In child welfare?
5. What is the role of non-Indigenous social work educators in reconciliation?

References

Adams, R. (2009). Being a critical practitioner. In R. Adams, L. Dominelli, & M. Payne (Eds.), *Critical practice in social work* (2nd ed.) (pp. 233–248). New York, NY: Palgrave Macmillan.

Agger, B. (2013). *Critical social theories: An introduction*. Boulder, CO: Westview Press.

Aronson, J., & Hemingway, D. (2011). "Competence" in neoliberal times. *Canadian Social Work Review, 28*(2), 281–285.

Barter, K. (2001). Building community: A conceptual framework for child protection. *Child Abuse Review, 10*(4), 262–278.

Baskin, C. (2016). *Strong helpers' teachings: The value of Indigenous knowledges in the helping professions* (2nd ed.). Toronto, ON: Canadian Scholars' Press.

Bellefeuille, G., & Schmidt, G. (2006). Between a rock and a hard place: Child welfare practice and social work education. *Social Work Education: The International Journal, 25*(1), 3–16. doi:10.1080/02615470500477797

Bennett, D., Sadrehashemi, L., & Smith, C. (2009). *Hands tied: Child protection workers talk about working in, and leaving, B.C.'s child welfare system.* Vancouver, BC: Pivot Legal Society.

Blackstock, C. (2016, October 26–28). *Rights of Indigenous children.* Keynote presented at the biennial Prairie Child Welfare Consortium symposium, Winnipeg, MB.

Blackstock, C., & Grammond, S. (2016, August 1). Reforming child welfare first step toward reconciliation: Opinion. *Toronto Star*. Retrieved from https://www.thestar.com/opinion/commentary/2017/08/01/reforming-child-welfare-first-step-toward-reconciliation-opinion.html

Bundy-Fazioli, K., Briar-Lawson, K., & Hardiman, E. R. (2009). A qualitative examination of power between child welfare workers and parents. *British Journal of Social Work, 39*(8), 1447–1464. doi:10.1093/bjsw/bcn038

Campbell, C. (2015, April). The intersection of social work education and regulation: A primer. Unpublished document, Canadian Association for Social Work Education. Retrieved from http://caswe-acfts.ca/wp-content/uploads/2015 /10/CampbellPrimer.pdf

Carriere, J., & Strega, S. (Eds.). (2015). *Walking this path together: Anti-racist and anti-oppressive child welfare practice* (2nd ed.). Halifax, NS: Fernwood Publishing.

CASWE (Canadian Association for Social Work Education). (2017, June 26). *Board of directors endorses a statement of complicity and commits to change* (Press release). Retrieved from https://caswe-acfts.ca/

media-release-board-of-directors-endorses-a-statement-of-complicity-and-commits-to-change/

Clarke, J., Aiello, O., Chau, K., Zakiya, A., Rashidi, M., & Amaral, S. (2012). Uprooting social work education. *LEARNing Landscapes, 6*(1), 81–105.

Coggins, K. (2016). *The practice of social work in North America: Culture, context, and competency development.* Chicago, IL: Lyceum Books.

Copenace, S. (2016, October). *Moving forward.* Panel presented at the biennial Prairie Child Welfare Consortium symposium, Winnipeg, MB.

de Montigny, G. (2011). Beyond anti-oppressive practice: Investigating reflexive social relations. *Journal of Progressive Human Services, 22*(1), 8–30. doi:10.1080/10428232.2011.564982

Dominelli, L. (1996). Deprofessionalizing social work: Anti-oppressive practice, competencies, and postmodernism. *British Journal of Social Work, 26*(2), 153–175.

Dominelli, L. (2002). *Anti-oppressive social work theory and practice.* New York, NY: Palgrave Macmillan.

Dumbrill, G. C. (2003). Child welfare: AOP's nemesis? In W. Shera (Ed.), *Emerging perspectives on anti-oppressive practice.* Toronto, ON: Canadian Scholars' Press.

Dumbrill, G., & Green, J. (2008). Indigenous knowledge in the social work academy. *Social Work Education: The International Journal, 27*(5), 489–503. doi:10.1080/02615470701379891

Earls Larrison, T., & Korr, W. S. (2013). Does social work have a signature pedagogy? *Journal of Social Work Education, 49*(2), 194–206. doi:10.1080/10437797.2013.768102

Este, D. (2007). Cultural competency and social work practice in Canada: A retrospective examination. *Canadian Social Work Review, 24*(1), 93–104.

Faith, E. (2008). Indigenous social work education. In M. Gray, J. Coates, & M. Yellow Bird (Eds.), *Indigenous social work around the world: Towards culturally relevant education and practice* (pp. 245–256). Burlington, VT: Ashgate.

Gockel, A., & Deng, X. (2016). Mindfulness training as social work pedagogy: Exploring benefits, challenges, and issues for consideration in integrating mindfulness into social work education. *Journal of Religion & Spirituality in Social Work: Social Thought, 35*(3), 222–244. doi:10.1080/15426432.2016.1187106

Gosek, G., & Bennett, M. (2012). A day's discourse among Indigenous scholars and practitioners about Indigenous child welfare. In D. Fuchs, S. McKay, & I. Brown (Eds.), *Awakening the spirit: Moving forward in child welfare voices from the Prairies* (pp. 23–36). Regina, SK: Canadian Plains Research Center.

Gray, M., & Coates, J. (2008). From "Indigenization" to cultural relevance. In M. Gray, J. Coates, & M. Yellow Bird (Eds.), *Indigenous social work around the world: Towards culturally relevant education and practice* (pp. 13–25). Burlington, VT: Ashgate.

Hart, M. (2002). *Seeking mino-pimatisiwin: An Aboriginal approach to helping.* Halifax, NS: Fernwood Publishing.

Healy, K. (2014). *Social work theories in context: Creating frameworks for practice* (2nd ed.). New York, NY: Palgrave Macmillan.

Higgins, M. (2016). "Cultivating our humanity" in child and family social work in England. *Social Work Education, 35*(5), 518–529. doi:10.1080/02615479.2016.1181161

hooks, b. (2000). *Feminism is for everybody: Passionate politics.* Cambridge, MA: South End Press.

INAC (Indigenous and Northern Affairs Canada). (n.d.). Indigenous peoples and communities. Retrieved from http://www.aadnc-aandc.gc.ca/eng/1100100013785/1304467449155

Ives, N., & Thaweiakenrat Loft, M. (2013). Building bridges with Indigenous communities through social work education. In M. Gray, J. Coates, & M. Yellow Bird (Eds.), *Decolonizing social work* (pp. 239–258). Burlington, VT: Ashgate.

Jennissen, T., & Lundy, C. (2011). *One hundred years of social work: A history of the profession in English Canada, 1900–2000.* Waterloo, ON: Wilfrid Laurier University Press.

Joseph, K. (2016, October). Imagining panel: Moving toward reconciliation in child welfare. Panel presented at the biennial Prairie Child Welfare Consortium symposium, Winnipeg, MB.

Joseph, R. (2016, October). Imagining child welfare in the spirit of reconciliation. Plenary presented at the biennial Prairie Child Welfare Consortium symposium, Winnipeg, MB.

Kelly, D. (2016, October). Imagining panel: Moving toward reconciliation in child welfare. Panel presented at the biennial Prairie Child Welfare Consortium symposium, Winnipeg, MB.

Kovach, M., Carriere, J., Montgomery, H., Barrett, M. J., & Gilles, C. (2015). *Indigenous presence: Experiencing and envisioning Indigenous knowledges within selected post-secondary sites of education and social work* (Report). Retrieved from http://www.uregina.ca/socialwork/faculty-staff/FacultySites/MontgomeryMontySite/Indigenous%20Presence.pdf

La Berge, C. (2016, October). Imagining panel: Moving toward reconciliation in child welfare. Panel presented at the biennial Prairie Child Welfare Consortium symposium, Winnipeg, MB.

Lavergne, C., Dufour, S., Trocmé, N., & Larrivée, M.-C. (2008). Visible minority, Aboriginal, and Caucasian children investigated by Canadian Protective Services. *Child Welfare, 87*(2), 59–76.

Leslie, D., & Cassano, R. (2003). The working definition of social work practice: Does it work? *Research on Social Work Practice, 13*(3), 366–375.

Lonne, B., Harries, M., Featherstone, B., & Gray, M. (2016). *Working ethically in child protection.* New York, NY: Routledge.

Macdonald, N. (2016, June 1). Sen. Murray Sinclair on truth and reconciliation's progress. *Maclean's.* Retrieved from http://www.macleans.ca/news/canada/sen-murray-sinclair-on-the-progress-of-truth-and-reconciliation/

McLaughlin, A. M., Gray, E., & Wilson, M. (2015). Child welfare workers and social justice: Mending the disconnect. *Children and Youth Services Review, 59*, 177–183. doi:10.1016/j.childyouth.2015.11.006

Milliken, E. (2012). Cultural safety and child welfare systems. In D. Fuchs, S. McKay, & I. Brown (Eds.), *Awakening the spirit: Moving forward in child welfare voices from the Prairies* (pp. 93–116). Regina, SK: Canadian Plains Research Center.

Morley, L., & Ife, J. (2002). Social work and a love of humanity. *Australian Social Work, 55*(1), 69–77. doi:10.1046/j.0312-407X.2002.00008.x

Payne, M. (2014). *Modern social work theory* (3rd ed.). Chicago, IL: Lyceum Books.

Pease, B., & Nipperess, S. (2016). Doing critical social work in the neoliberal context: Working on the contradictions. In B. Pease, S. Goldingay, N. Hosken, & S. Nipperess (Eds.), *Doing critical social work: Transformative practices for social justice* (pp. 3–38). Crows Nest, Australia: Allen & Unwin.

Pelech, W., Enns, R., & Fuchs, D. (2014). Collaboration or competition? Generalist or specialized? Challenges facing social work education and child welfare. In D. Badry, D. Fuchs, H. Montgomery, & S. McKay (Eds.), *Reinvesting in families: Strengthening child welfare practice for a brighter future* (pp. 243–263). Regina, SK: University of Regina Press.

Pierce, J. L., Hemingway, D., & Schmidt, G. (2014). Partnerships in social work education. *Journal of Teaching in Social Work, 34*(2), 215–226. doi:10.1080/08841233.2014.895477

Preston, S., & Aslett, J. (2014). Resisting neoliberalism from within the academy: Subversion through an activist pedagogy. *Social Work Education, 33*(4), 502–518. doi:10.1080/02615479.2013.848270

SFNSCI (Saskatchewan First Nations Family and Community Institute). (2017, August). *Voices for reform: Options for change to Saskatchewan First Nations child welfare*. Saskatoon, SK: Saskatchewan First Nations Family and Community Institute. Retrieved from http://www.sfnfci.ca/ckfinder/userfiles/files/SFNSCI%20Child%20Welfare%20Report%20Web%20(3).pdf

Sinha, V., Trocmé, N., Fallon, B., & MacLaurin, B. (2013). Understanding the investigation-stage overrepresentation of First Nations children in the child welfare system: An analysis of the First Nations component of the Canadian Incidence Study of Reported Child Abuse and Neglect 2008. *Child Abuse & Neglect, 37*(10), 821–831. doi:10.1016/j.chiabu.2012.11.010

Sinclair, R. (2004). Aboriginal social work education in Canada: Decolonizing pedagogy for the seventh generation. *First Peoples Child & Family Review, 1*(1), 49–61.

Swift, K. J., Good Gingrich, L., & Brown, M. (2016). The challenge of neoliberalism. In I. Taylor, M. Bogo, M. Lefevre, & B. Teater (Eds.), *Routledge international handbook of social work education* (pp. 382-393). New York, NY: Routledge.

Wong, Y. R. (2013). Returning to silence, connecting to wholeness: Contemplative pedagogy for critical social work education. *Journal of Religion & Spirituality in Social Work: Social Thought, 32*(3), 269–285. doi:10.1080/15426432.2013.801748

Yee, J. Y., & Wagner, A. E. (2013). Is anti-oppression teaching in Canadian social work classrooms a form of neo-liberalism? *Social Work Education: The International Journal, 32*(3), 331–348. doi:10.1080/02615479.2012.672557

Epilogue

H. Monty Montgomery

To the public, issues associated with Canada's child welfare systems appear to be remarkably intractable and impervious to well-intentioned reform efforts. For some time now, the landscape that springs to mind for taxpayers, service users, advocates, academics, and casual observers who consider matters relating to child welfare seems to have been indelibly shaped by ever-increasing rates of children in care, climbing costs, hollow promises of change, and disturbing testimonies of systemic dysfunction. Whether such perceptions are grounded in evidence-based facts, unsustainable anecdotes, or agenda-laden opinion is immaterial at this point; certainly, there is much bleakness, inequity, and hopelessness to see if that is the view that one's eyes have become accustomed to seeing.

But just as is the case with bedrock that has a steady stream of water crossing it, transformative change is working away at some of the foundational "truths" that practitioners, commentators, and the public alike hold about child welfare. It is through forums such as those presented under the auspices of the Prairie Child Welfare Consortium (e.g., biennial symposia, scholarly books) where some of the most insistent change is making itself visible. Indeed, the theme of the 2016 PCWC symposium—Imagining Child Welfare in the Spirit of Reconciliation—drew attention to the many ways that voices for change are responding to generations of young people who have been treated by people claiming to act in their best interests. The chapters included in this text were written by authors who are interested in furthering a reconciling agenda for child welfare practice through a discourse of change that shows signs of altering the Canadian child welfare landscape. If one looks beyond the discourse of challenges in child welfare, there is evidence that a lot of important work is being done on behalf of children, youth, and families in this country—and these narratives receive less attention than those documenting troubled outcomes in child welfare practice. Recognizing the need to draw attention to current work being done in the best interests of children, the PCWC continues to strive to share voices from the Prairies and beyond through our conferences and scholarly publications, including this book series.

Many Canadians have been anticipating meaningful change in child welfare for some time, and the democratizing effects of social media have created platforms for the exchange of ideas and the telling of truths that were previously cloaked in anonymity and shame. Some stories are not new, such as those—as First Nations Elders have long reminded those who would listen—of ancient prophecies of healing and reproach for settlers and Indigenous peoples alike. Other narratives have emerged through demands for social justice. The truth telling of the Truth and Reconciliation Commission of Canada, on Indian residential schools, and the National Inquiry into Missing and Murdered Indigenous Women and Girls has reopened and cleansed old wounds and created conditions for societal and personal healing. Yet other voices have been raised through lawsuits that have cracked open sealed doors and begun to enable justice and compensation for historically misguided practices such as the wholesale adoption of First Nations children into non-Aboriginal families. The legacy of colonization in Canada will continue to unfold.

Fortunately, many of our political leaders have heard the insistent voices of change, and real policy movement has begun to occur. Even when looking only at the years between the 2016 PCWC symposium in Winnipeg and today, one sees that some substantially revised and inclusive approaches to resolving persistent challenges are emerging. Examples can be found in the more equitable and accommodating funding models for First Nations child welfare and policing in First Nations communities that have been announced and are being implemented. Newfound energy has recently been poured into mechanisms for resolving jurisdictional disputes associated with providing care to children with special needs, and the backlog of "Jordan's Principle" cases awaiting resolution has been significantly reduced. Granting bodies such as the Public Health Agency of Canada and the Social Science and Humanities Research Council of Canada have recrafted criteria to be more inclusive of Indigenous experiences and oversight. These public bodies have committed themselves to funding important research that will document evidence of the incremental progress that is being made (e.g., through provincial and national incidence studies) and to identifying areas requiring additional emphasis over the years to come. Calls to action are being acted upon, and progress is being made to improve important relationships that have not always been experienced as egalitarian. Finally, requests for cross-disciplinary professional development on matters related to child welfare are being made and responded to across the Prairies.

A commitment to collaborating on matters of social justice and safety—one that was envisioned at the time of Confederation and the signing of the treaties—has been renewed and is gaining strength. Over the past two decades, the PCWC has borne witness to this spirit of change and has itself successfully accommodated the membership turnover and succession-planning challenges that naturally occur with the passage of time. We remain committed to change, to collaboration, to scholarship and knowledge exchange. The PCWC collaboration between the University of Manitoba, the University of Regina, the First Nations University of Canada, and the University of Calgary and our child welfare and community partners continues to evolve and grow. Returning to our theme of imagining child welfare in the spirit of reconciliation, we have indeed heard the echo of voices from the Prairies. The 2016 PCWC symposium provided an opportunity for Prairie child welfare providers, service users, and educators to come together to discuss how to move the TRC's recommendations on child welfare forward in a good way and in the spirit of reconciliation. We hope our symposium and this book will serve to continue the process of reconciliation and transformation. In our partnerships with child welfare jurisdictions in the Prairie provinces, our steering committee, and all our relations, we will continue walking alongside others as change agents for decades to come.

Abstracts

Chapter 1: Exploring Human Rights Approaches to Kinship Care Provision in the Prairie Provinces: Implications for Social Work Practice *by Daniel Kikulwe and Julie Mann-Johnson*

The global shift in focus to kinship placements as an option for abused and neglected children is in line with the 2010 United Nations Guidelines for the Alternative Care of Children. As the basis for these guidelines, the UN defines kinship care as a formal or informal family placement that includes the child's extended family or close friends. The UN Guidelines support and share a global vision for the placement of children in alternative care including family networks. This chapter focuses mainly on (1) an exploration of the core values undergirding the United Nations Conventions on the Rights of Children and the UN Guidelines regarding kinship placements; (2) in light of the UN's global vision of kinship placements, the existing child welfare legislations/policies used by the Prairie provinces to promote the concept of kinship care; and (3) the implications of this for social work practice and education.

Chapter 2: Working with First Nations Child Welfare to Build Professionalism *by Shelley Thomas Prokop, Laura Hicks, and Rachel Melymick*

The Saskatchewan First Nations Family and Community Institute (SFNSCI) works with Saskatchewan First Nations child welfare staff to develop standards and professional service training that are culturally relevant and applicable to their practice needs. In its development of standards and professional training, SFNSCI has utilized a co-operative approach that includes methods focusing on agency staff and community knowledge as the foundation of development. The approach begins with knowledge and a literature search of the communities and people involved, their histories, and their culture, as well as an understanding of child welfare in the community. Although a lengthy process, it ensures the training reflects and recognizes the communities and the realities of people served. This chapter shares SFNSCI experiences of successes and learnings using already developed practices, developing standards, and developing curriculum. The chapter will share some of the promising practices used by SFNSCI to develop and create ownership of culturally relevant training processes and products that enhance and build professionalism in First Nations child welfare in the province, while maintaining alignment to the SFNSCI vision, its mission, and the many First Nations cultures in Saskatchewan.

Chapter 3: Exploring Decolonization through Kinship Care Home Assessments *by Julie Mann-Johnson and Daniel Kikulwe*

The United Nations guidelines for alternative care supports the use of kinship care, and literature suggests that children placed in kinship care achieve positive outcomes. Literature also suggests that the experience for kinship caregivers is very different from adoption and foster care; however, assessment practice and policy do not reflect these unique elements. These elements, which influence the practitioner, process, policy, legislation, and systemic issues, can inform kinship home assessment practice, policy, and legislation. This chapter discusses the use and findings of a secondary data analysis to honour the voices of people who have shared their perspectives at public consultations and information-gathering events. This use of secondary qualitative data ensures that the voices of the Indigenous community are heard to influence policy and practice for these traditional kinship caregiving networks. The data analysis is grounded in anti-colonial and critical ecological frameworks to understand the impacts of structural colonization on Indigenous children and families through the current use of child welfare kinship assessments policy and legislation. Crucial elements in kinship care home assessment are identified for practice and for consideration in policy and program development.

Chapter 4: Aging Out of Care: The Rural Experience

by Anne Marie McLaughlin, Richard Enns, and Deena Seaward

This chapter explores the unique and underreported experiences of aging out of care of both rural youth and those who support them. Research examining the transition of youth out of care has focused disproportionately on the experiences of urban youth. Building on our recent qualitative investigation conducted in rural and northern Alberta—which asked what are the experiences of rural youth who are permanent wards of the government as they transition out of the care of the government, and what are the experiences of rural caregivers (foster parents and child welfare workers) who support them?—we highlight serious challenges as well as the opportunities that are frequently overlooked in designing policy and practices with a "one size fits all" approach. Our research uncovered rural-specific issues such as role ambiguity, resource inequity, and resource depletion but also broader systemic issues that hinder the healthy development and future success of youth as they leave care.

Chapter 5: Inappropriate Application of Parenting Capacity Assessments in the Child Protection System

by Peter Choate and Gabrielle Lindstrom

Child protection (CP) remains one of the powerful forces of the dominant culture operating within Aboriginal communities across Canada. An examination of many of the methodologies used by CP shows weak linkages to Aboriginal cultures and parenting practices. When assessed using parameters and definitions of "good enough" parenting from the dominant cultural perspective, Aboriginal parents will often have difficulty meeting the standards. Such important factors as residential schools, the Sixties Scoop, and intergenerational trauma are absent from or poorly reflected in the main models of child protection parenting assessment. This is further compounded by the actuarial or risk assessment approaches that would weight these experiences negatively. New approaches are needed, as seen from a consultation with six Blackfoot Elders that helps inform this chapter. In line with the Truth and Reconciliation Commission's calls to action, we argue that the First Nations, Inuit, and Métis peoples must be empowered to seek these new methodologies in ways that respect their cultures while still enhancing the protection of children.

Chapter 6: Listening in a Settler State: (Birth) Mothers as Paraprofessionals in Response to FASD *by Michelle Stewart, Lisa Lawley, Rachel Tambour, and Alexandra Johnson*

The Truth and Reconciliation Commission's calls to action outline the need for a fundamental reordering of how child welfare is enacted in Canada and draws into sharp focus the ways in which Indigenous children have been, and continue to be, impacted by settler colonialism through child welfare practices that aggressively displace children by stripping them from their birth families and communities. Contemporary child welfare practices continue to justify the forced separation of families and children. From residential schools to the Sixties and Millennium Scoops, programs and practices actively and continuously decentre Indigenous parents and their perspectives. Placing the perspectives of parents at the centre of the analysis, this chapter discusses the role of micro- and macroaggressions that facilitate structural racism and the strategies parents use to address these incursions. Grounded in qualitative research, this chapter focuses on the resiliency of families who are raising children with a complex disability and the perspectives of two mothers in particular as they discuss the challenges of identifying culturally safe(r) programs/practices and the strategies they deploy to protect themselves and their children from unsafe practices. We argue for parents to be treated as experts in the care of their children—to be treated as paraprofessionals—and focus on the unique perspectives of Indigenous mothers as paraprofessionals who actively push back against colonial sensibilities that implicitly and explicitly facilitate the effacement of Indigenous families through the displacement of Indigenous children.

Chapter 7: A Summary: On the Edge between Two Worlds: Community Narratives on the Vulnerability of Marginalized Indigenous Girls *by Marlyn Bennett and Ainsley Krone*

Abused. Trafficked. Exploited. Easy prey. Missing. Murdered. These days this litany of depressing descriptors dominates any media story about

Indigenous girls. Online, in print, on air, and in daily conversations, being young, female, and Indigenous seems to be synonymous with having a bleak existence and an uncertain future. Consider, then, how it feels to actually be a young Indigenous girl today. Growing up, you might not have heard stories of strength from the outside world. You know strong and beautiful women in your family and community, but when you step outside in the morning that is not the way the world sees you; your inherent value, the role you can play in the lives of those around you, is diminished, unacknowledged, dismissed. These ideas, combined with the stories youth tell us every day in our work as advocates, inspired a research project undertaken by Manitoba's Office of the Children's Advocate (OCA). We interviewed eleven Indigenous community leaders about the experiences of Indigenous girls in Manitoba. This chapter passionately highlights the need for access to culture and Indigenous knowledge and teachings, the role of a healthy community, and what is missing in Manitoba's current public structures.

Chapter 8: Factors Associated with the Child Welfare Placement Decision in Alberta
by Bruce MacLaurin, Hee-Jeong Yoo, and Morgan DeMone

The placement of children in care continues to be a primary child welfare intervention in Canada; however, it is generally regarded as a very intrusive and costly response to maltreatment. An estimated 68,000 children were in care in Canada during 2007—a 60 per cent increase from 1992. While placements are designed to ensure safety for children at risk, outcomes related to well-being, permanency, and family connection do not consistently support these decisions. Further research is required to understand which children, with what presenting concerns, benefit from what types of placement in Alberta. Secondary data analysis of the Alberta Incidence Study of Reported Child Abuse and Neglect (AIS-2008) was conducted to examine which child, household, and case factors were associated with a formal child welfare placement. Further analyses examined differences noted between kinship care and traditional foster care. The analysis shows that level of risk and younger age of children are associated with placement decisions, as well as with an overrepresentation of Indigenous children. These findings establish an important context for understanding placement decisions in Alberta given the current commitment to maintaining child and family connections and the priority placed on kinship care.

Chapter 9: A Strained Relationship: Southern Sudanese Communities and Child Welfare Systems in Two Urban Centres in Western Canada *by David Este and Christa Sato*

Between 2002 and 2009, Alberta became home to many Southern Sudanese who fled the ongoing civil war in their country of origin, the Sudan. As they adapted to Canadian society, this group of (primarily government-assisted) refugees faced challenges experiencing new entities such as the legal, education, healthcare, and social service systems. One of the most contentious relationships that emerged within Southern Sudanese communities was with the local child welfare system. Through a qualitative study involving in-depth, semi-structured interviews with twenty-two Southern Sudanese community members in Calgary and Brooks, Alberta, this chapter examines the participants' perceptions of and experiences with the child welfare system. Using a thematic analysis, the chapter explores the specific issues that contributed to the problematic nature of the relationship. In this chapter, we present a series of strategies recommended by the study's respondents, which they maintained are designed to improve the relationship between child welfare authorities and the Southern Sudanese community in the two respective urban centres.

Chapter 10: The Linkage between FASD and Homelessness for Individuals with a History of Child Welfare Care
by Dorothy Badry, Christine Walsh, Meaghan Bell, and Kaylee Ramage

This chapter focuses on the intricate link between fetal alcohol spectrum disorder (FASD) and youth leaving the child welfare system who move into unstable, tenuous housing and often experience homelessness as young adults. The needs of youth with FASD who are leaving the child welfare system are not well understood, and the vulnerability of these youth places them at increased risk for exploitation. The FASD and Homelessness research project focused on adults with FASD who experienced homelessness. We interviewed seventeen individual adults, at least half of whom had prior child welfare involvement. The need exists to develop policy and programs that support individuals in housing across the lifespan, and this chapter serves to illuminate challenges with a focus on policy and program recommendations to support better outcomes.

Chapter 11: The Development of a Training Video: Demonstrating Essential Skills for Child Welfare Practice

by Cathy Rocke and Judy Hughes

A recognized gap exists between the social work classroom, where knowledge and skills about practice are taught, and the field placements where students are expected to apply these skills. This chapter describes the development of a training video, instructor's manual, and student's manual for child welfare practice that are intended to reduce this gap. The idea for this project emerged from a SSHRC-funded research project that examined the experience of women within the child welfare system. To create the video, we brought together an actor, who portrayed two different mothers (based on anonymized copies of the research interview transcripts), and two experienced child welfare workers. The instructor's and student's manuals were developed collaboratively with the two child welfare workers to highlight the skills needed in this challenging social work field. Future plans for the use of this teaching resource are also discussed.

Chapter 12: Transforming the Classroom: Supporting Critical Change in Social Work Education in the Spirit of Reconciliation for Child Welfare *by Jennifer Hedges*

Child welfare workers are responsible for and accountable in providing a variety of services that require a vast array of knowledges and skills related to complex individual, family, and community situations. However, there is a gap in the research on how social work education programs are helping to prepare social workers to make a difference and be successful in this field of practice. Child welfare services are delivered through a highly legalized and bureaucratic system that presents unique challenges for social workers. Indigenous children and families and other racialized minorities are highly overrepresented, and there is a great need to develop and design effective, culturally appropriate ways to improve the preparation of social workers. The proper education and training of child welfare workers is one of the Truth and Reconciliation Commission's calls to action. Barriers continue to exist between anti-oppressive frameworks and practice. This chapter reviews the literature through a critical and Indigenous theory lens to explore the relationship between social work education and preparation for work in child welfare. A small pilot study is presented that involved interviewing recent social work graduates who are working in child welfare to gain their perspectives on both the strengths and the areas needing improvement in social work education. Key findings included the relevance of experiential learning and the need for more attention to self-care, cultural awareness, managing authority, media relations, peer conflict, and working within a complex system.

Contributors

Dorothy Badry, PhD, MSW, RSW, is an associate professor in the Faculty of Social Work, University of Calgary. She is on the steering committee of the Prairie Child Welfare Consortium (PCWC). Her research is on child welfare and fetal alcohol spectrum disorder (FASD), from prevention to intervention. She teaches an online course on FASD and Social Work Practice to social work students through the PCWC. She has received research funding from the Public Health Agency of Canada, First Nations and Inuit Health Branch, and PolicyWise. She is co-lead of the Education and Training Council under the Alberta FASD Cross-Ministry Committee and research lead focused on child welfare for the Canada FASD Research Network (appointed in 2016). She worked in child protection in Alberta for sixteen years before joining the University of Calgary. She has also been a member of the Canada FASD Research Network Action Team on Women's Health/Prevention since 2008.

Meaghan Bell holds a master's degree from the University of Calgary and over the past eight years has worked in the area of human services. Her work has largely been focused on research, policy, and evaluation in the areas of homelessness, fetal alcohol spectrum disorder, family violence, and health. Her professional experience includes positions with the Calgary Homeless Foundation, Hotchkiss Brain Institute, and Calgary Housing. Meaghan has also served as a member of the board of directors with Calgary Fetal Alcohol Network since 2014.

Marlyn Bennett, BA, MA, PhD, is a member of the Sandy Bay Ojibway First Nation in Manitoba. She holds expertise in Aboriginal child welfare, with a special interest in qualitative and photovoice research, including narrative digital storytelling among First Nations youth who have transitioned out of care toward adulthood. She has received many awards in recognition of her achievements in policy and research and has published extensively on matters related to First Nations child welfare. She is the chair and founding member of Animikii Ozoson Child & Family Services and is on the board of directors for Sandy Bay Child & Family Services. Marlyn is an advisory member of the First Nations Canadian Incidence Study (CIS) advisory committee and currently serves on the Manitoba College of Social Workers board of directors as a public representative. She is one of two assistant professors recently appointed to the new Master's of Social Work Based in Indigenous Knowledge Program with the Faculty of Social Work at the University of Manitoba. She is a mother to one daughter and resides in Winnipeg with her life partner, Mike.

Peter W. Choate, MSW, RSW, PhD, is a registered social worker, member of the Clinical Registry, and approved clinical supervisor for the Alberta College of Registered Social Workers. He is an associate professor in the Department of Child Studies and Social Work at Mount Royal University, Calgary. He is an expert witness in the area of parenting capacity (including risk, domestic violence, and addictions). He has been qualified on over 150 occasions in the Provincial Court of Alberta and the Court of Queen's Bench. Peter's areas of research include assessment of parents within child protection systems, practice errors in child protection linked to serious injury and death, fetal alcohol spectrum disorder, stigma and implications for frontline practice, and implementation of Truth and Reconciliation Commission calls to action within the practice of social work. He is a member of the Minister's Child Intervention Panel (Alberta), joining three other experts on this all-party committee of the legislature.

Morgan DeMone, BSW, RSW, completed her social work degree and worked with Bruce MacLaurin as a research assistant on several projects related to child welfare, including the Alberta Incidence Study of Reported Child Abuse and Neglect (AIS-2008): Select Findings. She received the Iain Cullen Ramsay Recognition of Excellence Award in Personal Achievement in 2014. She continues to pursue her social work interests working with children and families.

Richard Enns, PhD, RSW, is currently associate dean in the Central and Northern Alberta Region of the Faculty of Social Work, University of Calgary, in Edmonton. His teaching interests include the history of federal Indian education policy and the development of industrial and residential schools in Canada. His most recent research has examined federal policy following World War II, childcare standards of the day, the role of social work in the residential school system in Canada, and current reconciliation efforts. In addition, he has examined current issues in refugee and immigrant settlement in Canada and taught critical perspectives in mental health.

David Este, PhD, MSW, RSW, is a professor in the Faculty of Social Work at the University of Calgary. He obtained his PhD from Wilfrid Laurier University and MSW from the University of Toronto. The majority of his research has focused on aspects of the immigrant/refugee experience in Canada, such as the experiences of immigrant/refugee men as fathers and intimate partner violence. He has also conducted research studies that examined the health and well-being of people of African descent in Canada, HIV/AIDS service utilization by African newcomers in Calgary, and the mental health of men from Asian communities in Canada. David is co-author of one book and co-editor of three volumes. He has published several journal articles and book chapters focused on issues related to immigration and diversity.

Don Fuchs, PhD, is a full professor in the Faculty of Social Work at the University of Manitoba. He has conducted extensive research on fetal alcohol spectrum disorder and children in care in the province of Manitoba. A founding member of the Prairie Child Welfare Consortium, he currently chairs PCWC steering and e-learning committees and has co-edited all six books emerging from the biannual conferences held in Alberta, Saskatchewan, and Manitoba. Don has made significant contributions to scholarship and research in the Prairie provinces and has had a distinguished career as a social work educator, making valuable contributions to graduate education and supporting the development of the MSW in Indigenous Knowledge at the University of Manitoba.

Jennifer Hedges is a PhD candidate in the social work program at the University of Manitoba. Her thesis topic is exploring social work education for critical transformation of child welfare policy and practice. Jennifer worked for nine years as a child welfare protection worker in Ontario. She is currently assistant professor in the Faculty of Social Work at Booth University College. Areas of research interest have included pedagogy for clinical practice, GIS mapping in child welfare, use of psychotropic medications for children and youth in care, and student experiences of vicarious trauma. Jennifer is a member of the Prairie Child Welfare Consortium and e-learning committee and is passionate about learning and the transforming potential of education.

Laura Hicks, BSW, is Métis with roots in Portage la Prairie, Manitoba, but she grew up in Marquis, Saskatchewan. She has been employed with the Saskatchewan First Nations Family and Community Institute since December 2013. Her role as SDM consultant is to provide assessment and onsite support for child and family agencies implementing the Structured Decision Making (SDM) tool. Laura graduated with a Bachelor of Social Work degree from the University of Regina. Prior to being employed at the institute, she worked in the field of child protection and young offenders.

Judy Hughes, PhD, MSW, is an associate professor in the Faculty of Social Work at the University of Manitoba. Her continuing program of research centres on exploring the meaning of violence and violent acts for victims and perpetrators. In collaboration with others, she also completed interviews with child welfare workers and women who experience intimate partner violence and involvement with the child welfare system.

Alexandra Johnson, BA, is a master's student and a research assistant working on the FASD Research Project. She is a graduate student at the University of Guelph, having completed her undergraduate degree in the Human Justice program at the University of Regina. Her research interests include fetal alcohol spectrum disorder, cognitive disabilities, mental health, youth in transition, social support systems, and criminal justice.

Daniel Kikulwe, PhD, is an assistant professor at the University of Regina, Faculty of Social Work. His areas of academic interest include families, immigration, and child welfare practices and policies. The United Nations Convention on the Rights of the Child and its applicability to the global south, as well as kinship care trends in Canada, are an important focus of his work. He teaches a Prairie child welfare course on immigrant and refugee issues.

Ainsley Krone, MA, has worked as an advocate for children and youth for eighteen years, the last eight of those with the Manitoba Office of the Children's Advocate (OCA). Since spring 2017, she has served as Deputy Children's Advocate, helping to organize and oversee ongoing initiatives and pending expansions to the OCA's province-wide mandate. Prior to returning to Winnipeg, Ainsley spent ten years on the Sunshine Coast of British Columbia as a direct service youth worker and alternative education program developer. She holds an MA in Communication with a specialization in international and intercultural communications. Ainsley's work focuses on children's rights education and finding ways to amplify the voice of young people in the public sphere.

Lisa Lawley, Family Advocate, is with the Kermode Friendship Centre of BC and has done significant work with families of children with fetal alcohol spectrum disorder (FASD). As a mother, she brings her own family experience to this work. She has run the Circle of Life Mentorship Program in Terrace, BC, and has supported many initiatives of the Canada FASD Research Network. She is an ally who supports the creation of safe spaces for women to heal. Lisa had a key role in the FASD Justice and Reconciliation: Tough Questions, New Collaborations national symposium held in Regina in 2017, facilitating the holistic and culturally safe(r) approaches to program and practices.

Gabrielle Lindstrom (nee Weasel Head), MA, BA, a member of the Kainaiwa First Nation in southern Alberta, is an assistant professor in Indigenous studies with the Department of Humanities, University of Calgary. She is in the final stages of completing her PhD in educational research with a specialization in adult learning. Her dissertation research focuses on the interplay between trauma and resilience in the post-secondary experiences of Aboriginal adult learners. Additionally, her other diverse research interests include micro-credentialing for educational development, meaningful assessment in higher education, parenting assessment tools reform in child welfare, and anti-racist pedagogy.

Bruce MacLaurin, MSW, RSW, is an assistant professor at the Faculty of Social Work, University of Calgary. He was co-investigator on four cycles of the Canadian Incidence Study of Reported Child Abuse and Neglect and principal investigator for provincial studies in BC, Alberta, Saskatchewan, and NWT. His research and publishing focus on child maltreatment, child welfare, outcomes, foster care, and youth at risk. He has collaborated with government on a variety of child welfare initiatives and was on the expert panel for legislation review in NWT, the Office of the Child and Youth Advocate in Alberta, the Ministerial Panel on Child Fatalities in Alberta (Phase 1), the Ministerial Panel on Child Intervention (Phase 2), and the Auditor General of Canada Review of the Northwest Territories Child Welfare Services.

Julie Mann-Johnson, MSW, RSW, is field education coordinator and instructor with the University of Calgary, Central and Northern Alberta Region. She has worked most of her twenty-year social work career in various areas of child welfare practice. This experience has led her to be particularly passionate about supporting feminist and anti-racist practice as well as ensuring meaningful kin connections for children and youth within that system. In addition to kinship care and assessment of caregivers, her research interests include socializing social workers to the profession, fetal alcohol spectrum disorder, and community partnerships. She lives in St. Albert, Alberta, with her husband and teen girls.

Anne Marie McLaughlin, PhD, RSW, is an associate professor, Faculty of Social Work, University of Calgary. Her research interests are in the area of social justice and social work practice. She is knowledgeable in qualitative research methods, particularly grounded theory. Her prior practice experience includes extensive work in mental health and child welfare.

Rachel Melymick, BA, BSW, started working at Saskatchewan First Nations Family and Community Institute (SFNSCI) on September 8, 2015, as the second SDM consultant hired to provide training and onsite support for First Nations child and family services agencies using the SDM program. Rachel has a Bachelor of Social Work from the University of Regina and a Bachelor of Arts in Native studies from the University of Saskatchewan. Prior to being hired by SFNSCI, she worked in child protection as a protection worker and in various community-based organizations.

H. Monty Montgomery, PhD, MSW, is of Mi'kmaq ancestry, from the Eastern Shore area of Nova Scotia, although he has resided in Western Canada for most of his life. Monty has worked with provincial and First Nations governments and non-profit Aboriginal organizations over the past twenty years, and he is an assistant professor with the University of Regina, Faculty of Social Work, in Saskatoon. Monty has held positions as the executive director of the Saskatchewan First Nations Family and Community Institute and as the manager for program and policy initiatives at the Caring for First Nations Children Society of British Columbia. His professional interests are First Nations child welfare program development and practice; information technology/management for social work practitioners; and online distance learning with Aboriginal adult learners.

Kaylee Ramage, MPH, is a PhD candidate in Community Health Sciences at the University of Calgary. She holds a Master of Science in Public Health from the London School of Hygiene and Tropical Medicine. Kaylee is passionate about improving the social conditions in which we live, promoting women's health, and helping to restructure systems to empower women around health. She works on a variety of community-based research and evaluation projects related to fetal alcohol spectrum disorder, housing and homelessness, immigration, domestic violence, and pregnancy. Her dissertation explores the structural influences on pregnancy decision-making for girls with involvement in the child welfare system.

Cathy Rocke, BSW, MSW, PhD, is an assistant professor at the Faculty of Social Work at the University of Manitoba. Her current research program is focused on addressing and evaluating how to reconcile the relationships between Indigenous and non-Indigenous peoples in Canada both on campus and in the community through intergroup dialogue. Prior to her academic career, Cathy worked in both the education and social work fields, including many years as a child protection worker.

Christa Sato, MSW, RSW, recently completed her MSW in the Faculty of Social Work, University of Calgary, specializing in the area of community development. Her thesis research focused on the university experiences of second-generation Filipino males in Calgary. She served for three years as site coordinator for the Strength in Unity Project, which focused on the mental health and well-being of Asian men. Christa has worked on an array of projects focused on immigration, diversity, and social justice and has developed a strong research agenda in these areas. She is the research coordinator for the Woods Home.

Deena Seaward (Workun), MSW, RSW, has a BA in Criminology and is an addictions counsellor with Alberta Health Services, Edmonton. She has engaged in treatment programs with complex needs around intimate partner violence and substance use and has work experience in the areas of sex offenders, addictions, and family violence treatment. She has worked on program development in the areas of spousal violence and addictions and completed her Master of Social Work degree through the University of Calgary in 2017.

Michelle Stewart, PhD, MA, BA, is an associate professor in justice studies and director of the Community Research Unit at the University of Regina. As an applied anthropologist, Michelle focuses on community-engaged projects and partnerships focused on cognitive disabilities, mental health, and racialized health inequalities as they present in the criminal justice system. Her research addresses these social justice issues through policy engagement and direct work with stakeholders to address programs and practices to bring about better justice outcomes for all individuals. The Social Sciences and Humanities Research Council, Canadian Institutes of Health Research, Saskatchewan Health Research Foundation, Canada Council for the Arts, University of Regina, various provincial ministries, and the Canada FASD Research Network have supported her research. Since 2014, Michelle has been strategic research lead for justice interventions with Canada FASD Research Network.

Rachel Tambour is from Yellowknife, NWT, and is with the Tree of Peace Friendship Centre. Rachel has shared her experiences as a mother of a young man with fetal alcohol spectrum disorder (FASD), and she is a strong advocate and ally for children and families. Rachel had a key role in the FASD Justice and Reconciliation: Tough Questions, New Collaborations national symposium held in Regina in 2017, facilitating the holistic and culturally safe(r) approaches to program and practices. She continues to speak publicly on the topic of FASD in support of families and as an advocate for prevention.

Shelley Thomas Prokop, MCEd, a Cree woman from Beardy's & Okemasis First Nation in central Saskatchewan, has been a researcher in child and family welfare for over twenty years. She focuses on community-based approaches, process development, and ethical practices in her position as the program director at the Saskatchewan First Nations Family and Community Institute. Programs focus on developing resources and training for First Nations group home staff, prevention workers, First Nations caregivers, and protection staff. Programs are developed using a community-based model that includes those being served in the development of resources and training.

Christine Walsh, PhD, RSW, is a professor and associate dean (Research & Partnerships) in the Faculty of Social Work, University of Calgary. She is interested in conducting research that contributes to the understanding of violence across the lifespan—child maltreatment, violence against women, and abuse against older adults. She also conducts action-oriented, arts-informed, community-based research aimed at contributing to well-being and enhancing social justice for marginalized and socially excluded populations, including Indigenous peoples, immigrants, youth in conflict with the law, and those experiencing poverty and homelessness.

Hee-Jeong Yoo, BSW, RSW, is a Master of Social Work student at the University of Calgary and research associate with a focus on child welfare research. Her thesis research focuses on challenging Western notions of maternal identities using the narratives of mothers in child welfare. Her research interests are in child welfare, homelessness, and mothers involved in child welfare. She worked with Bruce MacLaurin as a research assistant on several projects related to child welfare, including the Alberta Incidence Study of Reported Child Abuse and Neglect (AIS-2008): Select Findings. Hee-Jeong is also a therapist with a public health agency working with individuals with acute mental health disorders.

Subject Index

G

J

K

Author Index

C

D